Modern Masculinity for the Conscious Man

Modern Masculinity for the Conscious Man

Making Sense in Troubled Times

MICHAEL RONIN

Published by Edge of Tomorrow LLC

Book Design by Kory Kirby
SET IN ADOBE GARAMOND PRO

ISBN 978-1-7367046-0-8 (paperback)
ISBN 978-1-7367046-1-5 (eBook)

Printed in the United States of America

Contents

Let me tell you why you're here. You're here because you know something. What you know, you can't explain. But you feel it. You've felt it your entire life. That there's something wrong with the world. You don't know what it is. But it's there. Like a splinter in your mind.[1]

— MORPHEUS

Introduction

Words are cheap.

Words are all around us. A cacophony of sounds, slogans, and statements competing for our attention, demanding that we react and rethink how we move through this world. And I'm about to throw a bunch more at you, dear reader. So much has been said already by so many people for so many generations. We've talked to, talked at, and talked around each other and, after all that time, we still find ourselves grasping for meaning despite all those words having been spoken. Ideas are plentiful and clarity is in short supply. If this book simply adds to that noise, I will have done you a disservice. But if I'm wrong about anything, hopefully you'll think I'm helpfully wrong.

This book is broad, rather than deep. Everything is more complex than can be imagined. Life is a deep analytical puzzle—we can only perceive a fraction of the truth of things which may have significant bearing on our lives. So inevitably, there is much material worthy of consideration that has been omitted so as to make this book manageable. The material I have included is, perhaps also, confusingly diverse.

The difficulty has been to simply pick those elements which are pertinent to masculinity because "everything is in everything," as one of my teachers used to say. So that means I have to include certain things that you might think out of place or irrelevant and include things which might have you scratching your head. I'll let you be the judge of that.

Although the content material I've decided to present may seem rather arbitrary at first glance, I consider it to be the most crucial and compelling and/or the least understood by conscious men. My hope is to draw connections through many ideas and offer my perspectives to those that seek the truth and live the truth through their own efforts. There's stuff about psychology, human development, human nature, human consciousness, mental health, societal norms, etc—everything that can serve to help or hinder conscious men in the modern age.

I discuss extensively intimate male/female relationships. While there are numerous books devoted to that specific subject, my contribution is to consider aspects of those relationships that really don't get talked about enough. These aspects are more likely to be things that conscious men either haven't yet recognized or encountered. Other authors have important contributions that have already been well documented. For example, if you want to read about attachment theory and its impact on relationships, you couldn't do better than read some of Stan Tatkin's work. So I won't repeat what he says, even though it's invaluable knowledge.

Much of the purpose of this book is to look at the pressures and obstacles men face in their lives in terms relative to their masculinity. I hope to offer some potential insights and observations which, now processed through the course of my life, may have some merit for a road map to a better life for other men. My aim is to promote active thought among my readers, and there will be topics, vocabulary, and intellectual elements that will require pause and contemplation for best effect—the things that adversely affect a man's life circumstances that he might not yet have considered fully.

A snapshot in time, this book is a temporary view of wisdom over many subject areas—a brief moment within an ever-changing global timeline. I would suggest extrapolating backwards in time from where you find yourself to appreciate and understand whatever timeline we've since gone down since its publication. The pace of change is quickening and, by the time you read this book, conditions and circumstances may well be different.

~

I've spent a large proportion of my adult life trying to see the world as it really is and coming to my own conclusions. Conclusions about everything I've been told or have learned from others. Most people, especially nowadays through their social media preferences, live in an echo chamber. Strangely, I find there aren't enough groups or people out there whose thinking is closely mirrored by my own. I find myself constantly and intentionally challenging my thinking by reading and reviewing stuff from all over the informational map. I digest as much as possible from as wide an array of rock-solid sources as I can, picking and choosing those that make the most sense to me, and then synthesizing it all into something coherent. As I ingest information and perspectives, I try to accept and acknowledge my own limited ability to fully understand everything and, instead, embrace a growth mindset, however flawed or imperfect I might be at any moment. I am at war with my level of ignorance.

I'm deeply concerned with society and our shared journey together as a species and in particular how it affects men. Even in western cultures, society is "not fit for human consumption." It in no way works for the benefit of the vast majority of people. I'm both fascinated and disturbed about how the world is screwed up, how it got to be screwed up, how I got to be screwed up, and the parts we all play in creating the best conditions for people and planet.

Something seems to have reached a tipping point in our collective consciousness, and people are becoming distressingly polarized and hysterical, if not basket cases. The causal factors for our predicament are, for the most part, available for those who care to look but are largely relegated to the fringe. More than this, I'm writing this book because so many people don't know they're being lied to. And they don't know that they are being manipulated and conditioned in such a way that distracts them from realizing their true nature[2] and living harmoniously with each other.

I feel bereft at the state of the world right now. I would say men and women are tearing themselves apart but that isn't quite true, as you'll discover. Because it's actually women who are tearing themselves away from men—some of them awarely, others unawarely—and mostly out of conditioned fear. I feel the cruelty of unconsciousness in this world and the harm it causes. This is the creature from the Black Lagoon that lurks unrecognized by most.

I'm also here to speak the truth which, by its very nature, is belligerent—because it stands squarely against a world built on comfortable misperceptions, mild deceptions, and outright lies. The uncomfortable truth stands squarely at the side of the conscious man as his ally in life. There may be moments you find yourself recoiling at some of the things I write. You'll find that I prefer to be direct rather than massage a point to make it softer and more palatable. I ask your forgiveness if I rely on declaratory statements more than you are comfortable with—they are mostly to make for streamlined reading rather than indicate a fixed mindset.

~

We are born into a world already vastly polluted with bad ideas, false narratives, faulty beliefs, hypocrisies, half-truths, and downright lies, to such an extent that we've lost sight as a species of what it's like to live

2 True nature is the truth of our nature. To return to this truth we must pursue a long self-reflective journey in which our shadow aspects, false narratives, trauma patternings and woundings are revealed, to be faced and integrated.

harmoniously. Much of this has been intentional. Often, the best way to give a false narrative is to present a small degree of truth but then surround it by falsifications. That modicum of truth confuses us into wondering if the rest could be true, or if all of it's false. I have found that, because of the level of disinformation and bullshit that's out there, it's been necessary to develop a skeptical mind. Skepticism is a skill that needs to be developed over the course of a lifetime in order to at least come close to seeing things as they really are.

What's important is to question prevailing narratives. All the time. And in fact, to adopt a default position of not believing any of it until otherwise proved. These narratives are embedded in the social and political control systems. While whole books could, and have, been written about these subjects, I'll be focusing on several fields of reference I feel are the most urgently in need of a fuller understanding.

This work is not presented as a one-size-fits-all solution to men's needs. It's more of a starting point for further contemplation, exploration, and discussion. Clearly, a lot of the focus of this book will reflect my own subjective conscience. I invite you to question it and see if there are aspects which you find serve you so that you can feel your own inner subjective truth. Stay open to your own views relative to your core or conscience, even when doing so threatens your own beliefs—and perhaps changing as a result of that inquiry. Whether you agree with my perspective or not, my hope is that you will develop as a highly self-guided person, a freethinker, a free-feeler, whose internal compass points to your *own* truly felt sense of "yes or no," rather than those of others.

I've also chosen the device of "archetypes" for some chapters. Modern Man, Modern Woman,[3] Divine Masculine, Divine Feminine,[4] the Divine Union, etc, are all archetypes which point to fundamentals and broad principles rather than stereotypes. You may be a man in your 20s, say, but that doesn't necessarily make you a "Modern Man," as I've described him.

---

3 Shadow aspects of femininity and masculinity in the modern age.

4 Femininity and masculinity at their most evolved. Or in their true nature.

Ultimately, please take what is useful to you and dispose of the rest.

~

Your journey is not the same as mine, and my journey is not yours. But if you meet me on a certain path, may we encourage each other.

– UNATTRIBUTED

This book is primarily for the younger man, (although I hope anyone, man, woman, or lizard-person will find in it something of interest). Older men might also find it useful in understanding the challenges and obstacles that younger men are facing in today's world—a world very much different from the one they grew up in. I am writing this from a straight male perspective but the thoughts and ideas expressed here may sometimes be applied to other non-normative relationships. Finally, I am offering my thoughts from the perspective of "modern, western, secular culture," what's called WEIRD (Western, Educated, Industrialized, Rich, and Democratic).

One of the advantages of being an older man is that I've been seasoned by time. I make no other claims—I don't have letters after my name, I haven't distinguished myself in the service of men, and I consider myself a philomath,[5] rather than a specialist in matters of male interest. Even though I've never met you, I care about you. My hope is that I can direct my own particular blend of skills and idiosyncrasies for your benefit.

~

When you come to a seemingly insurmountable problem, and it doesn't appear that there is a path forward, sometimes the path forward is the path back. Søren Kierkegaard, the Danish philosopher, once wrote,

5 A philomath is a lover of learning and studying and I love to uncover and discover things which are generally not part of the collective awareness. I'm not necessarily interested in becoming a subject matter expert, preferring instead to develop a broad understanding of a variety of subject areas.

"Life can only be understood backwards; but it must be lived forwards." Since I'm nearing the end of my incarnation, I feel I have a perspective about today's world compared to yesterday's that could prove valuable to younger men who consider themselves "conscious." Ever since I was in high school, I've been reflecting on the world around me, on how people relate with each other, and how it all hangs together, or not. I've also taken it a stage further and tried to understand the perspective of the generations before me, as I recognize that my own life span is just a blip in the history of human relations. As a younger man, I hope that you will take what I write "on advisement," so to speak, and simply use my perspective in reaching a fuller perspective of your own. Maybe you do or maybe you don't, but many young men think that things are normal. Fish don't know they're swimming in water—they're so surrounded by it's normalcy that they can't see it. Only by jumping out of the fish bowl do they appreciate its existence. Stuck as we are in the zeitgeist of our times, we're so surrounded by it that it's almost impossible to see or conceive it until we get outside of it—the most important and obvious realities are often those which are the least perceivable and understood.

Younger men haven't had as much time to reach a fuller understanding simply because they haven't been incarnated for as long, not because of any implicit deficit. Hopefully your pace of learning will be quicker than mine so that you can make more informed choices about your life. I'd like to invite you to be the first generation which seriously addresses the issues and challenges facing men and promotes solutions which meet their needs, and the women who love them.

We apply fight-or-flight reflexes not only to predators,
but to data itself.[6]

– CHRIS MOONEY

The Importance of Nuanced Understanding

Before the truth can set you free, it would be wise to ask yourself what programming, distortions, and illusions are holding you hostage. The predisposition of human beings currently is to explain complexities in rigid or simplistic ways. We live in a time when people generally no longer have subtle conversations or arguments. People are engaging in opposing monologues, yet calling this dialog. Dogma is winning out over data. Diatribe is winning out over reflection. The thinking is, if your position cannot be summarized in a sentence, there is little point in making it, since there is no patience nor interest for nuance or context. Everything has to be binary and for two sides to square off against each other. It's more about point-scoring, securing the agenda, and signaling one's tribal alliance. "Angry rhetoric seems to demand acceptance just because it is angry."[7]

People accept certain narratives because they find it unsatisfying to know the truth. Any empirical data which challenges (and potentially alters) their attachment to a particular set of ideas, values, or data points

7 Piers Benn (January 13, 2018). *"Freedom of Expression and the Flight from Reason."* Quillette. https://quillette.com/2018/01/13/freedom-expression-flight-reason/

leaves them feeling emotionally bereft.[8] So merely having a discussion is dangerous in the modern world where you're either "for us or against us." People are becoming almost singularly focused on "good behavior" and "bad behavior," and they want blood for those who stray too far into controversial territory. Points are scored and social prestige enhanced by attacking the enemy.[9] People don't examine the merits of an argument or thesis anymore. If a claim is made, there is no coextensive expectation that evidence be provided in support of that claim. The potency of their certainty is just the gateway drug to their dogma. They deem others contemptible if what they're saying challenges their world-view, regardless of any implicit veracity.

You could say it's human nature that when a number of people agree upon something, they coagulate into groups, big and small, which then exist in an echo chamber of their own singular rightness. It feels good to receive validation from those around them. There's this sense of belonging—of having found one's tribe. There is meaning in this maddening world.

But what we see around us is "confirmation bias on steroids"—people actively seeking to confirm what they already believe, while condemning contrary information and actively discrediting any opposing evidence out of hand. This sense of rightness is extrapolated outward towards "hostile" unbelievers who then must be converted or defeated so that there remains no chance of *their* perverted perspectives becoming pervasive.

~

Coming from a tradition of progressive politics, I've been shocked at how it has evolved in recent times. Declaring themselves "woke," the Left has moved almost entirely towards authoritarian, Stalinist-type

8 An example:
YouTube channel, Gary Orsum (January 1, 2021). *"Tim Pool Destroys Low Information Voter Hunter Avallone."* https://www.youtube.com/watch?v=_TiSP5E-o9Y. Note: whether someone is on the left or the right or neither, insidious narratives come from all angles.

9 Social psychologist, Amy Cuddy (forthcoming 2021). *"Bullies, Bystanders, and Bravehearts."*

politics. Unlike other political positions which also seek to influence the thoughts and opinions of others, the identitarian Left (commonly called "social justice warriors") wear the clothes of compassion and consideration while actively hounding and demonizing (and worse) anyone who raises even the mildest objection to seeing the world through their filter of "minority oppression." As a conscious male, this is important to be aware of because their allure is appealing to the naive and good-hearted. Who doesn't want to see a world more tolerant, just, and inclusive? Yet they use the tactics of bullying, assaulting, and othering anyone they deem contemptuous—liberally throwing around slurs, like misogynist, Nazi or racist, full of moral outrage and indignation. "Only a woman can talk about women's issues, only a black man can talk about racism, only a Muslim can talk about Islam!" Because how could a privileged, middle-aged, white man have any conception of their lived experiences and offer a perspective—"it's because of *his* ilk that we find ourselves here!" The novel, *Animal Farm,*[10] could not have been more prescient.

Most everyone has political position and yours can be whatever you want it to be. We do best as a society when we listen, agree or disagree, and move forward with good ideas not because they emerge from a tribal alliance but because they are as correct as can be determined.

How disagreement is interpreted and managed between individuals and groups is virtually at rock bottom. In a more enlightened social environment, there would be more tolerance for disagreement. We would come to recognize that, despite our differences, there exists common ground between parties. And we would use that common ground as a basis for constructing a world where we could coexist in relative harmony. Differences don't prevent us from being compassionate, friendly, and respectful towards each other. By treating others as human beings, worthy of respect and dignity, we create less stress, more connection, and greater cohesion as a species.

10 George Orwell (1996) *"Animal Farm."* Signet.

~

People love to rest within their self-satisfied moral architecture and view the world in absolutes of rightness and wrongness. "Culture is not your friend," the late Terence McKenna once said, because culture reflects the dominant proscriptions of others. These proscriptions rarely have your best interests at heart for your full flourishing as a human being. So as a conscious man, it's a good idea to ask yourself what morals, perspectives, narratives, ideas, and universal views have you embodied unconsciously? What was your parents' messaging? Your peer group's? Your school's? Your religious/spiritual teachers'? Your newsfeed? How much have you examined and kept, discarded, or refined?

An honorable scientist or rational thinker will change his mind on a dime, if given persuasive data. Reason and logic are excellent tools for confronting the conditioned ego. In the face of good, solid evidence, and if the rational mind is wearing the pants, the ego has no footing—delusion falls away.

Subjective reality is a perception of reality that is uniquely and solely based on an individual's subjective perspective. Reaching for an understanding of objective reality, however, requires extending one's perspective and perception wide enough to synthesize other coherent subjective realities.

To question our own perspectives must mean that we have to come face to face with either our inner resistance or that of others—of perceiving ourselves, or having others perceive us, as being wrong, bad, or shameful. We hold tight to these patternings because we're trying to avoid condemnation, both self-directed and from others, and the consequences that might follow. Without consciously intervening in the process ourselves, we would otherwise unawarely pass on unhelpful judgments to those around us, closing down more minds and hearts. The quest is for freedom by breaking outside of rigid personal subjective realities and the thought-constraints that shackle the mind.

Modern Masculinity for the Conscious Man

Part One

Being a Man

There are many ways of being a man;
mine is to express what is deepest in my heart.[11]

– E.M. FORSTER

11 E.M. Forster (1965). *"A Passage to India."* Mariner Books

1 Getting a Handle on Masculinity

We are in a relationship with life. We are in a relationship with ourselves, with others, with the planet, and with our beliefs, values, and concepts. And ultimately, we are in a relationship with nothingness which gives us our perspective as living, sentient beings. For a relationship to exist, there has to be a relator and a relatee. In a universe based on duality, one opposite cannot exist without the other. We have a tension between separateness and togetherness. Masculinity doesn't exist without femininity. This is why its necessary to define men in the context of their opposite, women, and which is why the focus of this book is in large part concerned with that relationship. That's not to say that men are uniquely masculine nor women feminine.

First let's acknowledge that there are different kinds of men and that just because most men are not John Wayne, James Bond, or LL Cool J, doesn't mean that they are not "real men." Neither is being a man simply embodying exemplary masculine traits. We are all a divine blend of water and fire, earth and air, yin and yang. Contained within men is both a masculine and a feminine essence, or energy. Most men are more masculine. Some have an eclectic mix of masculine and feminine traits. And a few have a stronger feminine essence. Integrating one's feminine essence is as important to a conscious man as it is to live from his masculine.

What we call source, or God, or the Infinite, can be considered "uninterrupted energy." That which is created from source energy is therefore an example of "interrupted energy." All organized designs of interrupted energy can be translated into terms of yin and yang—and "men and women" are pretty cool manifestations of it. The concept of yin and yang is derived from Taoist philosophy.

A mutual attraction and repulsion causes constant change, yet the two opposing forces are also complimentary. These forces are not equal, in the sense of being identical. There is a balanced asymmetry. The beauty of the yin yang is how one side simultaneously penetrates and surrenders to the other, and how an aspect of its opposite is contained within (the small circles). In psychology, the anima is regarded as the feminine part of a man's nature, and the animus refers to the masculine part of a woman's nature. Both sides of the yin yang form a perfect union without being perfectly identical.

This is why there is no simple, five-minute advice about how men and women are, or could be, in relation to each other.

In the Tao Te Ching,[12] Laozi refers to the feminine as being the great Mother—the mysterious, receptive, passive force (usually represented by the black part of the symbol). The masculine (the white part) is considered the active force and is the more easily perceived and prominent. Men and women both possess yin and yang characteristics. Ideally, both feminine and masculine keep each other in check. When one becomes too dominant, the other will expand until it too becomes too dominant, and then the other side will once more expand. Each regulates the other in a kind of dynamic equilibrium.

Men and women have their own style of "meeting the world." Men draw upon certain elemental energies which inform them of their nature and have been doing so unconsciously across all cultures, for all time. Masculinity is a penetrative energy which is outwardly directed. It's a force which alters, develops, modifies, and recasts its environment, for

12 Laozi, 6th-century BC Chinese sage

good or bad. Its opposite, femininity, receives, surrenders, and flows with change, wisely or unwisely. But masculinity doesn't penetrate the world for its own sake—it does so in reference to the feminine. Men who live only for their own benefit, live only half a life. As satisfying as their avocation or passion might be, there are certain groups of men who have decided not to have women in their lives, either because they perceive women as being a malevolent force, or because they have been passed over by women numerous times (see *The Single Man,* chapter *The Divine Union).*

We live in an age where men have fewer "traditional" interests, mostly without being shamed for them as being "gay" or "girly," as in the past. "Be a man!" All men are men. Some men are shamed by both men and women for "not being a man," either for not comporting themselves as a man who exhibits typical/desirable masculine traits, or who "puts the pussy on the pedestal," or who carries beliefs and values which are at odds with others, or who either cannot or will not meet a woman's expectations, etc. We never hear the opposite, "Be a woman!" which suggests that manhood is not automatically granted just by virtue of having a penis.

~

What does it mean to be a man? We could break this down into several masculine archetypes, such as the traits and values consistent with being a brother, a son, a father, or a husband (or equivalent). An archetype is a mental model that represents the fundamental ideas of the thing it is describing. This book explores two simple masculine archetypes, Modern Man and the Divine Masculine. The book, *King, Warrior, Magician, Lover,*[13] uses four archetypal male energies to contend that, to be confident and purposeful, a man should work to embody these higher aspects. For the authors of the book, the falling out of fashion of rites of passage signaled a misstep for society, as boys were less able to successfully transition to manhood.

13 Robert Moore and Douglas Gillette (1991). *"King, Warrior, Magician, Lover."* HarperOne

Traditional rites of passage of indigenous peoples teach a boy how to remain functional despite being in enormous pain—where he might be facing possible death and must do so without complaint.[14] These rites may teach him how to dissociate and ignore his body (which, regrettably, is the root of trauma). They may also teach the boy to see his life as "disposable" in the service of others (see *Patriarchy*, chapter, *Feminist Myths and Narratives* and *Evolutionary Programming*, chapter, *Modern Men*).

Rites of passage were instigated almost exclusively by the male members of the tribe. They represented the end of the childhood phase and start of the adult phase. The boy-turned-man realizes that he is his own protector and that he is now residing in a power he had not previously manifested. When he returns to the mother, he is no longer looking to her for nourishment or survival. He then realizes that he has the capacity to protect her. The boy in him has died and the man arisen. He then begins to listen to his own inner authority rather than hers. He is his own man. Joseph Campbell talks about the different cultures regarding rites of passage and what the common thread is—what he called the monomyth.[15] "A hero ventures forth from the world of common day into a region of supernatural wonder: fabulous forces are there encountered and a decisive victory is won: the hero comes back from this mysterious adventure with the power to bestow boons on his fellow man." Men love challenges and adventures which "test their manhood." So it could be argued that any challenge or adventure, which has a level of risk, is also a rite of passage, like hiking the Appalachian trail or taking a beat-up aluminum canoe solo down the Allagash River.

What are the persisting values that one would typically describe as deriving from men? How persistent would they be—over hundreds of years, thousands, tens of thousands? How has it changed? What might it change into?

An ideal alpha male might be described as being a conqueror, having

---

14 Jim H. "*5 Rites of Passage From Around The World.*" *Historic Mysteries.* https://www.historic-mysteries.com/disturbing-rites-of-passage/

15 Joseph Campbell (1991). "*The Power of Myth.*" Anchor.

regular and abundant sex with women, having notoriety/renown, commanding leadership and the respect from followers, competing with and dominating other men, expressing his frustration through anger rather than tears, etc. There's certainly an attachment to this archetype as reflecting an essential and aspirational aspect of maleness but I would suggest that it is ego-driven rather than derived from our true nature. It's true that we can see examples of these traits having been persistent over a long period of time (thousands of years) but, as I will describe later, the last few thousand years of humankind's progress have been founded on principles which are antithetical to our true nature and which have therefore produced traits and behaviors which are largely inconsistent with true masculinity. To make our way back to our true nature, our journey must be a conscious one that reveals to ourselves everything that we have become that we are not.

~

As a man, it's helpful to take an ideal male quality and use that as a signpost in his own life. He uses himself as the starting point.

There are many traits considered to derive from the yang, including industriousness, strength, courage, competitiveness, confidence, and decisiveness.

Take the trait of leadership—a man starts by leading himself. By not accepting the stories others write for him nor treading in the footprints of those he might seek to emulate, but crafting his own journey—taking control of his script, and believing in the idea of his own potential. He makes a practice of putting himself in circumstances where he needs to take control and make decisions, even if it directly affects no one but himself. Circumstances where he has the choice to give up or give in, and out of that develops the fortitude to continue. He may or may not then become a leader of others, but if he does, he'll then have the wherewithal to do so competently.

Discipline is another admirable masculine trait. Not to become rigidly disciplined, but to apply it to his life in a way that adds value and makes sense.

When a man is experiencing confusion and chaos, this might mean taking the time to fully process the situation, getting back up and getting back going, and executing a plan to get him from A to B. It is a way of applying masculine linearity along with strength of heart.

Finally, a man's spirit of independence is reflected in how his life is self-chosen. His "autonomy" is an attribute of a person who engages with the world as an active, reasoning, and conscious individual.[16] He is a law unto himself, hopefully without being a shithead.

For more on this, see the chapter, *The Divine Masculine.*

16 The etymology of this word: autos (self) and nomos (rule of law) conveys the meaning of self-rule. Frank Furedi (2011). *"On Tolerance: A Defence of Moral Independence."* Continuum.

2 The Biological/Socializational Narrative

Masculinity exists under two narratives—a biological narrative and a socializational narrative. We are born boys but must claim manhood. Masculinity is generally in a constant pursuit and defense of manhood. Girls do not have the same journey. When they mature, they automatically become women, without any need for self-justification or societal approval (although they face other pressures). In our society, a man has an expectation to constantly defend and assert his manhood, by subtle means (like how he holds himself) or overt means (like fighting for his honor or to defend those he loves).[17] This means that there is something profoundly impermanent about the male identity since it can be lost if he fails to live up to certain expectations. Of course, how much importance individual men place upon their sense of manhood varies. Some men bridle if their masculinity is questioned, others give it little consideration. In societies which provided a rite of passage to boys, expectations of manhood were largely predetermined. Nowadays, boys are left to figure it out themselves. On the one hand they can choose their own path but on the other they are often left with a sense of being adrift at sea, especially if they grew up

17 Growing up in the 70s/80s, my peers expressed mild homophobia in order to "demonstrate" their heterosexuality, and hence manhood.

either without a father in the house or one who provided little positive modeling. This can often produce aberrant behavior.

Modern boys are not mentored into adult life. As a result they usually go with whatever the current zeitgeist is. For Baby Boomers, it was have 2.4 kids with a good-looking woman who also shared an interest in his pastimes and to make and spend as much money as possible on material stuff. Nowadays, the good-paying jobs have all but evaporated, student debt hangs like a millstone around younger men's necks, and internet porn offers vicarious sex with whatever size, shape, or color they're into without the need for figuring out how to navigate the dating scene, relationships, and female psychology. They are not taught how to connect with a woman and her relationship issues while holding firm to their boundaries, without being defensive or offensive. They're also not taught when, how, and why they should get out of a poor relationship, and what one of those looks like. What a bad relationship looks like includes relational aggression in the form of emasculating communication, emotional blackmail, passive aggression, adult tantrums, and domestic violence.[18]

Having a respected mentor, father, or father-figure is an essential element of personal growth for the young man. That older man's mark of approval (or disapproval) for his behavior is the trellis that the young vine will climb. It is this early interaction with the respected elder that will help the young man develop his own code of honor (see *Code of Honor*, chapter, *The Divine Masculine*).

18 It's generally accepted that men are far and away the main perpetrators of domestic violence against women. In fact, approximately 1 in 7 adult men report having experienced severe physical violence from an intimate partner in their lifetime, compared to 1 in 4 women. And given the stigma associated with men being physically abused by a woman, the rate is probably quite higher. CDC's National Intimate Partner and Sexual Violence Survey (NISVS). 2018.

If someone tried to take control of your body and make you a slave, you would fight for freedom. Yet how easily you hand over your mind to anyone who insults you. When you dwell on their words and let them dominate your thoughts, you make them your master.[19]

— EPICTETUS

3 What does being a Conscious Man mean?

There are at least two major types of consciousness. One is relative consciousness (the standard type of ego consciousness or rational consciousness). The other type is unity consciousness—which has been the subject of attention from some of the world's greatest contemplative traditions, meditators, psychonauts, and spiritual explorers. My intent here is to predominantly consider the first (although the second interests me greatly and I'll say a little about it in my conclusion).

To take Epictetus's quotation further, we hand over our minds not only to those who insult us but also to those who charm us, beguile us, trick us, promise us, threaten us, or lead us. Even though we can experience life consciously, it seems we are largely predisposed to certain scripts, internal and external, which favor a state of unconscious thought and behavior. It has value as a survival mechanism where being part of the herd confers a degree of safety and protection.

19 Epictetus (2017). "*The Manual: A Philosopher's Guide to Life.*" Ancient Renewal.

~

Being unconscious is to lack free will—which is to be operating from a place of automation. From day one, we are programmed by our society, our culture. The impenetrable morass of entrenched narratives, beliefs, and reactive patterns attempts to conceal and cloud the innate clarity of our awareness.

Our society places an excessive privilege on external values—social status, wealth, power, beauty, possessions, etc. Those who are unconscious are individuals who have not questioned their programming to any great extent, and whose lives are strongly colored by those external values. The Mass Man, a term coined by Carl Jung,[20] is someone who typically experiences no force strong enough to challenge his preconceived reality—who receives his instructions from "authority" (which itself can take many forms) and automatically complies, without thought to the implications of his actions. His pathological obedience serves as a substitute for the difficult work of individuation and the building of character. The only principles by which he can judge his behavior is in answer to the question, "How should I comply?" He is the stormtrooper, the stickler for the rules, the low ranking official, the company man, the nice guy, the drone. He receives the ideological narrative *du jour* because he is defined primarily by what he is not. He is the walking dead (see *The Police and National Guard*, chapter, *Why You are a Slave*).

Having free will is to be capable of having one's own thoughts, rather than thoughts which have been internalized from prior conditioning by others. This is why we want to start an internal investigation. We need to get in touch with the *process* of our thinking and find ways to catch ourselves buying into falsities. Knowledge truly *is* power if we are committed to moving more towards free will and away from unconscious impulses. We want to investigate our belief systems, our limiting ideas about ourselves, and our thoughts. There are helpful questions to assist us

20 Carl Jung (February 7, 2006). *"The Undiscovered Self: The Dilemma of the Individual in Modern Society."* Berkley; Edition Unstated.

in this respect. Am I thriving as a result of entertaining my values, beliefs, expectations, and moral architecture? Just because I'm having a thought, what makes it my own? How many of my thoughts have been implanted or programmed into my head? Or have I fallen in love with an idea and adopted it for its desirability, rather than its truthfulness? My friend, Larry, loves his bumper sticker, "Don't believe everything you think."

This knowledge offers extraordinary benefits to those who can acknowledge, accept, and master their "wiring" to create a richer and more engaged experience of life. My hope is that by getting a handle on our unconscious thoughts and neurological patternings, our ego stages, and perhaps even tweaking some of the default-mode networks given to us by mother nature, we can become more effective and efficient in engaging with the world around us; with our relationships, and with ourselves. When our thoughts are generated by an alignment with our true nature, they are original and essential. Paired with self-awareness and free will, true nature emerges with an immediacy that is unaffected by our conditioned history. This can happen in a flow state, during meditation when the mind stops chattering, during a survival situation which demands focused attention, in a silent and deep state of intimacy with nature or the moans of our lover. When applied at the collective level, we make the world a better place by being the best version of ourselves and holding space for others to realize their own true nature.

Everyone views reality through a perceptual lens, creating a unique and personal point of view. Humans are a morally-complex bunch of beings. There's a little good in the worst of us and a little evil in the best of us. Shadow and light. "...the line separating good and evil passes... right through every human heart. And even in the best of all hearts, there remains...an unuprooted corner of evil."[21]

Even if the chances of the majority of humans rising above their core programming is close to zero, especially when there exist nefarious entities which hijack that programming for their own ends,[22] there is value in

---

21 Aleksandr Solzhenitsyn (2002). *"The Gulag Archipelago."* Vintage Uk.

22 Robert Cialdini (2006). *"Influence: The Psychology of Persuasion."* Harper Business; Revised edition. His book describes how humans have evolved behavioral shortcuts which businesses can manipulate.

achieving a moral victory over a physical one. If you believe that there are forces for "good," as well as forces for "evil," (however you want to interpret that word), then striving towards a more integrated human condition for oneself (and collectively) not only reveals opportunities to choose wisely one's fate, but also a responsibility to do so.

~

With only a small range of experiences and information, only a limited level of awareness can be achieved. When we ignore what's in front of us, blinded by the rigid narratives in our minds, we're moving through this life on automatic pilot, tragically failing to listen and interact with the world around us as it really is. However, with a broad range of experiences and information, an expanded level of awareness is possible. The more aware we are, the more our consciousness increases. The more things make sense to us, the better decisions we make. The more aligned we are with "what is," the less delusional or confused we become. When we see things as they really are, we become disillusioned. We become free from illusion—dis-illusioned. This is a good thing—and also it doesn't always feel very good.

For the conscious man, the unconscious is his playground. He becomes curious about stuff previously unknown to him which one day emerges from the unconscious soup. "Triggers," or emotional reactions, offer him the opportunity to become a private investigator—a P.I. of his own experience. An experience of an angry feeling, say, is then enjoyable because it offers him the chance to do good work by investigating its primal origins and pathways to the present-day catalyzing event. He realizes something true about his nature, or something that was obstructing him from seeing it. Upon "ego integration," his ego is not discarded but fully strengthened. He becomes "autonomous" through having integrated his shadow aspects and emotional states (called, ego death) and ultimately becomes an emotional master (without being emotionless).

He asks himself about the processes that influence his sense-making.

"How does my mind actually work? By what processes do I form beliefs, make decisions, reason, and think?[23] What *is* the most optimal way to reason and think (or a way to make good-enough decisions quickly)? How literate am I in recognizing how cognitive biases might color my perception?"

There may have been times when a conscious man has held to a particular thought, value, or idea in his life with a passionate certainty. And was then stunned at finding himself wrong. Sometimes 180 degrees wrong. When presented with new information, he changed his mind. Even better was to ask himself why he was so certain to begin with? Down which rabbit hole did he go to reach such erroneous conclusions? He then might begin a self-authoring process where the internal mechanisms which were initially faulty and led him astray can then be reprogrammed or removed.

Certainly, for a conscious man, what he believes at the age of 25 will probably be modified by the time he reaches 50. And this is to be celebrated. Those ideas and beliefs that he held as a younger man seemed so obvious and certain at the time and behind which he stood passionately.[24] A strong indicator of whether or not a man has been seized by a particular narrative is if he is outraged, offended, or disgusted by "the other side." He has absolute certainty that he is right and they are wrong. The most likely scenario is that he is a product not of his own thinking, but has been hijacked by someone else's agenda.

So attachment to a particular viewpoint, idea, or mental map is unwise. Better to hold a particular "truth" and then try to continuously challenge and change it with better information.[25] These would be "proto-truths."[26] Proto-truths are the best working model of reality, currently available, without which forward progress would not be optimal or even possible.

---

23 These might include a basic understanding of game theory, decision theory, or deductive logic.

24 It's highly unlikely that we can can name a single belief that we currently hold which we know to be wrong (unless by an act of cognitive dissonance).

25 Seek out commentators, guides, teachers, etc who approach their work earnestly and with great conscientiousness and clarity yet come from conflicting perspectives. Notice where they agree and disagree. Then explore the differences. The result is to be the owner of a mind that can embrace nuanced thought.

26 Edward de Bono (1977). "*The Happiness Purpose.*" Random House UK.

They allow us to not so easily dismiss other people's ideas. Most of the time, we are slightly wrong and they are slightly wrong—we just have to make sense of the temporary confusion, await new information, or embrace a paradox. The key is to neither accept nor reject someone's entire train of thought but to look for partial truths across many different propositions, from the far left to the far right, the far ups to the far downs.

~

Many consider that it is the brain itself that generates consciousness. The mechanisms by which it does so are still largely a mystery, even given our advances in neurology. Our conscious experience at every moment, and all of the content that comprises that experience, is a result of brain processing. Different brains process that information differently. In fact, of the 7.8 billion human brains on planet Earth, no two see the world identically. "Never do we find two eggs or two leaves or two blades of grass in a garden that are perfectly similar. And thus, perfect similarity is found only in incomplete and abstract notions."[27] You would think that at least a few might—especially since seeing reality as it really is would prove more helpful the more accurately it is perceived. As much as my ego would like it to be the case, there is not one reader of this book who would agree with every argument I put forth.

The brain offers a view of reality based on our experience of being. The physical and social environments, as well as the way we constructed models of understanding earlier in life, crucially interact to mold our perception of reality. The home environment, and society more broadly, will shape the mind of man as he matures. Cultures and societies morph and change but are largely maintained by this process. As one generation passes the baton to the next, belief systems and behavioral norms are either maintained or challenged by the march of time.

It's useful to imagine what our true natures might be, where we are

27 Gottfried Wilhelm Leibniz (1989). Primary Truths—"*Leibniz: Philosophical Essays.*" Hackett Publishing Company; 1st edition.

free of societal conditionings; free of those drives which are not essential to our well-being. How can we recognize the unconscious aspects of our nature in our behavior?

If you ask yourself, "Why do I say this?" or "Why do I do this?" or "Why do I think this?" and the answer is "I don't know," then that indicates a level of unconsciousness in that particular area. A conscious man would be able to (or mostly be able to) answer those questions with some depth and clarity. He'd also be curious about any deficits he became aware of and correct himself until resolved to a fuller sense of knowing. There's no shame in answering "I don't know." If any shame exists, it is in choosing to remain ignorant where an opportunity to learn exists. One's own ignorance is cause for celebration, as an opportunity for growth! This is an opportunity to find out why he's been feeling, thinking, behaving, and acting in an unconscious way. Being conscious, a man recognizes and realizes who he really is.

~

There exists within us an intrinsic aspect, just as the image of an oak tree is inherent in the acorn. We start out in life on the path to realizing what is encoded in our beingness. This is our true nature. From our first steps, we are trained to ignore and repress difficult truths until we find them harder and harder to see at all. As a conscious man, you've been transcending your unconsciousness, biases, and ignorance. You've been taking apart your psyche piece by piece, determining what is conditioned by others and by your own belief/value systems, and coming into alignment with your own true nature. We take our story into our own hands and become speakers from the heart. And in an ongoing sense, we must stand guard at the door of our minds.

The world can place pressures on the way we might live our lives. Every time we step outside the front door, we are are being judged and evaluated by people who have been programmed and conditioned to regard others in a certain light and expect certain behaviors and "duties." There is an unspoken expectation of conformity which can either be helpful (like not urinating in the grocery aisle) or unhelpful (like being ridiculed for wearing/not wearing a face covering in the time of a pandemic). But we also put pressure on ourselves. We place so much of our identities on collective ideas of labels and limits—what it means to be a certain person—and become afraid to step into our authentic nature.

When you become conscious, one of the first things that comes to your realization is why you remained unconscious up until now. Being conscious means that you have to be present with your condition; how you are feeling; what beliefs and meanings you've been carrying; what thoughts are there and even what thoughts are not.[28] This can frequently leave one feeling vulnerable and adrift.

The choice for conscious men is to commit to the path of self-awareness above all. Our projections, fears, our own limiting thoughts, would otherwise influence our capacity to bring in useful information from the world around us. Messages that are received by us are largely colored and distorted because they are coming through our own subjective perceptual reality. So the more aware of our own perceptual reality we are, and the more we have broken outside of it and can actually see things as they really are, the better of a channel for these energies we will be. By challenging and stretching our perspectives, no matter how uncomfortable they may be, the less likely misinterpretation of any kind will occur.

~

Being conscious is a step on the path to self-actualization. In a sense, I'm intentionally conflating actual consciousness with complex thought, as a device. You can be conscious but not fully-realized. According to Swiss psychologist, Carl Jung, the ultimate self-realization is the integration of the unconscious into the conscious. "Until you make the unconscious conscious, it will direct your life and you will call it fate." A self-actualized

28 Fortuitously, I don't have an inner critic. It took me quite a while to realize I didn't have certain patterns of self-destructive thinking and was baffled that others did.

man, ideally-speaking, is someone who has achieved all he can by using all of his powers and potentialities—to fulfill himself according to his own internal design, to form himself as his own architect, and represent his work. Being conscious requires a certain degree of introspection and contemplation in order to create awareness and to see things as they really are, both within and without. The superficial details of life are observed without becoming attached to them.

How do we become conscious as to our essential, true nature? Doing our inner work, or spiritual work, is essential to finding our true sovereignty and then living according to our own particular design. Once we start to "unbelieve" our conditioning and we unlearn our limitations, we discover unlocked powers waiting for us. We form self-knowledge from within, by walking the walk. We end up choosing a perspective which truly serves us and choosing that perspective with our conscious free will. Not that this is without pain. "It takes courage to endure the sharp pains of self-discovery, rather than choose to take the dull pain of unconsciousness that would last the rest of our lives."[29]

Our work means that we need to awaken inside of, and in spite of, the environments in which we are enmeshed—any environment that has an impact on our lives—the political environment, spiritual environment, economic environment, social environment, even the environment environment! It might be easier to sequester oneself in a cave, yet for almost everyone this is neither desirable nor possible. The process of developing the mind as a conscious witness to one's own interiority, that of others, and to the external world, is essential. To be free of limitations/delusions—the things that we believe ourselves to be, the things we are limited to, or to those things we believe we are limited in discovering or feeling…a conscious man has to learn from life's lessons.

---

29 Marianne Williamson (1996). *"A Return to Love: Reflections on the Principles of 'A Course in Miracles.'"* HarperOne; Reissue edition.

I suppose the woman wants to live her own life; and the man wants to live his; and each tries to drag the other on to the wrong track. One wants to go north and the other south; and the result is that both have to go east, though they both hate the east wind.[30]

— HENRY HIGGINS

4 The Differences between Male and Female "Operating Systems"

In recent times, sex differences in thinking abilities were thought to be due to socialization practices and that the belief that there were fundamental cognitive differences between the sexes was due to mistakes in prior research, bias, and prejudice. Yet gender differences are not exclusively derived from social or cultural norms—men and women do indeed run on different operating systems, like Macs and PCs. To the casual observer they look pretty similar in terms of their functionality. But "beneath the hood," there are key differences. Physical dimorphism between men and women is plainly obvious (we divide most sporting activities based on the premise that men would otherwise largely dominate a particular field). Behavioral dimorphism is less obvious but nevertheless has a body of evidence behind it.

Problems arise when men and women relate to each other as if talking

30 George Bernard Shaw (2005). "Pygmalion." Simon & Schuster.

to someone of their own sex. In terms of how the sexes process information, men think a woman is just a curvy type of man, and women think a man is just a hairy type of woman. But we input, process, and deliver information differently. Both female and male intelligences are desirable but conflict can arise from differently aligned interpretations of reality. Ultimately, this does not mean that the sexes shouldn't be given equal opportunity to demonstrate their abilities in areas traditionally favored by their opposite. Over the last few decades, there has been a significant equalization of sex roles in society, and this has produced a degree of liberation for both sexes. Men can make great preschool teachers (I used to be one!) and women can make great physicists. But this is unusual. Recognizing and accepting the differences between the two could mean that both could be comfortable, accepting that one sex is more likely to perform better in some circumstances and not others, without anything being written in stone. Seeing this as a cause for celebration would cut out much of the heartache, misunderstandings, and acrimony between the two. But because of this equalization in roles, we seem to be under the impression that men and women are basically the same. Yet, objectively speaking, there is clearly a difference in how men and women perform and behave based in large part on their respective biologies and psychologies.

Let's take a look at the objective fact that men have historically outperformed women across many different terrains of achievement. Now why is this and why does it hurt so much to make mention of it? It hurts me to bring it up because I recognize that women, like men, need to be validated—to feel that their contributions have merit. My sense of fairness is affronted because I value women as much as I do men and I would much prefer the historical record to show greater equality in this regard. Generally speaking, I don't think it's particularly helpful to highlight male versus female achievement. But women have had, conservatively, fifty years to redress this imbalance and if the differences were societal, you'd expect the performance distributions to look more similar today because attitudes and access to education have changed. Yet with all the attention paid to equalizing educational opportunities,[31] men still display a wider range of intellectual ability. Indeed, men are likely to be more smart *and* more stupid than women. The intelligent ones make history and the less intelligent are invisible (men predominate the bottom of the socioeconomic ladder). Nobels and dumbbells. Feminists have not demonstrated any interest in this distinction; they have merely concerned themselves with the lack of female presence in the upper echelons of society. By all appearances, they are envious of apex males—because those at the bottom are either invisible or contemptuous, and feminists are not pushing for parity with them. Men, for the most part, care about producing results. And whoever is going to produce those results is who they want on the team. Or whoever can empower others on the team to produce results, we want *them* on the team—man or woman.

The brain has evolved different sorts of intelligence in men and women. Yet it's inevitably hard to parse out what is biological and social because intelligence[32] reflects what one's field of interest is and how intensely studied it is. In general, men are drawn towards what they are good at, what they have access to, and what will earn them money and status. Whilst women are drawn to what they are good at, what they have access to, lifestyle choices, and work which brings them into contact with people where communication skills are prized. The confusion lies in what is socially conditioned and what is not. The neuroscience of sex differences suggests that there are neural circuits which regulate certain innate behaviors. In utero, our brains are marinaded in either testosterone or estrogen which predisposes men and women to specific behavioral traits.

For men, their brains are predisposed to systematic thinking, deductive functioning/ logical analysis, working memory, and spacial awareness. They

31 Parity was reached in 1980, when as many women as men were attending college or university in the United States.

32 "In general, men have approximately 6.5 times the amount of grey matter related to general intelligence than women, and women have nearly 10 times the amount of white matter related to intelligence than men. Grey matter represents information processing centers in the brain, and white matter represents the networking of—or connections between—these processing centers." Richard Haier (et al.), Professor Emeritus, UC Irvine (March 2005), *"NeuroImage Volume 25, Issue 1."* Pages 320-327.

are more predisposed to focusing on "things." A great example of this is the world of competitive chess. There are no male-only tournaments, only mixed or female-only. In fact, women can expect to earn proportionately more prize money by sticking to female-only tournaments than they could in mixed tournaments. And in world rankings, the top female player is currently ranked 84th, overall.

Female brains are better-suited to multitasking, verbal ability, noticing details (including subtle emotional cues), organizing, recalling information from long-term memory, intuition, and emotional thinking/nurturing. They are also more predisposed to empathy, loving, and social connections. Her brain is more holistic; his is more specialized.

Both men and women are capable of embracing traits of their opposite but, for the most part, simply prefer to operate from their own paradigm. For example, females are generally less interested in leadership than males but many have excelled in other areas (Maria Montessori,[33] being a personal favorite).

Men and women also communicate with each other using "different languages" in relationships but because we are speaking in English we think the other person knows what we mean. For example, approval and disapproval are commonly used to try to control a man's behavior. It rarely works—the man just feels judged. He is not susceptible to approval and disapproval in the way that women and girls are. Being a "good girl" or conducting herself in a socially acceptable way in accordance with what others think is of greater importance to her. "Behaving" means less to a man than it does to a woman.

33 Maria Tecla Artemisia Montessori was an Italian physician and educator best known for the philosophy of education that bears her name, and her writing on scientific pedagogy.

Part Two

Feminist Myths and Narratives

You can resolve to live your life with integrity. Let your credo be this: Let the lie come into the world, let it even triumph. But not through me.

— ALEXANDR SOLZHENITSYN

5 Why Focus on Feminism?

There has historically been an antagonistic relationship between men and women that's often been called "the battle of the sexes." The argument has been that, for millennia, women have always been on the losing side. Yet over the past 50-60 years, there has been a war where only one side has shown up. Women have been attacking men far more vociferously and brutally, to the detriment of men rather than to the service of equality. Yet it is only the wrongs that men do that are front and center in our collective consciousness. There is a wall of vitriol directed at men which is allowed and celebrated.

Feminism has two distinct facets. The first is a set of claims about empirical facts (the reality of male-female relations). The other is a set of claims about values (how those relations should be organized). The argument is that women have been treated differently to men, historically, in a way that has systematically disadvantaged them. And, in spite of the positive changes women have experienced in recent times (the right to vote, the right to own and pass on property, access to birth control, the right to occupy traditionally male jobs, a more level playing field in business, politics, and domestic life, etc), that they remain significantly disadvantaged. Indeed, in spite of these barriers having been removed and advancements made, they contest that there remain a variety of social forces which are still discriminatory.

I was a feminist for 30 years. I was happy to give strong support for women's equality—one in a long line of male voices dating back to even before John Stuart Mill.[34] Appealing to my innate sense of fair play regarding perceived injustices suffered by women, as I was told there were, I was seduced by feminist ideology. I'm now highly critical of the movement. There came a time when I felt conned by feminism which presented injustices which were simply and factually false. It also highlighted desirable rights for women but singularly failed to talk about responsibility and how women had contributed to social inequality and what, if any, obligations they had to society and to men. I view feminism harshly but remain pro-woman. The theme often is, "if you're against feminism you must be against women and their struggles for equality." I am for women. And I am for men—for both sexes realizing their full potential as human beings. But I also see key differences in men's and women's "operating systems" so the concept of equality has to embrace these differences for the full flourishing of each to emerge. It has to be nuanced.

I am choosing to focus on feminism for the simple reason that most of the issues facing men these days stem from feminist ideology and its real-world implications. Feminism masterfully passes itself off as a social good in a way that makes invisible and insidious the harms it does. It can do so because, as a society, there is an assumption that femininity (and, by extension, women) is inherently full of goodness and beauty—indicating a presumed moral superiority. By contrast, men are considered inherently problematic (if not toxic) and must be tamed and subdued so as to reverse past transgressions, and to then step off the plate.

A few such issues men face include a lack of support if you're a victim of domestic violence, denial of employment or promotion owing to positive discrimination policies, punitive settlements in divorce courts, and denial of access to children by the family courts. Consciousness involves seeing things as they really are and the feminist movement adversely

34 John Stuart Mill (1806-1873). Male feminist and philosopher. In 1866, he became the first Member of Parliament to call for women being given the right to vote.

affects men's life circumstances, which is why it's important to address this at the outset. I no longer want to silently acquiesce to a culture where I, and most people, submit to lies about systemic female victimization and male privilege.

Feminist ideology has been seeping into every aspect of life, from news media, to social media, to politics, to education, to Hollywood, etc. Its foundation is fundamentally anti-male, defining men down to their lowest common denominator, and is antithetical to the full and natural expression of healthy masculinity. There exists a pressure to conform to its demands and a social conditioning expected of men, which men need to guard against in order to exist in their true nature.

~

Women who consider themselves feminists are not necessarily malicious—just uninformed. Or more accurately, misinformed (as opposed to feminism itself which is both malicious and wantonly misguided in so many respects). On one end of the spectrum are what might be called "equity feminists," who advance the political and social notion that both men and women be treated as equals.[35] This is what most people think of when they hear the term, "feminism." Most women who are fair-minded, and think of themselves as feminists, are equity feminists. Essentially, they are coffee house feminists who don't feel particularly oppressed. These feminists would probably not place a lot of resistance at the suggestion that they are, rather, an "equalist" or a humanist, or an egalitarian (instead of simply a positive alignment to the feminine and a less positive alignment to the masculine). They do tend to believe that feminism "owns" the concept of equality and therefore if someone is an anti-feminist, they must be against female equality and must be suspected of malintent towards women. At the other end of the spectrum are "gender feminists" or "radical

35 Equity feminist, Christina Hoff Sommers, published a the book, "Who Stole Feminism?" (Simon & Schuster, 1994) which claimed feminist activists and authors were employing bogus facts and what she called "myth-information" in charging that women in western culture as being brutally oppressed.

feminists," who happen to be the main drivers of the movement in the 21st century, so-called third (and fourth) wave feminists. They have a set of scholarly theories and philosophies which are harmful to the fabric of a harmonious society, sometimes willfully and knowingly so.

A third type of feminist operates in the shady area between coffee house feminists and activist feminists. They are the judicial feminists (judges, lawyers, and law professors) who have the generally uncritical and unconscious support of coffee house feminists, and who have rather closer ties with radical/activist feminists. They litigate change as social engineering by targeting key institutions in the system to favor/advantage women over men. Where they cannot get the law changed, they change the way existing law is interpreted.

~

First-wave feminism fought for women's right to vote. Second-wave feminism fought for sexual/reproductive rights, workplace and home life equality. Third-wave feminism focuses intensively on, what most people would consider, trivial or mild examples of bias or sexist behavior (mansplaining,[36] manspreading, manterrupting, micro-aggressions, mildly blue jokes, mild objectification, air conditioning favoring men's biology, etc). They spend their energy trying to determine how women are victims in every minute aspect of life—a form of catastrophizing where even the smallest perceived slight is blown out of proportion to its impact. They also embrace "intersectionality" which views certain "oppressed" minorities as allies to receive uncritical and unconditional support.[37] They are aggressively critical of "The Patriarchy," a concept which I will later deconstruct.

In social institutions, judicial feminists have changed public policy to unfairly favor women over men, simply because they declare themselves

36 When feminists use the term "mansplaining," they are basically telling men to shut up.

37 In Rotherham, UK, feminists remained silent in the name of multiculturalism as, for more than a decade, gangs of Muslim men targeted 1400 children for sexual abuse, http://www.answeringmuslims.com/2014/08/1400-children-sexually-exploited-in.html

"oppressed" in some way (affirmative action hiring, female-only scholarships, explicit attempts at female-only hiring, female-only workshops and classes, family law, college campus tribunals, etc). I will go on to demonstrate how this is untrue.

Third wave feminism plays into the irrational, dysfunctional, and disordered psychology of modern women who have grown up in an irrational, dysfunctional, and disordered world. These are women (plus their white-knight male allies, as such was I)[38] who irrationally believe themselves to have been harmed by a supposedly patriarchal society intent on their subjugation. Their behavior is to shame and demand, absent of any self-reflection.

Their preferred means of propaganda is by phrases, slogans, and memes, such as #Malegaze, #RapeCulture, #TimesUp, #BelieveAllWomen, #MaleViolence, which coffee house feminists can absorb without putting too much thought into their veracity.

Male feminists are targeted with #HeForShe. They, and other progressives, hear the siren song of feminist messaging and want to help create a world free of aggressions and oppressions against women. Their blind nobility only serves to further enslave them to an agenda of special treatment for women and, ultimately, female supremacy. I woke up to this fact and I would urge other male feminists to do likewise. Good men have always provided strong voices for women's equality—it's time they become strong voices for men's equality too.

Feminism is a slippery beast because it is essentially incoherent. It's definition shuffles this way and that depending on the desired ends. On the one hand, the politics of feminism claims that women are as equally able as men and should therefore have equal representation in all (desirable) aspects of life (for example, congress, corporate boards, etc). On

38 Those more active in the feminist movement could be considered "brownshirts;" I.e. thugs who enforce the feminist line on their erstwhile brothers. Feminist women confer a provisional status on male feminists with the underlying message being "You're not quite as bad as other men." Their very identities are controlled by feminist women. Given the opportunity of hearing and accepting a logical deconstruction of the feminist narrative and of challenging their own sense of being, these men must first contest with their primal drive of fear of rejection and the consequent loss of belonging, acceptance, admiration, and love.

the other hand, feminists insist that double standards should be applied which favor women, in the interests of justice and equality (for example, different rules for each gender when having a drunken sexual encounter on college campus). The reality is that feminists have little interest in gender equality.

~

Tribal mentality has been present in human social arrangements probably even before the emergence of modern human beings. This mentality reflected the shared interests and close personal experiences of its members and was by and large a good thing, both from a survival perspective and caring/bonding perspective. But in modern times, this band mentality can be used as a mechanism for unconscious control, playing on the more noble motivations of individuals who listen to their hearts but not their heads. Political and social movements habitually identify a common enemy. The more that feminists can claim that there is an enemy against women, and identify that enemy as men in general, or the Patriarchy, the more funding and support they receive and the more antagonism is generated. I'll go on to show how attacks on men and "male culture" are unwarranted.

Ultimately we need to value and respect each other as people rather than as labels, with the only form of discrimination being according to the content of our characters—our virtuous nature, or the lack of it. You might think that goes without saying but that's not how it's playing out. Feminism has never been a spiritual path after all—it is an ideological movement. It has simply paid lip service to a more just and fair world without being willing to question its own contribution to the global pain-body.

Our goal should be not to redefine masculinity, but to abolish it.[39]

— ROBERT JENSEN

6 Toxic Masculinity

When we hear the term, "masculinity," what comes to mind is no longer a positive image of men being the best they can be. In fact, the term itself seems to now be permanently coupled to the word, "toxic." We are constantly being bombarded in the media with tropes, depictions, and images of men which portray them as "toxic."

A lot of what passes for "toxic masculinity" is simply masculinity that certain women don't like. When guys are being guys, having fun with each other, being at ease with each other, being playful and not harming anyone, not all women are attracted to that energy. Men gather together because it is safe to be themselves without being policed by women. Yet some of those women, rather than walking away to do their own thing, decide to engage in a war of emasculation (see *Emasculation,* chapter, *Modern Women*).

The term "toxic masculinity" suggests something fundamentally wrong and bad about masculinity, and therefore men—that they are incorrigibly flawed. At best, it suggests that the qualities associated with being male are symptomatically harmful to society and to women in particular. It

39 Robert Jensen (2007). *"Getting Off: Pornography and the End of Masculinity."* South End Press

paints all men with a broad brush that they are born bad, and that they should strive to overcome their toxicity to join the human race, the idea being that they are subhuman. The term is a feminist-invented control mechanism to reduce men to passivity and powerlessness.

To quote Lisa Wade from Occidental University, "If we're going to survive both President Trump and the kind of people he has emboldened, we need to attack masculinity directly. I don't mean that we should recuperate masculinity — that is, press men to identify with a kinder, gentler version of it — I mean that we should reject the idea that men have a psychic need to distinguish themselves from women in order to feel good about themselves...The problem is not toxic masculinity; it's that masculinity is toxic."[40]

This sort of sludge is hateful, bigoted, and intellectually dishonest from someone who is deemed qualified to teach at college level.

When called out for such an excessive and repugnant stance, and in a typically manipulative way, other feminists defend their use of the term "toxic masculinity" as a benevolent way of saving men from their negative aspects, and that sadly the existence of violent, dominating, emotionally closed men is proof of men's toxicity. My argument is that such negative aspects are rooted in trauma, wounding, and absent or abusive parents—not masculinity (see chapter, *Wounding and Trauma*). In fact, rather than women needing to be protected from masculinity, it's more accurate to say that women need to be protected from the lack of masculinity. Men who hurt women have a lack of embodied masculinity which results in aberrant behaviors. What this also means is that feminists are endangering women by diminishing men and masculinity.

Any push-back against any invented toxic male trait is itself considered to be a glaring example of toxic masculinity. So all talk of "bad behavior," or simply behavior which doesn't have the feminist stamp of approval, can then be avoided and reduced to the simplistic assertion that

40 Lisa Wade, Associate Professor, Sociology, Occidental University (November 7, 2017). *"The Big Picture,"* public symposium, co-organized by Public Books and NYU's Institute for Public Knowledge.

men who do "bad" things do so because they are male. Since men are viewed as oppressors, making them gentler, more passive, less assertive, less aggressive, quieter, etc, would mean that women would magically have less issues to face.

~

Men tend to act on and shape the world around them, be they engineers, farmers, politicians, CEOs, inventors, crab fishermen or septic system technicians. This means that, whatever the state of their organism, their inner life, they tend to project into the world either a certain level of good or a certain level of dysfunction (usually a mixture of both, since the global economic system they operate within brings with it a significant and inevitable level of dysfunction—see chapter, *Why You are a Slave*). Deeply unhappy men tend to have an unhealthy impact on the world. They prefer structures which are hierarchical and dominating where they can control others and control their environment. Because their impact is materially observable, it is given much more attention than the more covert dysfunctional female influences. It's far easier to see the devastating influences of tortured, driven men racing to exploit a natural resource and who care little about the devastation they leave behind (e.g. wildcatter, Daniel Plainview, played by Daniel Day Lewis in the movie, *There Will Be Blood*).

Less obvious are the verbal and emotional abuses that leave these men feeling less than whole. The mother whose love was conditional, who was emotionally absent, or who demanded love and attention from her boy in order to assuage a hole in her heart. These leave no scars on the external world, just the internal world. Tortured, driven men are not born—they are products of their past. And exhibiting maladaptive behaviors doesn't make them an inherently toxic person—it makes them a product of their social environment, half of which is populated by women.

There is no doubt that many men exhibit antisocial behaviors. There are plenty of obnoxious, cruel assholes. But condemning men for being fundamentally toxic is like blaming the patient for the disease. Men who use aggression, domination, petty anger, and violence in service of their own vapid concerns either have no moral compass or have not successfully learned how to control themselves. Some have little concern for their fellow human beings, no love in their hearts, no honor. It is the compass that is faulty, not the man. In this age, the real toxicity is in feminist or gynocentric narratives which poison the minds of women against men. These then produce female behaviors which emasculate and alienate men who then are of no use to women, nor even themselves.

Yet do not women also have certain characteristics which when used wrongly have a toxic effect on society? The short answer is "yes." In one study, *Child Maltreatment 2013*, mothers were found to be twice as likely to abuse their offspring as fathers.[41] No one seems to be suggesting that this is an example of toxic femininity. I should say, more accurately, that *literally no one* seems to be suggesting that this is an example of toxic femininity! This is how one-sided the attack on men has become. This sad state of affairs has nothing to do with women's toxic nature but likewise stems from adverse childhood experiences and from our so-called civilized existence (see chapter, *Trauma and Wounding*). Primarily female-perpetrated crimes are not considered a direct result of being female in the same way that men's are. When a criminal act occurs, many women don't see a criminal—they see a man. Women get a free pass on such grievous behavior where men would otherwise be vilified (see *Sentencing Disparities*). We see these women as an "exception." Indeed, they are offered consideration and understanding.[42]

41 P. 49. Table 3–14 Victims by Relationship to Their Perpetrators reveals 125,829 victims at the father's hands and 252,426 victims at the mother's hands.
Children's Bureau (Administration on Children, Youth and Families, Administration for Children and Families) of the U.S. Department of Health and Human Services. *"Child Maltreatment 2013."* https://www.acf.hhs.gov/sites/default/files/documents/cb/cm2013.pdf

42 Kimberly Key (November 2016). *"Why is Child Abuse on the Rise?"* "I think it also screams out that mothers need help. With the rise of single mothers and tougher economic times often necessitating the need for two-income producing parents, there may be some added burdens placed on mothers to juggle work and raising children." Psychology Today. https://www.psychologytoday.com/us/blog/counseling-keys/201611/why-is-child-abuse-the-rise

Another aspect of male toxicity is the assumption that men and boys are emotional pygmies in need of reconstruction. There are countless claims from society in this respect, from TV shows, advertising, the education system, the family court system, to mental health services,[43] etc, that men are stunted in how they observe and process their emotions. It's true that men generally differ in ways they cope with emotions. This is seen as bad. The expectation is that men recognize and emulate the "superior" emotional-processing of women. Men are depicted as being unable to form an awareness of their emotions—sensing inwardly, feeling the feeling, and verbalizing their experience. Yet studies have shown that males and females are equal in terms of emotional responsiveness, but report and act on what they feel differently.[44] Women process their emotions by talking them out. Men do so by solving the problem that is causing them distress, or promoting solutions which cause them to be happy. Neither process is always right or always wrong. Some women may talk in circles for literally years (I married one!) about how they feel about something without taking steps to change their situation. Some men push away uncomfortable feelings by pushing away the thing that is causing those feelings. At best, these are not indicative of toxicity, just unskillfulness. At worst, it reflects a society which shames men for not expressing their emotions—and then shaming them when they do; when they open up and are vulnerable and are then called pussies.

Women, more and more, have exhorted men to express their emotions and men have learned the consequences of so doing. Being vulnerable is a gift to those that receive the blessings of an open heart. Sadly, many men have learned that those vulnerabilities may be weaponized against them. Indeed, more widely, the world doesn't particularly care about how men feel—it just cares about their utility. We've come to learn that both

43 Ronald F Levant, William S Pollack (2003). *"A New Psychology Of Men."* Basic Books.

44 Yoshiya Moriguchi et al. (April 2013). *"Sex differences in the neural correlates of affective experience."* National Institute of Mental Health.

women and other men can't be trusted with something so valuable as our emotional life. So the lack of verbalization should not be mistaken for the lack of its presence. "Man is the victim of an environment which refuses to understand his soul."[45] Happily, there are more and more men's groups where men can go to express what's alive in their hearts and be received by other men in sacred trust, who want nothing but the deepest good for each other.

What's missing is a healing perspective—an emphasis on men and women treating each other with compassion, kindness, and respect, and how to produce a culture which fosters well-adjusted human beings.

You can call masculinity many things. It can be unconscious, uninformed, unaware, wounded, defensive, immature, etc. But its essence is not a toxic product from which women need to protect themselves. It's not a gateway drug to violence. Men are people too and, ultimately, men are as deserving as women. It's shocking to have to assert this reality.

---

45 Charles Bukowski (1984). "*Tales of Ordinary Madness.*" City Lights Publishers

If you are a white male, you don't deserve to live. You are a cancer, you're a disease, white males have never contributed anything positive to the world![46]

— NOEL IGNATIEV

7 Male Privilege

Women have been told for years that the history of our culture is the history of male privilege. Yet, certainly for the last fifty years, girls and women have been given every encouragement to go for what they want and to expect to be supported in their efforts. Even before then, men had been open to admitting women into traditionally male professions and encouraging them to flourish. While receiving all this positive societal encouragement and being able to reach goals according to their ability, they've simultaneously been fed a diet of supposed historical male oppression and privilege which continues even to this day. Men and women have achieved substantive equality. There are no rights, encoded in law, enforced by the judicial system, which specifically advantage men above women.

We have this idea that, for centuries, men could vote and could steer society while women couldn't. This is completely untrue. But the women's suffrage movement (the winning of the vote for women) presented an illusion of women fighting back against men to regain equal standing.

46 *"Mass. College Professor: White Males Are A Cancer And Must Die, Urges Students To Kill Themselves."* Truth and Action. http://www.truthandaction.org/mass-college-professor-white-males-are-a-cancer-and-must-die-urges-students-to-kill-themselves/

In fact, women's suffrage in the UK was achieved shortly after male suffrage, subsequent to World War I. Men who went to war, who died in the trenches, so that women might live.

Women currently comprise about 56% of the workforce, up from under 35% in the early 1950s. Women drive the majority of consumer/household spending, estimated at approximately $40 trillion.[47] They control more than 60% of all personal wealth in the U.S,[48] purchase over 50% of traditional male products, including automobiles, home improvement products, and consumer electronics.[49] Approximately 40% of U.S. working women now out-earn their husbands.[50] If women were an oppressed group, suffering from male privilege, they would be the first oppressed group in history to be able to shop in a mall where the vast majority of stores there were geared towards their needs, not their oppressor's. No one ever mentions the spending gap (only the purported "wage gap"). Who has the privilege—he who earns, or she who spends? Data may not be reliable, but estimates are that women account for 70%-80% of personal spending.

In 56 of the largest developed nations, boys and young men are lagging academically. College attendance is falling, which is not surprising since reading and writing skills, which should have been acquired at high school, have shown a marked decline.

~

The once-despised bigotry and racism against minority groups has found a new home in vilifying white men for all social evils. Most people subscribe to the notion that people should not be judged on the basis of skin color, gender, race, religion, etc. And Dr. Martin Luther King Jr. rightly

47 Michael J. Silverstein, et al. (2009). *"Women Want More: Updated Findings on the World's Largest, Fastest-Growing Market."* Harper Business.

48 Federal Reserve, MassMutual Financial Group, BusinessWeek, Gallup

49 Andrea Learned (2004). *"Don't Think Pink."* AMACOM.

50 U.S Bureau of Labor Statistics, 2009

exhorted people to judge others by the "content of their character"[51] rather than the color of their skin—to judge someone by the totality of their personhood. The importance of judging individuals on their merit, their community involvement, their wisdom and compassion, their work ethic, their virtues, has been replaced by identity politics which places nominated "victim groups" by social hierarchy. No longer are people's socio-economic circumstances the determining factor in assessing their needs and suggesting social remedies. You just have to be in an identified and socially-sanctioned "oppressed" group.

Some males are privileged in terms of power and money. The vast majority are not. In many parts of the western world, male unemployment in impoverished communities has been systemic for generations. This inter-generational welfare dependency culture has principally affected middle-aged men who used to be able to rely on low-skilled manufacturing jobs which were once plentiful but have since been off-shored. These men have suffered, not just financially, but socially as well, often experiencing family breakdowns, suicides, addictions, and both petty and serious crime. The defeatism and disadvantage they experienced has been passed down from father to son. There are millions of men at the bottom of the rung of society who are suffering, yet are invisible.

~

Women's groups follow a double standard: When women lag behind men, that is an injustice that must be aggressively targeted. But when men are lagging behind women, that is a triumph of equity to be celebrated.[52]

---

51 Dr. Martin Luther King Jr's address, *"I Have a Dream,"* delivered at the March on Washington for Jobs and Freedom. August 28, 1963.

52 Dr. Helen Smith (2014). *"Men on Strike: Why Men Are Boycotting Marriage, Fatherhood, and the American Dream - and Why It Matters."* Encounter Books.

Men have sacrificed and crippled themselves physically and emotionally to feed, house, and protect women and children. None of their pain or achievement is registered in feminist rhetoric, which portrays men as oppressive and callous exploiters[53]

— CAMILLE PAGLIA

8 Patriarchy

The definition of patriarchy floats around in many directions. Many feminists use it to mean whatever they want it to mean in any situation where doing so can underscore a complaint about men by using this meta-narrative. The premise is that patriarchy is so evidently true, it cannot even begin to be challenged.

A core aspect of "actual" patriarchy involves passing down property and titles from father to son, generation to generation. In this sense, we can see that it simply doesn't exist in modern society. Only monarchies and some billionaires of the ruling elite continue its practice. Even under this paradigm, the goal was not to oppress women, per se, but to ensure plundered resources remained in the family line (which might also include women). There is nothing commendable about this form of patriarchy but its "victims" included both disempowered men and women.

53 Camille Paglia (July 25, 1993). *"Challenging The Male Mystique."* The Washington Post. https://www.washingtonpost.com/archive/entertainment/books/1993/07/25/challenging-the-male-mystique/31b3a4da-3b8b-4f11-9252-01058c385a99/

Patriarchy, in a broader sense, is about male power, where men make the rules to benefit men at the expense of one half of the human race—women. This is one of the key concepts taught in gender studies courses all over the world. It's the power to decide what to do and who gets to do it. It tells the story that all men have power over all women, enforced by violence or the threat of violence. Yet a simple examination of the lives of all but the most powerful men clearly demonstrates that we, both men and women, are essentially powerless. We don't even have the ability to control our own lives—the vast majority of us need to work for someone else to earn money, usually in jobs we don't like.

Many women seem to confuse the existence of male-dominated professions with Patriarchy. They take it as evident that since men mostly comprise the boards of Fortune 500 companies and Congress they therefore must have arrived at their positions with nefarious intent against women. They refuse to entertain the idea that male preferences for these positions are strongly linked to human biology. Indeed, rather than being refused entry to these professions, women are actually being incentivized to do so, yet their numbers remain small.

~

Historically, in order to survive, men and women have had to adopt certain strategies. Women were required to bear and raise children (oftentimes losing their lives in childbirth) and maintain the home. Their own personal fulfillment came a distant second. The feminist movement then framed this dynamic as discrimination against women by men. But men were expected to be disposable in war. And to work to protect and provide for those women and children—a point they ignore. Society was "comfortable" with men being maimed, mutilated, and dying on the battlefields and the factory floor. Men were, and are, expected to physically defend their loved ones from armed assailants to the point of sacrificing their own lives. Who gets out of bed to investigate the strange noise? The concept of disposability is hidden in plain view. It is so deeply ingrained into the warp and weft of our culture, that we barely recognize its existence. To be disposable is to not be coming from a place of power. How can disposable men be patriarchal? It's important to recognize and speak about the concept of male disposability because its omission from gender discourse is truly noteworthy. The reason is that society provides social validation for those men who sacrifice themselves as being honorable, selfless, and good—selfless in the sense of having a self vastly less worthy of preservation.

Being the breadwinners, men would earn money that would be spent, not on themselves, but their family. Feminists considered the increased earnings of men as proof of male power and privilege, rather than seeing men as having social expectations and pressures to earn more money at the expense of time spent away from loving connection with their women and children. No one who feels pressured and obligated to do something can be said to be coming from a place of power. Power is about having the freedom and opportunity to do what you want.

So society oppresses both men and women. Much is made of the fact that lack of access to resources means that some women have to sell their bodies. But so too do men. But since there's little demand for gigolos, they can only sell their labor, often at the expense of their bodies, their mental health, and their lives. "A disproportionate share of fatal work injuries involved men relative to their hours worked in 2010."[54] But our moralistic view of sex workers and female victimhood carries greater moral weight than male disposability.

~

The term "patriarchal" is also used to pillory men at the interpersonal level. Men and women understand and wield personal power in different ways, sometimes with harsh intent. The description of "patriarchal" power, here, is simply a description of the way in which wounded men wield

54 U.S. Bureau of Labor Statistics. https://www.bls.gov/iif/oshwc/cfoi/cfch0009.pdf

power—through aggression, domination, and "going in all guns." There is a wounded "matriarchal" style of wielding power too which involves backstabbing, verbal manipulation, and using their sex appeal, of which men are too polite to make mention. Where men try to break people's will, women try to bend people's will. Both are abhorrent.

If society is patriarchal, then there must surely be social mechanisms for men to consider and implement ideas for the subjugation of women. As far as I can tell, there are none. In the 21st century, what constitutional or civil rights do men have that women don't? I am a man and I don't recognize myself as someone who seeks to get or maintain unfair advantages over women. Nor do I recognize my male friends or family as seeking and celebrating such a privilege. Have you, dear reader, ever been invited to a group or organization which spends time devising ways to make society more man-friendly, more male-dominant? Do you have any friends/acquaintances who have? Do you, or anyone you've heard of, appeal to your local congressional representative to change the law to favor men? Certainly, you can get specific religious or racist groups which have a component of misogyny but, on a societal scale, men are not actively devising ways to oppress women. The same is not true in reverse (see *Divorce and Family Court,* below).

Men have become a lot more compassionate in response to historical requests/demands from women. The level of male-perpetrated domestic violence is at an all-time low. Looking back at old movies from 50, 60, 70 years ago, the leading man/good guy would have no compunctions about spanking his woman to keep her in line.[55] It was a normal thing and didn't really raise any eyebrows unduly. It's hard to believe, looking back at it. But just imagine men 50 years from now, men looking back at us. I imagine they would say, "You let her get away with *that*? And you just took it?"

55 For example, *McLintock*! movie, starring John Wayne. 1963.

Equal pay for equal work. It's common sense. It's also overdue. Let's close the gap and let's do it now.

– JOE BIDEN, 2020.

9 The Wage Gap

What feminists want you to believe is that women are systematically discriminated against in how much they are paid compared to men. 77 cents to the dollar (and curiously, a few other amounts) is often cited. The first thing to say is that sex discrimination is illegal; it's actually unlawful to pay women less for equal work. With the law on their side, you would expect lawsuits to be plentiful. They're not. And it's not because the fabled patriarchy has rigged the system so that they would never win in court.

What the proponents of this narrative are doing is essentially adding up all the money men make and taking the average, and all the money women make and averaging that, and pointing at the difference. In this simplistic manner a wage gap (it's actually an earnings gap) materializes.[56] This simple wage gap is regularly, systematically, and misleadingly used to advance the feminist public policy agenda without giving the real reasons for the disparity. For instance, more women than men work part time, women tend to leave the labor force to have a child or look after elders, women choose lower-paid employment for lifestyle reasons more

56 Derek Thompson (May 30, 2013). *"The Biggest Myth About the Gender Wage Gap. The real gap isn't between men and women doing the same job. It's between the different jobs that men and women take."* The Atlantic. https://www.theatlantic.com/business/archive/2013/05/the-biggest-myth-about-the-gender-wage-gap/276367/

than men (who focus more on pay, typically),[57] women value non-wage benefits more than men do, plus a few other variables. This is why they earn less overall.

Logically, if women were doing the same job as men for less money, there would be no incentive for companies to hire any men (who would have to be paid more) since this would adversely effect their bottom line. Why pay a sex premium? The only other explanation would be that companies are unconcerned about losing money and are deliberately paying men more because of a commitment to advantaging men over women, and over profits. The shareholders of the company, who would otherwise expect profit maximization, would likewise have to be okay with this arrangement. What it boils down to is that there are numerous variables for the wage gap which have nothing to do with discriminating against women or that there is systemic sexism that is causing women to make less money. Men get paid more because men work more.[58]

Women have been riled up by this propaganda which has been debunked time and again. But because of how quickly memes spread through social media, repeating the message over and over, this has now become the narrative. The truth is far more nuanced. So why does it persist? Why do feminist advocacy groups, having been shown the data, knowingly perpetuate this misinformation?

Absurdly, feminists will even go so far as to suggest that women should be paid more than men.[59]

---

57 Actually, in my view, men should take a page out of women's books and make more fulfilling career and life choices which suit their character and life-purpose more closely.

58 They also have a higher retirement age than women in 35 countries. There are no countries where women have a higher retirement age than men. What was the Patriarchy thinking!

59 Jessica Valenti (4 November, 2014). *"A radical fix to the world's wage gap: why not just pay women more – and pay men less?"* The Guardian. https://www.theguardian.com/commentisfree/2014/nov/04/world-wage-gap-pay-women-more-men-less

In the radical feminist approach, masculinity is the behaviour of the male ruling class and femininity is the behaviour of the subordinate class of women.[60]

— SHEILA JEFFREYS

10 Gender Studies

With "soft" sciences like sociology, anthropology, political science, psychology, and non biology-oriented gender studies, it's much easier to manipulate research than it is in the "hard" sciences, like astronomy, chemistry, or physics. This makes it much easier for ideologues to push an agenda rather than seek objectivity. Students are taught what to think, rather than how to think (rather than how to coherently challenge assumptions and structures). Since these fields have a strong impact on setting cultural narratives and determining social policies, this can adversely affect the lives of conscious men.

The notion of studying gender in relation to human society is a worthy ambition—understanding men's and women's psychological and emotional make-up and how they interact in their professional and personal lives. Some of the most rigorous studies on the subject have come from university sociology departments and the New Male Studies journal.[61] These soft science researchers who strive for objectivity deserve kudos. However,

60 Sheila Jeffreys (2014). *"Gender Hurts: A Feminist Analysis of the Politics of Transgenderism."* Routledge

61 New Male Studies - An International Journal. http://newmalestudies.com/OJS/index.php/nms/index

Gender Studies, as currently formulated, is ground zero for the feminist movement. It's not a scholarly department so much as an ideology mill.

The primary purpose of Gender Studies programs across colleges in North America is to be the activist arm of the feminist movement—to advance feminist ideology. There is no actual interest in looking at the subject from a variety of viewpoints and being evidence-based. There are key premises that are made which are not subject to scrutiny or challenge (e.g. patriarchal power, toxic masculinity, male sexual and physical violence deriving from a sense of male entitlement, male privilege, etc). The assertions are that we live in a patriarchal society where all men have systemic privileges which are denied to all women, and therefore necessitate that men should recognize and check their privilege and commit themselves to assisting, or getting out of the way of, women rising to achieve "true equality" (as defined by feminists).

"Colleges have now become privileged finishing schools for girls. Except rather than teaching manners, they teach women that men are the enemy and men are treated as such on campus..."[62]

In Gender Studies classes, males in general are portrayed in stereotyped ways to foster contempt—as sexual aggressors, jocks, chauvinists, predators, pedophiles, dead-beat dads, etc—and as targets of insults and condescension in all aspects of our culture. Two Canadian scholars, Paul Nathanson and Katherine Young, documented the presence of misandric concepts and the professors who promote them.[63] Male students' views are given short shrift or even dismissed with sarcasm should they challenge the narrative put forth in these classes. At a certain point, the male students learn to sit in silence rather than face the inevitable ridicule. It soon becomes apparent that only pro-feminist viewpoints are acceptable discourses in class. Examining the ways males are disadvantaged in society is considered preposterous because males have "male privilege" and even if there is a grudging acknowledgment about an incontrovertible

62 Dr. Helen Smith (2014). *"Men on Strike: Why Men Are Boycotting Marriage, Fatherhood, and the American Dream - and Why It Matters."* Encounter Books.

63 Paul Nathanson and Katherine Young (2006). *"Spreading Misandry: The Teaching of Contempt for Men in Popular Culture."* McGill-Queen's University Press.

fact where men have it worse, it is because "patriarchy disadvantages men too." This sets up the logical fallacy, Begging the Question.[64] Gender studies professors have all the traits of cult leaders. They demand extreme loyalty to the doctrine of feminism. Criticism is not tolerated. And they have no shame.

Thankfully, it isn't considered correct to teach contempt for women in colleges and popular culture. The fact that we unquestioningly accept the rhetoric around toxic masculinity means that the presence of "hate studies" (dressed up as Gender Studies) amounts to teaching contempt for men as an acceptable and mind-bogglingly grotesque reality.

These academic departments are not concerned with the sort of objective, intellectually rigorous inquiry one might expect to find at a university—they are morally motivated. And although they are ground zero, the portrayal of men's shortcomings, the Patriarchy, etc, can easily be found across other college courses and society more broadly—the media, the educational system, the legal system, in politics, in medicine, in dating and sexual activity. They have sought to, and have been successful in, radicalizing students into seeing the world through a particular moral lens, the result of which adversely impacts the lives of men and boys as the effects ripple outwards into society.[65]

---

64 Men are misogynistic and bad because feminism teaches us that men are misogynistic and bad. Therefore if you, as a man, object to feminism, you are misogynistic and bad.

65 Perhaps the most famous example of an ideologically obsessed administration was Bret Weinstein's constructive dismissal at Evergreen State College where he objected to an event which insisted that white students leave campus for a day (to talk about race issues). He stated, "one's right to speak — or to be — must never be based on skin color."

Hollywood brides keep the bouquets and throw away the grooms.

– GROUCHO MARX

11 Divorce and Family Court

Marriage is currently at an incredibly low rate, not seen since 1860, with four in ten Americans believing it to be obsolete.[66] Research indicates that 25% of millennials are unlikely ever to be married.

Why is this? Cohabiting and sex before marriage are now considered acceptable where they used to be taboo, and people have found it generally desirable to remove these social limitations. Yet perhaps the most compelling reason for the decline in marriage is how a subsequent divorce can destroy lives. Divorce rates are considered high (some estimates put them at 50%)[67] and horror stories abound about the quality of relationships prior to divorce and the subsequent legal nightmares which followed them. Since no-fault divorces became legally codified, they allowed one spouse, usually the wife, to divorce her husband for any reason or no reason. This meant that men could be separated from their belongings, home, and children through literally "no fault" of their own. The term "divorce rape"

66 *"The Decline of Marriage And Rise of New Families."* Pew Research Center (November 18, 2010). https://www.pewsocialtrends.org/wp-content/uploads/sites/3/2010/11/pew-social-trends-2010-families.pdf

67 Federal funding for the collection and publication of marriage and divorce statistics was discontinued in 1996 and, as a result, accurately determining the rates of divorce in the US is problematic.

has come into common parlance to reflect how men are being shafted in family court by their ex-wives and pitbull lawyers who take them to the cleaners. Women are regularly encouraged to file restraining orders/reports of abuse on their husbands as a legal strategy,[68] knowing full well the man's innocence. This gets him away from the children, away from the house, and gives her legal leverage. It is considered normal legal strategy. But it also abuses the very system designed to protect vulnerable individuals against abuse.[69] Women who game the system are committing relational abuse by proxy.

It might be expected that judges should rule neutrally on all matters of law before them and treat all parties with fairness and equal consideration. But the evidence indicates that there is an anti-father/pro-mother bias on the part of judges which plays an enormous part in court settlements.[70] In California, for example, a 1994 report showed that family courts awarded sole custody to ex-wives 49% of the time compared to just 12% for fathers (joint custody was only granted 25% of the time).[71]

At best, the marriage/divorce scenario is about whether two self-concerned individuals can work out their differences and stay together agreeably or part amicably. But if children are part of the mix, these two egocentric adults have an additional responsibility—they must hold the best interests of their defenseless and impressionable offspring above their own base needs. Historically, because the man was the breadwinner of the household, he was invariably granted custody of children in a divorce as he had the necessary financial means to ensure their material well-being

68 SAVE (2010). *"What is the Cost of False Allegations of Domestic Violence?"* Courts issue 1.5 million false or trivial temporary restraining orders every year. In half of those cases, no physical violence actually occurs. There are on average 700,000 false charges of domestic violence each year in the U.S. 85% of these, target men. Women are believed without proof. https://www.saveservices.org/pdf/SAVE-Cost-of-False-Allegations.pdf

69 Joseph E. Cordell (September 23, 2011). *"Order Of Protection: And Justice For All?"* Huffington Post. https://www.huffpost.com/entry/order-of-protection-and-j_b_974970?guccounter=1

70 Tom James (November 2013). *"What Judges Really Think About Fathers: Responses to court-commissioned judicial bias surveys."* Transitions Journal of Men's Perspectives. Vol. 31 Issue 4. https://ncfm.org/wp-content/uploads/2013/11/Transitions-Issue-4-v-FINAL.pdf

71 Malcolm M. Lucas Chief Justice (November 1994). *"California Family Court Services Snapshot Study. Report 5. California Family court Services Mediation 1991. Visitation with Children: A Followup of Court Mediation Clients."* http://www.courts.ca.gov/documents/r05rpt.pdf

going forward. In 1896, Ernest B. Bax wrote, "It has always in England been laid down as a fundamental law based on public policy, that the custody of children and their education is a duty incumbent on the father."[72] The best interests of the child were given little consideration in those days. Yet even around the turn of the twentieth century, the mother was increasingly becoming the default parent given sole custody of the child, with the father being required to maintain "the children as well as [the mother] out of his property or earnings, and has the added consolation of knowing that they will brought up to detest him." And still, the best interests of the child were not sufficiently considered.

Children raised by single parents tend to end up poorer, less well educated, and frequently have emotional deficits. They are many times more likely to face problems of addiction and have sexual issues than children from intact homes. Some studies have indicated that 80-90% of adults who are incarcerated came from single-parent households. Boys are especially susceptible to the absence of a father in their lives. A whole book could be written on the subject. And indeed one has. Highly recommended is Warren Farrell's, *The Boy Crisis*.[73] If masculinity was truly toxic, then those children growing up without fathers would exemplify standards of behavior an order of magnitude better than of those who had come from intact households.

~

Men love others more than they love themselves. They'll sacrifice their own health and happiness in order to provide comfortable, safe and loving environments for their women and children. Any man who's ever been used by a woman, for whom he gave everything, knows what it feels like. He thought that his life and actions meant something, and then found out that it really didn't mean anything to her. And once she had strip-mined him of his resources, both inner and outer, she disposed of him—his

72 Ernest B. Bax (1896). *"The Legal Subjection of Men."* http://www.embscomputerart.com/pdfs/e.bax.legalsubjectionofmen.pdf

73 Warren Farrell (2019). *"The Boy Crisis: Why Our Boys Are Struggling and What We Can Do About It."* BenBella Books.

usefulness coming to an end (divorced men kill themselves eight times more than divorced women). Yet we live in a world where *men* are told they are toxic and patriarchal.

Divorce has become a celebrated weapon in the arsenal of feminism because it creates thousands of personalized battles of the sexes every day, with the National Association of Women Lawyers declaring no-fault divorces to be "the greatest project the NAWL has ever undertaken."[74] Fathers who try to organize to seek redress to inequitable family laws, such as Fathers for Equal Rights, are painted as "anti-women" and misogynistic ranters.[75] Yet these fathers, now simply "uncle daddies," rarely receive the empathy they deserve as having been deprived of the joys of being an equal presence in the lives of their children and with little to no say in how they are raised.

---

74 Baskerville, Stephen (2007). "*Taken Into Custody – The War Against Fathers, Marriage and the Family.*" Cumberland House.
At its convention in 1947, the National Association of Women Lawyers voted to draft and promote a bill that would embody the ideal of no-fault divorce and described its efforts to promote the passage of no-fault divorce laws as "the greatest project NAWL has ever undertaken."

75 Kelly Behre (June 13, 2014). "The Fathers' Rights Movement Undermines Victims of Domestic Violence." New York Times. https://www.nytimes.com/roomfordebate/2014/06/13/fathers-rights-and-womens-equality/the-fathers-rights-movement-undermines-victims-of-domestic-violence

Domestic abuse is a form of communication fueled by personal insecurities, temperament, economic, educational or lack therein, physical and psychological conditions.

– ASA DON BROWN

12 Domestic Violence

There was a time when there were few resources for men and women who had experienced domestic violence. Women were consoled and perhaps given advice on how to handle the situation, and if they were lucky enough could count on friends or family to provide a safe haven if things got too bad. Men who were beaten by their wives were subject to ridicule, and no empathy or assistance was offered because it was laughable that a bigger, stronger man could allow himself to be beaten by a woman. The situation has changed enormously for abused women who can count on support and sympathy, and for whom domestic violence shelters now exist. The situation is largely the same for "battered" men who still can expect to find little sympathy from society.[76]

Erin Pizzey opened the very first shelter for battered women (in London, 1971). She also recognized that men too suffered from domestic violence, often at the hands of the same women who were seeking shelter. These men and women came from a culture of family violence rather than gendered violence. She attempted to open shelters for men too but

76 NPO Blog (2014). *"Researcher: What Happens When Abused Men Call Domestic Violence Hotlines and Shelters?"* National Parents Organization. https://archive.is/nLLs6

was undermined by second-wave feminists of her time. Pizzey had death threats from feminists, her dog was killed, and she had to leave the country for her own safety.

Feminists continue to push the narrative that men are the primary perpetrators of domestic violence and yet studies show gender-symmetry, with increasing data on significant male rates of injury and death.

According to the Centers for Disease Control (CDC),[77] men do more damage than women when they become violent but women resort to violence more often than men. But their favorite m.o. is to use psychological aggression and coercive control, which they do far more than men. These types of behaviors include false allegations, possessiveness, jealousy, gaslighting, threatening to withhold access to children, verbal and emotional abuse, and demands for certain types of behavior (like not seeing men friends).

	Male Victims (estimated)	Female Victims (estimated)
Any severe physical violence	2,266,000	3,163,000
Slapped, pushed, or shoved	5,066,000	4,322,000
Any psychological aggression	20,548,000	16,578,000
Coercive control	17,253,000	12,689,000

As can be seen, partner abuse of men by women is practically as common as the reverse, and yet receives little to no public acknowledgment or sympathy, nor government intervention.[78] We have the Violence Against Women Act, 1994, but no male equivalent. Apparently, there is no need for any male gender distinction to be made. Instead the overwhelming narrative is of male perpetrators and their female victims, contrary to the verifiable truth. This perpetuates the "man bad, woman good" story which gives strength to the general anti-man sentiment of our times. It also provides high levels of funding to feminist organizations to attack

77 CDC (2010) *"National Intimate Partner and Sexual Violence Survey."* https://www.cdc.gov/ViolencePrevention/pdf/NISVS_Report2010-a.pdf

78 Joan Arehart-Treichel (3 August, 2007). *"Men Shouldn't Be Overlooked as Victims of Partner Violence."* Psychiatric News. https://psychnews.psychiatryonline.org/doi/full/10.1176/pn.42.15.0031a

a problem which is not gendered and for which they are not looking for actual-world solutions.

Everyone has the human right to defend themselves from violent behavior. Men and women alike. Except men, when being confronted by a violent woman, have to contend with the cultural taboo that it is "always wrong to hit a woman." This gives women free reign to celebrate how "empowering" it is to attack men violently.[79]

The origins of domestic violence can be found in generational family abuse, not gender abuse. And as such, it is treatable. With the focus on male perpetrators, violent women are ignored. They never receive the therapeutic interventions they need to confront their own programming and break the cycle of violence. These women are both addicted to violence and to receiving violence, "...a battered person is the innocent victim of another person's violence; a violence-prone person is the victim of their own addiction to violence."[80] This does a massive disservice to the men and children in their lives, and to the resolution of violent women's personal pain.

Domestic violence in the form of physical abuse by men has been thoroughly stigmatized, thankfully. In the past, it was relatively acceptable. It was a tool to keep in check a woman's shadow aspects which manifested as relational violence.[81] But this meant that she repressed those aspects for fear of punishment. Neither did she process them, at least not with men. There was a stand-off. Without this tool of coercion, men are no longer able to keep women repressed (the #MeToo movement perhaps being a delayed backlash). It's good that men are no longer able to "physically correct" a woman but this has left women with an open playing field to get away with outrageous behavior, unchecked. As women get "crazier" and more masculinized by feminist messaging, more domineering, men are lacking

---

79 Tracie Egan Morrissey (8/28/07). *"Have You Ever Beat Up A Boyfriend? Cause, Uh, We Have."* Jezebel. https://jezebel.com/have-you-ever-beat-up-a-boyfriend-cause-uh-we-have-294383
Also:
YouTube channel, Roma Army (December 8, 2020). *"THIS is why men DONT come forward!"* https://www.youtube.com/watch?v=2dmd37PgT5U

80 Erin Pizzey (1982). *"Prone to Violence."* Hamlyn (UK).

81 Old black and white movies often show a guy slapping a woman to "bring her back to her senses."

the resources, the backbone, and the bite to stand up for themselves and their children. Men have received a strong, social correction indicating disapproval for physical aggression towards women. There is not, nor is there likely to be a strong counter-movement, a #HeToo movement, which would hold women to account for their own historical abuse against men (particularly emotional abuse). Men are reluctant to claim victim-status in the way women do. This is why female abuse, in all its different forms, is relegated to the shadows.

A reputation once broken may possibly be repaired, but the world will always keep their eyes on the spot where the crack was.

— JOSEPH HALL

13 #MeToo and Sexual Abuse

I certainly stand with victims of sexual assault and sexual harassment, whether they're men or women. No matter how much compassion and genuine integrity and concern inspired the #MeToo movement at its inception, the sad reality is that the direction it has gone has been very dangerous for the fabric of male/female relations. It's efforts have been to shame and emasculate men publicly not just for criminal but also non-criminal offenses, large and small.

The focus of attention around the treatment of women has been on the continuum ranging from mildly sexist quips[82] to rape itself. It should be noted that the definition of rape foolishly no longer means penetrative sex without consent—it could be anything on this continuum, such has been the influence of feminist reprogramming. A man can rape a woman with his eyes, even.[83] Feminists, or women who are conditioned by feminist rhetoric, appear to be as equally outraged about bad jokes as they are

82 Ruth Marcus, Deputy editorial page editor (May 3, 2018). *"She called his elevator joke offensive. He called her complaint 'frivolous.' Who's right?"* Washington Post. https://www.washingtonpost.com/opinions/she-called-his-elevator-joke-offensive-he-called-her-complaint-frivolous-whos-right/2018/05/03/43ba4084-4ee1-11e8-af46-b1d6dc0d9bfe_story.html

83 Esha Gupta, Bollywood actress. "This guy was literally raping me with his eyes. He was requested to behave thrice and then leave..then eventually 2 guards had to be around me..even the security cam can confirm this..who is this future rapist," Her Instagram and Twitter accounts.

about genuine rape to the extent that they'll go after anyone's reputation. Acknowledging that this continuum even exists can get you into trouble. Matt Damon is a case in point. He made the benign and rational reflection that, "I do believe that there's a spectrum of behavior and we're going to have to figure — you know, there's a difference between, you know, patting someone on the butt and rape or child molestation, right? Both of those behaviors need to be confronted and eradicated without question, but they shouldn't be conflated, right?" He was vilified for such a remark and realized that, had he not immediately apologized, his career would be in jeopardy of being run off the road by the #MeToo bandwagon.[84]

The court system is no longer the preferred place to solve legal grievances where alleged sexual abuse is concerned. Women are increasingly choosing social media, as their preferred mechanism, to allege wrongdoing. It is less costly, omits that pesky need for evidence, and has speedier results in bringing a desirable outcome for the accuser. The accusation doesn't have to be in the least way true. If you want to ruin a man's reputation, lose his job, and be vilified by men and women alike, social media (and even mainstream media) will deliver the goods and the woman will be lauded for her bravery in coming forward. It should always be born in mind that, in the court of public opinion, there are no rules of evidence, as there are in a court of law, so greater care needs to be exercised on a personal level before a rush to judgment. The power imbalance in terms of the moral judgment of men clearly lies with women and the troops they rally (be they male or female), and how you walk through life is proscribed by their agenda—and you will risk paying a price if you ignore it.

#MeToo has become a movement for the large-scale disposal of men who may or may not be legally guilty of a crime. The sympathy lies with the "victim" who is believed by default (#BelieveHer). It's now so bad,

84 *"Sexual Harassment Isn't a Joke - Remove Matt Damon from Oceans 8."* Signed by 28,748 people. The Petition Site. https://www.thepetitionsite.com/441/501/676/sexual-harassment-isn%E2%80%99t-a-joke-remove-matt-damon-from-oceans-8/
"Success! The all-female reboot of Oceans 8 turned out to be the empowering film we wanted — with Matt Damon's cameo left on the cutting room floor. Thanks to everyone who signed and held Damon accountable for his thoughtless and sexist comments about Harvey Weinstein and the brave silence breakers of the #MeToo movement."

it's almost like it is an axiom of human existence. Her heroism is seen to redress an uncaring society's perception of her as powerless, voiceless, helpless, and vulnerable. Gone is the presumption of innocence and due process for the man who is not considered to be worthy of consideration—whose perspective is either suspect or unwanted. The repercussions can be immense for him. Everything he's worked for can be stripped away with relative ease. His reputation as a good and decent human being will be destroyed. And he will have little recourse. This is not just hyperbole—it's happening all around us. More and more men are recognizing that they are just one accusation away from reputational and career ruination. The accusation need be for only the mildest impropriety to receive condemnation and retribution. These are men who have never been charged with a crime, who are fired, kicked out of college, or compelled to resign from leadership positions in their community based solely on having been accused of sexual misconduct.

Conversely, there is no standard of ethical behavior to which women are equally held accountable. In practice, a false-accuser has fewer repercussions, socially and legally. When a woman makes life-destroying accusations against a man, and then is asked for proof of his wrongdoing, being insulted at being challenged to supply evidence is itself evidence of her lack of maturity and non-accountability. Equally, those offering uncritical, slam-dunk sympathy and support bear much of the responsibility for enabling this behavior. Good men are often the first to offer empathy to the alleged victim. They experience a large degree guilt for not having prevented the situation, whether they could have or not, that they feel down to their bones that they should have. They feel they should have made a better world where such a thing was impossible to occur. It's not logical, as it reaches down to their instinctive protective responses. In large part, this is why the #MeToo movement has been so powerful. And in large part, it has thrived because men care about women more than they care about the truth, or the effects on other falsely accused men.

~

So let's take one of the largest offenders, the poster boy villain of the #MeToo movement, Harvey Weinstein.[85] Hollywood film producer, Weinstein, was ousted from Miramax after a number of accusations that he pressured women for sexual favors. This was essentially held up as an abusive male and a classic example of toxic masculinity—as if there were no gray area here. Yet, as always, life is complex, messy, and nuanced. But to consider his debacle in such a light would spoil the morality play. Weinstein, being in a position of power, leveraged that power for sexual benefit. Being rich and famous and in a position to turbo boost a starlet's career is, for better or worse, part of the Hollywood culture—mixing sex with business for access to resources produced by men. There is a quid pro quo where men use power to get sex and women use sex to get power. Many women enthusiastically pursued relationships with this man and consequently enabled him. They also stayed friends with him for years afterward and then went on to call him out.[86]

Of the 100+ women who made allegations against him, only two complainants went to trial. One, Jessica Mann, had continued to have sexual relations with Weinstein long after the instances when she claimed to have been abused.[87] Alexandra Canosa, a producer in his company, claimed to have been sexually assaulted and raped by Weinstein on numerous occasions. Yet over the time frame in question, several years, she sent him hundreds of affectionate emails, including one the day after he was alleged to have raped her.[88] "Both complainants, though now

85 Praised by Michelle Obama as a "wonderful human being" and a "good friend." Careers in Film Symposium. November, 2013.

86 In fact, there had hitherto been no police reports or criminal charges brought up against him.

87 Adamqqq. *"Weinstein 11-29-18 Motion [to Dismiss]."* https://www.scribd.com/document/394703598/Weinstein-11-29-18-Motion-Wm

88 Kayla Brantley (September 9, 2019). *"Netflix producer suing Harvey Weinstein 'sent HUNDREDS of affectionate emails to the disgraced movie mogul - including one saying "I'm thinking about you" just a DAY after he allegedly raped her'."* Daily Mail. https://www.dailymail.co.uk/news/article-7442217/Netflix-producer-suing-Harvey-Weinstein-sent-HUNDREDS-affectionate-emails-disgraced-mogul.html

willing and eager to see Weinstein given a lengthy sentence, maintained a friendly relationship with him for years."[89]

In response to the Weinstein revelations, creator of the DKNY clothing line, Donna Karan, was ripped apart for even daring to suggest that women "have to look at [them]selves and question how [they] are presenting themselves and their sexuality."[90] It's apparent that certain Hollywood women leveraged their sexual value for career advancement, to the detriment of other women who did not accept what Weinstein, and others like him, had to offer. They were in a position where they were making a choice by choosing a career over their own dignity and self-worth. Yet they never fell under the spotlight outside of their victim status, needing a couple of decades, apparently, to process their trauma before complaining about it.[91]

In the #MeToo hysteria of the time, few people cared about how the jury might be protected from being swayed by the public blood lust. Indeed, Judge Burke "did everything he could to facilitate the transmission of anti-Weinstein news and sentiment to the jury. Casually dismissing the scale of the media campaign and its potential impact on the jurors, the judge ignored an important legal precedent."[92] He refused to recuse himself from the case for this apparent bias.

~

There have always been badly behaved men—men who are not particularly nice to women in romantic or sexual relationships. They used to be called cads. The women end up feeling used. I can't say I like them either. But that doesn't make them sexual predators; it makes them indifferent and

89 YouTube channel, StudioBrule (February 4, 2020). *"The #MeToo Trial Of The Century - The Fiamengo File Episode 113."* https://www.youtube.com/watch?v=Rh26i1yMOEU.

90 Donna Karan, DKNY fashion designer. CinéFashion Film Awards, 2017

91 Men who use their power to coerce women into sex with threats of career consequences for not doing so are another ball of wax. Whether Weinstein used this method or not is unknown to me.

92 Eric London (February 26, 2020). *"The New York Times gloats over the destruction of "the Monster"* Weinstein." World Socialist Web Site. https://www.wsws.org/en/articles/2020/02/26/wein-f26.html

uncaring assholes on the one hand, and human beings who are alienated from their own humanity on the other, usually through having lacked a well-rounded, loving childhood. If you're a woman and you wind up with such a man, forgive him and leave him.

But nowadays, if women perceive that they've been treated poorly after a consensual relationship, it's often recharacterized as abusive, even if no criminal abuse took place. Sex with men can become rape simply because the woman chooses to regard it as such—perhaps 40 years later. Bari Weiss, Staff Editor at The New York Times, argued that the #MeToo movement had moved from "uncovering accusations of criminal behavior" to "criminalizing behavior that we previously regarded as presumptuous and boorish…In a climate in which sexual mores are transforming so rapidly, many men are asking: 'If I were wrongly accused, who would believe me?'...Women are no longer human and flawed. They are Truth personified. They are above reproach," she wrote.[93]

This suggests a lack of accountability in their putting up with bad behavior, as if women have no agency to make other choices. It also means that any man who has (not even necessarily) behaved badly and ended a relationship badly, with the woman feeling that he didn't treat her well, if he has any kind of public profile or professional reputation, he can face ruination because he is automatically presumed guilty until proven innocent. What's little-considered is that the falsely accused are victims as well. We're faced with the idea that we should listen and believe women's stories when they come forward with accusations of abuse. And we do, because it plays directly to the male psyche which wants to protect women. This means we are biased and deaf to the appeals of men who are isolated and in agony having been falsely accused.

#BelieveHer was the slogan of the #MeToo crowd and should have no place in or out of court. If the presumption is that the alleged female victim is telling the truth, this automatically means that the alleged male

93 Bari Weiss (November 28, 2017). *"The Limits of 'Believe All Women."* The New York Times. https://www.nytimes.com/2017/11/28/opinion/metoo-sexual-harassment-believe-women.html Post-script. Bari Weiss has since resigned from the NY Times citing the failure of the paper to move away from established orthodoxies. https://www.bariweiss.com/resignation-letter

perpetrator carries the burden of proving his innocence—there is a presumption of his guilt at the outset. "[The number of sexual allegations] plays a role in the court of public opinion. It should not play a role in the courthouse."[94] This is completely antithetical to the basic principles of either social fairness or jurisprudence which have historically underpinned how we organize ourselves collectively. We have, instead, a snarling lynch mob.

~

How about Louis C.K? He also fell victim to the #MeToo witch-hunt. His crime was to ask women if he could masturbate in front of them and, when they consented, he did so. This was not a matter where women were physically coerced—these were consenting adults who failed to have an adult conversation with him after realizing it wasn't what they were into. The concern was that he was putting female comedians in situations where they felt obliged to agree and where he could help or hinder their career, depending on how they responded to his proposition. My understanding is that he had been requesting this favor even before he was famous and that he failed to appreciate how his emergent fame could shift the power dynamic. Once he was accused of impropriety, he gave a full and frank apology.[95]

But this was just red meat to the #MeToo vigilantes and, ever since, he has been hounded, disparaged, and unpersoned. In a civil society, one would imagine that there is a "pathway to redemption for sinners" but this no longer appears to be the case. Nothing short of death by permanent ostracization is permitted—a cancel culture. Years after the apology, it's still not socially acceptable to attend his events or laugh at his jokes.[96]

---

94 Donna Rotunno, Harvey Weinstein's lawyer. YouTube channel, Sky News (March 11, 2020). *"Weinstein's lawyer: 'His accusers are guilty of a lot of things.'"* https://www.youtube.com/watch?v=foT7VtupDBs&feature=emb_logo

95 Elahi Izadi (November 10, 2017). *"Louis C.K. responds to sexual misconduct allegations: 'These stories are true'."* The Washington Post. https://www.washingtonpost.com/news/arts-and-entertainment/wp/2017/11/10/louis-c-k-these-stories-are-true/

96 Radheyan Simonpillai (October 3, 2019). *"Disgraced comic Louis C.K. gets a standing ovation in Toronto."* NOW Toronto, NOW Communications Inc. https://nowtoronto.com/culture/comedy/louis-ck-toronto-yuk-yuks-2/

~

The common thread in the #MeToo movement is that these transgressions are all coming from men. Men are the perpetrators. So men are the problem. No scrutiny is ever placed on the women's role in these men's lives (they are pure, helpless victims). And on the flip side, never do female perpetrators of sexual or domestic violence ever fall under serious scrutiny—because they are female, and "females don't do that sort of thing."

The teenage son of a family in Pennsylvania faced considerable repercussions when five girls at his high school falsely accused him of sexual misconduct. He ended up being expelled from school, losing his part-time job, had to endure the stress of court appearances, was held in a juvenile detention facility, and was also held under house arrest. He had done nothing. It was all just a vindictive act on the part of the girls—they terrorized him because they knew they could. Finally, one admitted, "I just don't like him...I just don't like to hear him talk...I don't like to look at him." The girls were never held to account for their actions and the boy went on to receive psychotherapy for the ordeal he had to endure.[97]

People have been raping and lying about having been raped since time immemorial. The number one reason why a woman may falsely allege having been raped is so that she can get revenge against a man in her life that has crossed her in some way. She may also do so for one of a number of other reasons. She may have a mental illness or is suffering from depression. She may want to extort the guy. She may have regrets about the sex. Or she may want attention and sympathy. Clearly, false allegations of rape do immense harm, not simply to the man but to all women who are genuinely victims of rape. At some point, there may well be a zeitgeist of disbelief after only a few false accusations become widely known and skepticism spreads about legitimate accusations.

~

97 Wendy McElroy (October 17, 2018). *"Is it time to punish false accusers?"* The Hill. https://thehill.com/opinion/civil-rights/411905-is-it-time-to-punish-deliberate-false-accusers

Increasingly, rape shield laws function to prevent cross-examining the alleged victim, resulting in the accused not being able to fully defend himself. What little evidence there is to gather, to demonstrate consensual sex between adults, is being excluded from the court (most sex happens behind closed doors with little means to prove consent). Evidence like text messages proposing and agreeing to sex are deemed inadmissible, since consent could have supposedly been withdrawn after the messages were sent. A woman's sexual history is inadmissible in court but a man's isn't. Neither are her previous false allegations of sexual assault.[98] If the accused is innocent, there are fewer and fewer mechanisms by which he can prove it.

Rape and sexual assault can occur without witnesses, and often does, which makes proving rape difficult. But are women more deserving of justice than men? Is it more just to believe a woman and risk an innocent man going to jail? And is it better to have an innocent man going to jail than risk a potential rapist walking the streets? And why is it that a man is a "rape apologist" when he doesn't automatically #BelieveHer and favors due process and a fair trial?[99] The justice system can never deliver justice perfectly in this world. And the American justice system is a long, long way off from being perfect. But the point is to aim for continuous improvement to something perhaps approaching perfection. The justice system (at its best) is meant to convict only those who are guilty beyond reasonable doubt and to prevent mob rule. Both of these cornerstones are becoming increasingly and worryingly absent.

There are institutional arrangements in place which are aimed to ensure the rights of all parties are maintained, however poorly it might happen in practice. When it does happen poorly in practice then, we need to be good citizens and demand improvements. For victims for whom sexual assault happened behind closed doors, I absolutely understand their desire

98 Sonia Hickey & Ugur Nedim (July 13, 2020). *"Complainant's History of False Sexual Assault Allegations is Inadmissible."* Sydney Criminal Lawyers. https://www.sydneycriminallawyers.com.au/blog/complainants-history-of-false-sexual-assault-allegations-is-inadmissible/

99 Cotwa (June 27, 2013). *"Is Respecting the Presumption of Innocence 'Rape Apology'?"* SAVE (Stop Abusive and Violent Environments). https://web.archive.org/web/20150521082533/http://www.saveservices.org:80/2013/06/is-respecting-the-presumption-of-innocence-rape-apology/

to be able to share their story and find compassion or resources where concrete evidence to proceed to prosecution does not exist. Yet in doing so publicly, in a climate where the woman is believed, the man's reputation and legacy can be obliterated.

~

I consider rape and other forms of sexual assault to be crimes heinous enough to warrant significant societal sanctions. Actual rape is a nightmare situation for women. Yet a woman has more agency protecting herself from rape and sexual assault by doing what her grandmother did, and avoiding potentially dangerous situations, than a man does from avoiding a false allegation. For example, drinking in moderation is wiser than drinking to excess. Being too wasted to knowingly consent to sex means she is unaccountable for her actions and leaves herself open to being targeted by a predator. It also avoids that pesky problem of having to falsely accuse a man of rape when she wakes up the next morning horrified by her actions.

There are "bad" women in the world. This has always been true and will always be true. They are angry, alienated, and vindictive—and they just want to harm something, to change something, even if it produces a negative outcome, because that's what they feel is all they have left. This mentality deserves our pity, if not our compassion. If we are ever to mitigate the effects of their behavior, we need to understand this.

Ultimately, the #MeToo movement reveals that there is no objective definition of sexual harassment. If particular behaviors are either unwanted or perceived to be sexual harassment, then so they are. A man's intention, the context, or his actions count little when compared to a woman's supposedly fragile nature.

I'm actually not at all concerned about innocent men losing their jobs over false sexual assault/harassment allegations[100]

— EMILY LINDEN

14 Rape Culture

Rape is considered a gendered problem where men are the perpetrators. Females also rape men but this is difficult for both men and women to wrap their heads around. "Statistics on sexual harassment from the Department of Justice suggest that over 1.5 million women and 834,700 men are raped and/or physically assaulted annually by an intimate partner in the United States."[101]

To live in a rape culture of female victims, one must accept that the reality that raping women is pervasive and normalized—in which rape is condoned and implicitly or explicitly approved. Yet culturally, we take rape so seriously that it was the last non-lethal capital crime in the USA for which perpetrators could receive the death penalty.[102] Rape as a cultural norm has never been present[103] (see also *Consent, Living Together Harmoniously,* chapter, *Conclusion*).

100 Teen Vogue columnist and UnSlut Project founder, Emily Lindin, via Twitter (November 21, 2017).

101 Branka Vuleta (February 16, 2020). *"32 Disheartening Sexual Assault Statistics for 2020."* Legal Job Site. https://legaljobsite.net/sexual-assault-statistics/

102 Coker v. Georgia, 433 U.S. 584 (1977), held that the death penalty for rape of an adult woman was grossly disproportionate and excessive punishment, and therefore unconstitutional under the Eighth Amendment to the United States Constitution.

103 Recommended viewing: Janice Fiamengo (2016). *"When Feminists Control The Past - TFF Episode 53."* YouTube channel StudioBrule. https://www.youtube.com/watch?v=PIXjDFmC44o

Rape cultures do indeed exist. There have been many occasions in war zones where both men and women were victims of rape; where it was used as a tool to humiliate and pacify a population. Rape of street boys in Pakistan and Afghanistan is also common. Sex trafficking (rape for profit) is horrific and represents a callous indifference to humanity.

If rape culture is not present in US society more broadly, perhaps it exists in pockets? Prison is a good example. Here a high number of men are raped in US prisons due to public and penitentiary indifference.[104]

But let's take a step back. When we think of rape, we imagine it means some form of penetrative sex (usually by a man). But nowadays the meaning has become much more loosely defined. Indeed, according to judicial feminists, it is what most others might consider nothing more than regret after unsatisfactory sex, where even kissing and non-sexual touching can be sexual assault and can result in PTSD.

How about on college campuses? Apparently we face an epidemic of rape and sexual assaults in colleges across the USA. For several years, feminists have been clamoring that the chance of a woman getting sexual assaulted or facing an attempted sexual assault while attending college was about one in four or five. If true, no parent would send their daughter to college. It turns out, the yearly Association of American Universities' Campus Climate Survey (which set off the whole rape culture panic) did not ask college students directly if they had been raped or sexually assaulted, as you might suppose but rather asked a series of questions which sought to highlight unwanted sexual contact. It asked about whether men had ever "expressed displeasure" or criticized her attractiveness, about moving in for a kiss too soon on a date, about not obtaining consent at every stage of a potential sexual interaction.[105] Despite the low respondent rate to the

104 Interestingly, sex offenders are violently targeted to a greater degree by other inmates who recognize their crimes as being too heinous to stand without further punishment. This also gives a lie to there being a rape culture tolerated by men.

105 It wasn't so long ago that rape was considered an act of violent power over a woman (penetration was the mechanism by which it was done). There was a marked distinction between rape and sex—it was not seen as a "sexual act" for sexual gratification. The modern interpretation conflates sex and rape to the extent that a man's natural self-expression through seduction/sex is akin to rape.

study and equivocation of the authors of the report as to its accuracy and veracity, it cannot therefore be extrapolated that 25% of women are getting sexually assaulted or raped on college campuses. Yet politicians[106] and the media have used its findings to push a false narrative of a rape epidemic. In fact, other studies, when confined to just ascertaining incidences of rape and sexual assault (as commonly understood), find that they have remained largely static since 1987.[107] In fact, according to the Bureau of Justice Statistics, there has been a more than 60 percent decline in sexual violence against females from 1995 to 2010.[108] RAINN (the Rape, Abuse, & Incest National Network), which describes itself as the nation's largest anti-violence organization, in its letter to the White House Task Force to Protect Students from Sexual Assault, lamented the "trend towards blaming 'rape culture' for the extensive problem of sexual violence on campuses" and that, "Rape is caused not by cultural factors but by the conscious decisions, of a small percentage of the community, to commit a violent crime."[109]

Young men are required at several colleges to attend mandatory do-not-be-a-rapist seminars. And should a young man become angry at the feminist messaging that "all men are potential rapists," this simply indicates that he *is* a potential rapist, as his "violent" response forewarns.[110] If you're a young man in college, you could easily find yourself in front of a tribunal (their kangaroo court, lacking any real form of due process)

---

106 The Whitehouse (April, 2014). "*Not alone: the first report of the White House Task Force to Protect Students From Sexual Assault.*" [instituted by President Obama]. https://www.justice.gov/archives/ovw/page/file/905942/download

107 Koss MP, Gidycz CA, Wisniewski N. "*The scope of rape: incidence and prevalence of sexual aggression and victimization in a national sample of higher education students.*" J Consult Clin Psychol. https://publichealth.arizona.edu/sites/publichealth.arizona.edu/files/JCCP1987.pdf

108 Michael G. Planty, Ph.D., Lynn Langton, Ph.D., *Bureau of Justice Statistics*, Christopher Krebs, Ph.D., Marcus Berzofsky, Dr. P.H., Hope Smiley-McDonald, Ph.D., (February 7, 2013). "*Female Victims of Sexual Violence, 1994-2010.*" "*RTI International*." Bureau of Justice Statistics. https://www.bjs.gov/index.cfm?ty=pbdetail&iid=4927

109 RAINN letter to White House Task Force to Protect Students from Sexual Assault (February 28, 2014). https://www.rainn.org/images/03-2014/WH-Task-Force-RAINN-Recommendations.pdf

110 Eleanor Harding (November 22, 2015). "*Campus zealots hound student out of lectures and bars with shouts of 'rapist' after he dared to question the effectiveness of rape 'consent workshops'.*" Daily Mail. https://www.dailymail.co.uk/news/article-3329659/Campus-zealots-hound-student-lectures-bars-shouts-rapist-dared-question-effectiveness-rape-consent-workshops.html

where your continuing education and future work life could be ruined by an unsubstantiated, even anonymous, complaint. The point is to enable colleges to "investigate" and try rape cases, since judicial feminists consider that there are not enough convictions in the criminal court system. In a jury trial, unless there is clear evidence to the contrary, juries generally do not convict where there is just a "he says, she says" narrative. The college tribunals have allowed a shift of the balance away from the criminal standard to a far more improper standard of proof. And since we don't have college tribunals for other serious crimes like, say, murder, why on earth are they permitted to adjudicate rape cases? On the flip side, if a real rapist is caught and tried, why is he summarily expelled rather than facing jail time?

If one can point to any harmful, demonstrably provable, gender-based culture on college campuses, it would be that there is a calculated culture of institutionalized antagonism towards the lives of male students.[111]

Judicial feminists have no desire to see justice in the court room. A woman must be believed, even if it means an innocent man going to jail. "I'm really tired of people suggesting that you're somehow un-American if you don't respect the presumption of innocence, because you know what that sounds like to a victim? Presumption: You're a liar."[112] For Law professor, Wendy Martin, even a reversal of the presumption of innocence in law is apparently a price well worth paying.

To men, it would seem that fabricating a fake rape account would be such a pathological act that unless there was some glaring inconsistency in a woman's account, we would naturally believe her. Yet, according to the FBI, between 1.5% and 8% of rape accusations were later found to be false.[113] Thousands of innocent men's lives have been ruined by false accusations, imprisonment for crimes they did not commit, and a lifetime's

111 YouTube channel, StudioBrule (May 22, 2020). *"Betsy DeVos Drank the Feminist Kool-Aid - The Fiamengo File Episode 121."* https://www.youtube.com/watch?v=E2Plc98xql8&feature=emb_logo

112 Stuart Taylor, et al. (September 30, 2008). *"Until Proven Innocent: Political Correctness and the Shameful Injustices of the Duke Lacrosse Rape Case."* St. Martin's Griffin; First Edition. A quote from Wendy Murphy, Professor, New England School of Law (p. 166).

113 Brent E. Turvey, Criminologist (July 22, 2017). *"False Allegations: Investigative and Forensic Issues in Fraudulent Reports of Crime."* Academic Press; 1 edition.

stigma of being a sex offender. If we truly lived in a rape culture, how could this occur? A rape culture is meant to laud and protect rapists, isn't it?

If women want rape to continue to be given the concern it justly deserves, then there arises a responsibility to seriously sanction those women who make false accusations[114]—perhaps with a punishment equal to what the man would have received had she been a genuine victim, and perhaps by being registered as sex offenders. Just how one meets the constructed mendacity of "rape culture" is quite another matter.

114 Asche Schow (July 17, 2020). *"She Made 12 Prior False Accusations Of Sexual Assault. An Australian Court Ruled They Can't Be Used Against Her."* The daily Wire. https://www.dailywire.com/news/she-made-12-prior-false-accusations-of-sexual-assault-an-australian-court-ruled-they-cant-be-used-against-her

Law without reason is criminal.

– CRISS JAMI

15 Sentencing Disparities

"Research published in the Journal of Criminal Justice suggests that courts tend to go easier on women compared to men in some aspects of criminal proceedings."[115] Women receive lesser sentences and more leniency for equivalent crimes as men and are more likely to avoid being charged in the first place.[116] They are twice as likely as men to avoid being incarcerated.

The gender gap in sentencing is about six times as much as the gap in sentencing between whites and blacks.

Why should there be any sentencing disparity between the sexes, if we want to live in a world where men and women are treated equally before the law?

When feminists start asking for extra jail time for women, perhaps their claim for wanting equal treatment with men can be seriously entertained.

---

115 Avery Appelman (December3, 2015). *"Do Women Receive Shorter Jail Sentences Than Men?"* Appelman Law Firm. https://aacriminallaw.com/do-women-receive-short-jail-sentences-than-men/

116 Sonja B. Starr (August 29, 2012). *"Estimating Gender Disparities in Federal Criminal Cases. University of Michigan Law and Economics Research Paper, No. 12-018."* University of Michigan Law School. https://papers.ssrn.com/sol3/Delivery.cfm/SSRN_ID3291458_code572410.pdf?abstractid=2144002&mirid=1

Dictionary definition of feminism:
1 : the theory of the political, economic, and social equality of the sexes
2 : organized activity on behalf of women's rights and interests

16 But Feminism is just about Equality...

I spent my 30 years as a male feminist believing this was so and believing that a fairer, kinder world was possible once the inequalities between the sexes had been addressed. I've been on women's marches and automatically favored any and all social and legislative efforts which sought to redress any perceived imbalance. I cared about women's issues. And I still do today. But my understanding is now far more nuanced. My own internal bias favored women's voices above men's because of the ongoing injustices I believed they experienced as a group. Had I heard any rebuke of feminism coming from a man, I would have instantly judged him to be defending his privileged position and trying to muddy the water. So it wasn't until I heard such a rebuke coming from the mouth of a *woman,* Karen Straughan,[117] that I started to question my belief paradigm. I can now hear men's pain where before I was deaf.

It should be noted that most women agree with the simple dictionary definition. They assume that there must still be areas where women are less equal than men, are glad that feminists are actively fighting for equality, but are too busy focusing on other aspects of their lives to give it further attention.

---

117 Youtube channel, Karen Straughan. The older videos are more informative.

So not all feminists are man-hating female supremacists. But the movement is so infused with exactly this sentiment (and has been since its earliest days) that it inevitably filters through to the zeitgeist.

Here are some quotes from leading or high-profile feminists both recent and historic.

> *Women have always been the primary victims of war. Women lose their husbands, their fathers, their sons in combat.*[118]
>
> – HILLARY CLINTON

This is another example of "male disposability." Men losing their lives is of secondary significance.

> *I feel that man-hating is an honorable and viable political act that the oppressed have a right to class-hatred against the class that is oppressing them.*
>
> – ROBIN MORGAN, EDITOR, MS. MAGAZINE

> *Women, though saved by the noble sacrifice of men, were in the equally hard position of having to see the ship go down.*[119]
>
> – UNNAMED SUFFRAGETTE

> *I want to see a man beaten to a bloody pulp with a high heel shoved in his mouth like an apple in the mouth of a pig,*[120]
>
> – ANDREA DWORKIN

> *The proportion of men must be reduced and maintained at approximately 10% of the human race.*[121]
>
> – SALLY MILLER GEARHART

---

118 17 November, 1998 speech that Hillary Clinton (as First Lady) delivered at a conference on domestic violence in El Salvador

119 New York Times, circa 1912, in response to the sinking of the Titanic

120 Andrea Dworkin (1993). *"Mercy: A Novel."* Four Walls Eight Windows.

121 Sally Miller Gearhart, tenured professor at the University of San Francisco (1992). *"The Future—If There Is One—Is Female. Reweaving the Web of Life: Feminism and Nonviolence."* New Society Publishers.:266–284. In her essay, she considered the best option to reduce the male population was by male infanticide. But because this would be a hard sell, she favored advances in medicine so that women could have sex-selective abortions. She is also the inspiration for the present-day slogan, The Future is Female.

I believe that women have a capacity for understanding and compassion which men structurally do not have. Does not have it because he cannot have it. He's just incapable of it.

– BARBARA JORDAN, FEMINIST AND FORMER US SENATOR

The male is a biological accident. The Y male gene [sic] is an incomplete X female gene. That is, it has an incomplete set of chromosomes. In other words, the male is an incomplete female – a walking abortion, aborted at the gene stage. To be male is to be deficient, emotionally-limited. Maleness is a deficiency disease and males are emotional cripples.[122]

– VALERIE SOLANAS

To call a man an animal is to flatter him; he's a machine, a walking dildo.[123]

– VALERIE SOLANAS

All men are rapists and that's all they are.[124]

– MARILYN FRENCH

It cannot be assumed that men are bound to be an asset to family life, or that the presence of fathers in families is necessarily a means to social cohesion.[125]

– HARRIET HARMAN, PATRICIA HEWITT

Assume that all men are rapists.[126]

– LINDA SNECKER

Just imagine switching genders on some of these quotes. Consider this: "To call a woman an animal is to flatter her; she's a machine, a walking sex doll." Can you imagine the justifiable outrage? Have you ever heard something so vile coming from a man's mouth? Yet men's humanity is ignored because men are the problem.

122 Valerie Solanas (1968). *"The SCUM Manifesto."* Phoenix Press. SCUM stands for Society for Cutting Up Men.

123 Valerie Solanas (1968). *"The SCUM Manifesto."* Phoenix Press.

124 Marilyn French (2009). *"The Women's Room: A Novel."* Penguin Books.

125 Harriet Harman, Patricia Hewitt, senior ministers in Tony Blair's governments. New Feminist Review, 1992

126 Linda Snecker, Swedish Member of Parliament. 2019

Perhaps it might be imagined that modern feminism is the problem. Yet even first wave feminism was rooted in misandry.[127] It campaigned for a "bachelor tax." By withholding themselves from marriage, bachelors were considered to be depriving unmarried women of a claim on their income. Then there was the White Feather movement where groups of women roamed the streets looking for men of an age for conscription (for World War One). They would pin a white feather on any such man out of uniform to pressure, shame, and humiliate him for not enlisting in a war which killed millions in the trenches. Second-wave feminists, like Gloria Steinem and Betty Friedan, shamed those women who adhered to traditional female roles by defining what constituted both a feminist and femininity itself (also shaming men by proxy). Women's task was to usurp the male role not focus on, say, motherhood where her special qualities were hidden from the wider world, unlauded. You could even say that second-wave feminism was misogynistic.

There were some milestones that feminist consciousness expedited. Until the 1974 Equal Credit Opportunity Act, a woman was unable to apply for a credit card under her own name. She had to have a joint credit card with her husband. Viewed through today's lens of hostility towards men, surely this was a clear example of Patriarchal oppression! Yet, as always, there is nuance. Here the law was catching up to a changing world. Husbands had previously been expected to bankroll their wives—men were the breadwinners and women were the home-makers. Women had for decades been able to access in-store credit in the days when credit cards didn't even exist. Companies like Woolworth's were all too pleased for the wife to run up a hefty line of credit—the husband was expected to make good the money owed. Indeed, the courts ruled that it was the right of the wife to run up debt without prior approval from her husband.

Feminism is about raising women above men, not equal rights. It's

127 Misandry is the hatred of, contempt for, or prejudice against men or boys in general. Misandry may be manifested in numerous ways, including social exclusion, sex discrimination, hostility, gynocentrism, belittling of men, violence against men, and sexual objectification.

the gender equivalent of demanding a white ethnostate. Because, where women have it better than men, there is never any effort by them to redress the balance in favor of men (one example being for child custody arrangements which serve the child by acknowledging the value of the continuing equal presence of the father in the child's life). Judicial feminists want women to be treated as a special class with special laws enacted for them. For example, they argue that women should be allowed to murder men.[128] This reflects a version of equality, called "substantive equality," rather than "formal equality," usually reserved for very specific circumstances under law. The phrase "men and women should be equal" is no longer the standard. Instead, because women could never hope to rival men's privilege or power under any circumstances, it is argued they should not be held to the same standards and require special laws of their own.

~

Feminism's focus, more and more, is to re-educate, reprogram, and remake men. You could even compare their efforts to the regressive efforts to turn gays straight through conversion therapy, and which hearkens back to times when homosexuality was seen as a mental illness.

Psychologist, Ronald Levant wrote, "The new psychology of men has emerged over the past 15 years within the larger fields of men's studies and gender studies. Informed by the academic breakthroughs of feminist scholarship, the new psychology of men examines masculinity not as a normative referent, but rather as a problematic construct. In so doing, it provides a framework for a psychological approach to men and masculinity that questions traditional norms of the male role and views some male problems as unfortunate byproducts of the male gender role socialization process."[129]

128 Elizabeth Sheehy even argued in her book, *Defending Battered Women*, that they would be doing a public service by murdering men because men are inherently violent and the legal system did nothing to factor this in.

129 Ronald F. Levant (June 1996). *"The new psychology of men."* Professional Psychology: Research and Practice.

Or this…

"But the means justifies the end here. Of course saving the planet would justify the castration of 25% of the population. Sounds terrible, right? But if we would cut off your dicks, you would be just fine. We have to stop men from governing so they give the power to us women. Will they do that voluntarily? [Student - 'No']. We have to help them with selective castration. And if we cut off the balls of male babies at birth, not only will they no longer be able to have sons but they also wont develop the hormones to give them physical strength. And I've got my own idea of an alternate world. [Student - 'How?']. I don't think I have to explain it. It's called The Matriarchy."[130]

When was the last time you heard a man call for the sterilization of 25% of all female babies? If we existed in a patriarchy, such misogyny might be expected. But it just goes to show that the world we live in is far more misandric[131] than misogynistic.

#KillAllMen is an acceptable hashtag[132] since it has no social repercussions for those who use it. No one loses their job or are banned from social media platforms, etc, as would be the case if the hashtag #KillAllWomen were used.

Indeed, for a man to speak out against unfair treatment by women is to invite condemnation and ridicule. All feminist talking points will be thrown back in his face, his masculinity questioned as being a whiner. His reputation and career may well be at risk, too (taking the examples of

---

130 Carlos Cuesta (6/6/2019). *"Una concejal del PSOE en Canarias a sus alumnos de la ESO: "A los niños hay que castrarlos al nacer.""* Aurelia Vera, a school teacher and city council member in the Canary Islands town of Puerto del Rosario, Spain. From a student recording, reported in OKDiario newspaper. https://okdiario.com/espana/concejal-del-psoe-canarias-sus-alumnos-eso-ninos-hay-que-castrarlos-nacer-4211669

131 Misandry—the hatred of, contempt for, or prejudice against men or boys in general.

132 Ashe Schow (August 9, 2018). *"Vox's Ezra Klein Defends "Kill All Men" Twitter Hashtag."* Daily Wire. https://www.dailywire.com/news/voxs-ezra-klein-defends-kill-all-men-twitter-ashe-schow

James Damore[133] and Alessandro Strumia,[134] to name but two). Women in a position of some power have rather more latitude to dissent from the feminist orthodoxy. They may receive some invective but are unlikely to suffer some calamity. *And yet they don't say anything.* Can you think of any powerful woman who has challenged the much-refuted wage gap narrative? Championed for more women to be in male-dominated jobs such as refuse collectors, sanitation workers, or crab fishermen? Insisted women serve the same time as men for the same crime? That women die in equal numbers to men in times of war? Suggested that, while unfortunate, workplace deaths should be more evenly balanced male/female? Asked why women's needs are visible but men's needs invisible? In counterpoint, high-powered men regularly advocate for the advancement of women, even at the expense of men.

Objectively speaking, feminists care little about equality of the sexes. Since there is actually nothing left to fight for, they care only to keep feminism relevant by shaming and blaming men for the way they feel about their position in society—a cultural war on men. Feminism, it can be surmised, is a powerful hate movement dressed up as a movement for equality. It has engineered a hatred of men as dominators and oppressors whose single aim is to control women. Men are the enemy! They are toxic! They underlie everything that's wrong in society! They are barely human!

The question arises, should men shoulder the responsibility to stand up to this movement for female supremacy? Or should women? Currently, men don't know how to say no to women because of their need for validation, uncritical support, and the "provide and protect" mentality which blinds them. And women don't know how to say no to women because

133 Fired from Google for authoring the memo, *"Google's Ideological Echo Chamber. How bias clouds our thinking about diversity and inclusion."* 2017. See YouTube channel, American Enterprise Institute, *"Google Memo: Beyond the culture war."* https://www.youtube.com/watch?v=tu4tB9W3xFo&feature=emb_logo
Also, FiredForTruth.com, Damore's website.

134 Theoretical particle physicist fired from CERN for demonstrating that women were being advantaged over men in physics.
See YouTube channel, StudioBrule, *"Physics Under SJW Attack: The Case of Alessandro Strumia."* https://www.youtube.com/watch?v=sOCIke7zLMo
Also, Alessandro Strumia (April 16, 2019). *"Why Are Women Under-Represented in Physics?"* Quillette. https://quillette.com/2019/04/16/why-are-women-under-represented-in-physics/

of in-group bias.[135] How willing would women be, as a group, to reveal the deception of feminism which might then challenge their position as being "the better sex?" That being said, it is much easier for a woman to stand up to a woman (or male feminist) at the interpersonal level. But if a woman takes a public stand as an advocate for men's issues, she will be hounded and demonized.[136]

The collective voice of women is a good deal more powerful than the collective voice of men. The men's rights movement would never have as much impact as an (anticipated?) she-for-he movement simply because society is more interested in solving problems which adversely affect women—i.e. the collective, unintegrated pain of women which has an adverse effect on their lives.

Feminists have successfully broken the assumption of good intent that men have towards women. The repercussions for societal relations are quite frightening for the wellbeing of both sexes, should it continue to rule the day.

135 Rudman LA, Goodwin SA, *"Gender differences in automatic in-group bias: why do women like women more than men like men?"* Department of Psychology, Rutgers, The State University of New Jersey, Piscataway, NJ, USA. https://rutgerssocialcognitionlab.weebly.com/uploads/1/3/9/7/13979590/rudmangoodwin2004jpsp.pdf

136 YouTube channel, Roma Army (January 2, 2021). *"I Am A Female Mens Rights Advocate & Society Hates Me For It."* https://www.youtube.com/watch?v=maYWF_jzpBA

♫ *When a man loves a woman*
Can't keep his mind on nothin' else
He'd change the world for the good thing he's found
If she is bad, he can't see it
She can do no wrong
Turn his back on his best friend if he put her down ♫[137]

— PERCY SLEDGE

17 Gynocentricism

Gynocentricism[138] is a natural facet of human history. As a matter of species-level survival, women's needs were given top priority. In terms of procreation, a woman can produce only a handful of progeny whereas a man can spread his seed far and wide. This means that there is an asymmetry between the sexes in terms of importance in creating a baby. Theoretically, men are less important since a few men can impregnate all available women of childbearing age.

In order to ensure reproductive success, men have given women protection from harm, provision of resources, and guidance as fathers, brothers, leaders, and lovers. At the species level, it was necessary for women to be more self-interested, for men to recognize their dominant claim over men's needs, and to sacrifice their own needs for the greater good.

This expectation of service to the feminine has continued down through

137 Percy Sledge (1966). "*When a Man loves a Woman.*" Produced by Martin Greene and Quin Ivy.

138 Gynocentrism n. (Greek, γυνή, "female" – Latin centrum, "centred") refers to a dominant or exclusive focus on women in theory or practice; or to the advocacy of this.

the ages. And today, at the practical level, women are naturally the objects of greater sympathy and welfare than men. They are treasured. Very few men understand they are in many ways considered less worthy than women, and how the law and social norms reflects this. Even if they do understand it, they see it as a mark of a man not to complain and kick up a fuss. They suck it up. They may even create some dark humor around the personal injustices they have suffered. A case in point is a woman's expectation that it is "her body, her choice." Yet if a woman makes a unilateral choice to become pregnant and bring a baby to term (the father having no say in the matter), she cannot then claim that he support her financially. Yet the court system does not reflect the responsibility of independent women making autonomous decisions about their bodies, and to shoulder the consequences of those decisions. She would be awarded some form of child support, regardless of the father's absence of choice in the matter.

When looking at their positive actions in society, we can observe that women are given positive feedback, and men's respective efforts are played down. When women act in a negative way, society's response is neutral, and men's comparable actions are held in a negative light. Gynocentricism leads to distorted ways of perceiving reality, measuring worth, and applying fairness.[139]

Some examples. When men work harder and longer for more money, their efforts are played down because they are doing less work in the home. When women excel at education, they are celebrated for their achievements which are attributed to their female qualities. Men's considerable academic achievements are just a given, and are not seen as a reflection of their male qualities. Women's higher number at colleges is celebrated as a social good. Yet declining rates of men at colleges are met with a yawn and, if noticed, is expressed as a problem of masculinity. Firefighters used to be called "firemen." This descriptor was seen as gender-specific and therefore unfair. Yet the vast majority of firefighters are still men and their

139 This is also known as the "Women-are-wonderful effect." *"The Women-Are-Wonderful Effect (We Don't Live in a "Culture of Misogyny")."* Because it's 2015. https://becauseits2015.wordpress.com/2017/06/10/the-women-are-wonderful-effect-we-dont-live-in-a-culture-of-misogyny/

heroism as men exhibiting desirable male behavior (protection) is made gender-neutral by the term, firefighter—as if to imply that women contribute equally.[140] In domestic violence cases, male victims are ignored, as are female perpetrators, even though the rates of violence are comparable with neither sex having a monopoly. Almost exclusively, the focus is on male perpetrators and female victims.

Girls are made of "sugar and spice" and boys are made of "snips and snails and puppy dog tails."[141] You could say that, as a species, we are "vagazzled."[142]

For most of human history, the human race had a comparatively low population level. It was by no means a given that we would become the dominant species. Our numbers and impact on this planet have now reached a level where we can safely say that we have exceeded our biological imperative and won the race (if we don't now annihilate ourselves). There is no longer a societal need to put women first and, instead, recognize that men are people too, deserving of as much empathy as women. Indeed, society is ignoring gaping wounds in men in order to tend to paper cuts in women. "What's the worst that could happen if we all collectively decided that men were no more disposable than women, and women were no more valuable than men?"[143]

---

140 Inga Korolkovaite (2016). *"48 Firefighters Who Risked Their Lives To Save Animals."* Bored Panda. https://www.boredpanda.com/firefighters-rescuing-animals-saving-pets/?utm_source=duckduckgo&utm_medium=referral&utm_campaign=organic
"In honour of these brave men and women, we at Bored Panda have put together this list of firefighters saving pets." The list reveals only men.

141 Robert Southey. *"What Folks Are Made Of."* The complete stanza of this old poem reads, "What are little girls made of, made of? What are little girls made of? Sugar and spice and everything nice; that's what little girls are made of." And, "What are little boys made of, made of? What are little boys made of? Snips and snails and puppy-dog tails; that's what little boys are made of."

142 Dazzled by vaginas

143 Karen Straughan (February 7, 2013). *Feminism and the Disposable Male."* A Voice For Men. https://avoiceformen.com/feminism/feminism-and-the-disposable-male/

Equal opportunity is good, but special privilege is better.

— ANNA CHENNAULT

18 Equality of Opportunity versus Equality of Outcome

The United Nations defines gender equality as a world where "women and men, and girls and boys, should enjoy the same rights, resources, opportunities and protections." Yet their focus is solely about women's equality[144] and the perceived opportunities and protections needed by women to supposedly redress society's wrongs. There are many areas where men have less favorable outcomes compared to women but let's take one area—employment—where feminists claim redress is needed to advance the cause of women.

Let's say that, indeed, women do need a more equitable deal here. As a society, do we want equal numbers of men and women across all business, social, and political realms? More female politicians? More stay-at-home dads? More female engineers? So that eventually both genders had equal representation in terms of numbers in any and all aspects of day-to-day life? Would this lead to greater social happiness and social cohesion? If the answer is yes, then all well and good. This would be "equality of outcome."

Or do we want the same opportunities, as well as challenges, for men

144 *Gender Equality - The Unfinished Business of our Time.* https://www.un.org/en/sections/issues-depth/gender-equality/

and women, and for those men and women to decide where their interests lie and to make free choices according to their talent, their natures, and their dispositions? This would be "equality of opportunity."

These two concepts are hotly contested with very few people admitting that we have neither—and what we have are horribly distorted versions of each.

When you hear feminists advocating for the needs of women, they solely focus on the upper echelons of society—more female business leaders, politicians, scientists, scholars, etc. Here, they have traditionally demanded equality of outcome (although the cry increasingly is for men to step aside, as "the future is female").[145] Just imagine the next president, male or female, announcing to the nation that s/he was going to implement social programs to increase female participation rates to 50% across the board. That would mean:

- 32,864 more female pest control workers (which would mean 32,864 fewer male) to bring the number up to 39,500 out of a total of 79,000 for both sexes.
- 575,000 more female grounds maintenance workers (and equally fewer men); 664,000 of each sex for a total of 1,328,000.
- 27,492 more female logging workers (and equally fewer men); leaving 29,000 men and 29,000 women for a total of 58,000.
- 96,810 more female telecommunications line installers and repairers (and equally fewer men); leaving 105,000 men and 105,000 women for a total of 210,000.
- Or 32,305 more female refuse collectors (and equally fewer men); leaving 45,500 men and 45,500 women for a total of 91,000.[146]

Strangely, feminist leaders are not calling for these social changes. It seems feminism caters only to upper class or upper-middle class women—elite women. These elite women appropriate the experience of women of

145 Would it be acceptable for whites to say, "the future is white?" Or men to say, "the future is male?" Such statements would rightly be considered bigoted.

146 *(2018). "Household Data, Annual Averages, Employed persons by detailed occupation, sex, race, and Hispanic or Latino ethnicity."* US Bureau of Labor Statistics. https://www.bls.gov/cps/cpsaat11b.pdf

lower socio-economic status in order to further their own interests. By pointing to women's oppression in other parts of the world, it allows these socially privileged women to maintain that they are also oppressed. A type of victimhood appropriation.

~

Job preferences appear to be strongly linked to human biology. When given equal opportunity to select a career of their choosing, men tend to select jobs centered around things and women around people; systematizing professions and empathizing professions. In 2010, a Norwegian documentary,[147] receiving the Fritt Ord Award, explored why this was the case in what was then the most egalitarian society on Earth.[148] Sociologist, Harald Eia, found that, paradoxically, the more egalitarian the society was, the greater the divide in job selection by sex. 90% of nurses in Norway were female and 90% of engineers were male, despite both sexes having had the same opportunities in education and no barriers of entry to either profession based on sex. Given equal opportunities, both sexes showed traditional gender behavior. Conversely, in less developed countries, lifestyle choices were a luxury that many could not afford and both sexes gravitated to the better-paying jobs, creating a more equal outcome.

Even when considering the possibility of social conditioning and reinforcement of traditional gender roles from society more broadly, Eia cited studies which clearly demonstrated how toddlers and babies in their first months, when given free choice of feminine toys and masculine toys, and with no adult guidance, invariably chose toys associated with their particular sex.[149] Professor Trond Diseth at Norway's National Hospital

---

147 YouTube channel, Jurij Fedorov (September 14, 2014). *"Hjernevask (Brainwash) 1/7 - The Gender Equality Paradox."* https://www.youtube.com/watch?v=E577jhf25t4
Hjernevask ("Brainwash"), NRK1, 2010.

148 World Economic Forum.

149 Gerianne M. Alexander, Teresa Wilcox Rebecca Woods (1 July 2008). *"Sex Differences in Infant's Visual Interest in Toys."* Springer Science and Business Media. http://www.psy.fau.edu/iclab/pdfs/2009-Alexander-Wilcox-Sex-differences-in-infants-visual-interest-in-toys.pdf

Department of Child Psychiatry surmised that when "children are born with a clear biological disposition, as far as gender identity and behavior is concerned, then environmental influences either increases or decreases that behavior."

If gender and gender-based life choices are largely inherent, then trying to organize a society based on equal participation across all domains would be to deny our humanity, serving neither sex.

So is there any merit to "equality of outcome?" Equality of opportunity simply does not exist in a balanced sense for all human beings. We are not born equally blessed with intelligence, innate athletic ability, or rich parents. Those who are less than average are condemned to live a poorer life unless measures are taken to help them to maximize their potential and enjoy material equality. Most proponents of equality of opportunity are happy for there to be winners and losers but are displeased when those losers create societal problems owing to their diminished agency.

In terms of social well-being, I believe the principle of "reasonable accommodation" might be applied to good effect. The term is most commonly used when adapting workplace practices to help people with disabilities, who would otherwise perform equally well as those who were fully-abled. Given a modest investment of time and resources, a society can make the choice to enable people to meet their potential, especially when doing so would bring them an increased satisfaction and sense of well-being they might not have otherwise been able to achieve by themselves. So if a woman needed extra assistance to realize her dream of becoming an engineer, or a man a nurse, then a compassionate society would help them realize that vision, as long as both would be assessed on merit at the time of hiring.

Such is not the case presently, where many companies and institutions hire to "virtue-signal" their commitment to diversity at the expense of competency. Equity hiring practices in the workplace should mean that if you have two candidates of equal merit, you would choose the one which would permit the school/business/government department to accomplish its equity mandate by hiring the candidate who belongs to a minority group which has historically been discriminated against. This sounds like a very reasonable position. In practice what happens is that a mindset develops which positively favors the minority applicant (women are considered a minority) at the expense of the more qualified one, often with subtle, or even overt, pressure from senior staff. This has been ongoing for probably the last 20 years, resulting in diminished competencies across many fields. It also diminishes women by suggesting they don't have to be anything other than passable in their job—they just have to be female. Ideally, what is desirable is a world which holds women (and other minorities) to a standard of competency rather than affording them top jobs and special dispensations/perks simply because of being the proud owners of a uterus.

Part Three

Modern Women

God created man and, finding him not sufficiently alone, gave him a companion to make him feel his solitude more keenly.

– PAUL VALÉRY

In the next two chapters, I'll demonstrate how both men and women have, regrettably, become stunted in their maturation. For this chapter, additionally, I'm choosing to focus on those aspects typified by modern women which conscious men need to realize and appreciate which, through misapprehension, would otherwise bring them low. Behind my words, though, there is no blame, judgment, contempt, or malice. The sad state affairs we find ourselves in today has been decades, if not millennia, in the making. And modern women are simply the recipients of a legacy of maladaptive behaviors of both men and women through the generations in response to inhumane socio-political conditions.

A woman reading this chapter may find it objectionable but will have her answer to the question, "Where have all the good men gone?" A Google Trends search for the term, "dating tips," shows a marked downward trend since 2004. Although not gender-specific, it suggests a social environment where men are becoming progressively less interested or dispirited with the whole dating scene.

To reiterate, the following two chapters are not meant to demean or chastise today's generation of men and women and paint them unfairly with a broad brush. I also offer a critique of traditional men and women. Rather than preface each sentence with "some women" or the majority women" or "not all women" (which would make everything just a clumsy mess), I'll be more declarative, and leave the reader to figure out the valency of my assertions in respect to their own lived experience or observations. Ultimately, I aim to set the backdrop for the work to be done to improve interpersonal relationships with each sex (see *The Divine Union*).

A woman possessed by the animus is always in danger of losing her femininity.

— CARL JUNG

19 The Subversion of the Feminine Essence

Society systematically programs women to move away from their true nature, which is love, at its core. What we are left with is a feminine essence inside every woman which has been buried alive. Modern women smile far less these days, favoring instead either a "resting bitch face" or an impenetrable, cool, "I'm out of your class" expression. They are afraid of being perceived as a softy, a push-over, a doormat which they believe a smile transmits, rather than simply accepting the feeling of being soft around the edges. Women who smile infrequently receive less positive connection in their lives and feel less happy without ever knowing why.

Feminism has done a disservice to women (so too have legacy religions which deeply suppressed female wisdom). If feminism's aim was to take women back to an empowered state of being, it has wholly failed. The movement initially challenged women to compete in all aspects of life that were traditionally male-dominated. The equality they demanded was equality of masculinity—not equality of femininity *with* masculinity. The result has been that women have developed strongly integrated male approaches to life, functioning more from a male psychology—an animus-possessed persona. At its most basic, it simply produced two sources of taxable earnings in the household without even doubling the wealth (as the last two generations have found out by an ever-tightening belt). Despite their gains, modern feminism (third wave and fourth wave) paints the picture of a modern woman without agency—a victim, who is in a battle to the death with a fabled Patriarchy and all men who would be its favored beneficiaries.

Whereas girls have not had, to my knowledge, traditional rites of passage in the same way some boys had, they nevertheless had to step from being a girl to a woman. For her, it was more about the embodiment of her sexuality and the flowering of her heart energy. Our modern-day culture wants women to be valued more for her achievements, rightly or wrongly. The question is, does it serve her? Does it acknowledge and speak to her essential nature as a woman? Clearly there are many women occupying many previously male-dominated positions in society (and I'm not pushing for a return to the past) but are most living in their integrity? A woman naturally lives more from her body, in her body, and in the Now. So if society values achievement, she will start to divorce herself from her organism in order to meet its expectations.

Women are in a never-ending cycle of working, striving, and competing, in greater numbers than ever in the workplace. For women from lower socioeconomic circumstances, they may need to work at more than one job and barely make ends meet. They are so exhausted that they've neglected caring for themselves, they have little time for creative expression, and the world is just not fun. When their masculine energy dominates their lives, women can lose touch with themselves and their needs. They either martyr themselves in a relationship or expect their intimate partner to put her own needs first and foremost.

Many modern women almost have a sense of disdain for their feminine side and are, for instance, incapable of receiving. Even when they receive positive appreciative attention, they perceive it as aggression or harassment. They are inhibited in opening up and expressing their femininity in the presence of a man. This is an unnatural state resultant from women having been shamed, embarrassed, diverted, distracted, or programmed into repressing their femininity. This is mostly by her mother (although her peers exert great influence). The mother is the gatekeeper to womanhood and the girl imbibes her mother. Her relationship with her mother becomes her relationship to the world and with herself—her self-image, her body, her attitude towards men, sex, money, etc.

There are now a plethora of women's groups which claim to support "womxn" in reconnecting with their femininity but many are deeply unaware that they are operating out of the masculine. Many advance the notion that she needs to be a strong, powerful, warrior goddess. They support and condone female entitlement (#TheFutureIsFemale) or baby-girl bullshit and they dress it up in pseudo-spiritual New Moon circles, yoni ceremonies, etc. This has produced a plethora of entitled "yogini princesses" believing themselves to be transcendent goddesses. With "the future being female" and their sense of superiority affirmed, they call in the masculine to "do his own work" and to rise to join them. What many women fail to realize is that their softness, their yin, is their most powerful force. Being a deeply feeling, loving, compassionate woman is sadly given little credence in modern times. Yet this force can heal the world. But many of these groups arise in resistance to men—and are, in fact, antagonistic towards them and the supposed patriarchy which they believe exists to serve them. In fact, the presence of an open-minded, fully present, and accepting man (or men) at such gatherings would help women learn to release fear of unleashing their divine feminine essence in the company of men in general.

For feminist women, the problem is compounded. These women are in resistance to their own femininity under the guise that they are "for femininity." They reject the traditional view of femininity and hence throw the baby out with the bathwater.[150] If cooking for the family chained her to the stove, then cooking duties had to either be shared or come out of the microwave in the form of TV dinners—no matter if the woman herself truly enjoyed her role. If being a home-maker meant being dependent on

150 Amy Glass (2014). *"I Look Down On Young Women With Husbands And Kids And I'm Not Sorry."* Thought Catalog. https://thoughtcatalog.com/amy-glass/2014/01/i-look-down-on-young-women-with-husbands-and-kids-and-im-not-sorry/

a man, then shame on her for not being capable enough to earn a living—no matter if she relished the idea of her man being the provider because of the way it felt of having someone who loved her taking the time and energy to support her physical needs and wants.[151] Second-wave feminists demonstrated their rebellion by dressing like men, burning their bras publicly, and adopting male behavior in the workplace as a way of rejecting their femininity (and don't get me started on third wave feminists!). The feminist narrative confuses women because they advocate for consigning certain beliefs and practices to the trashcan—beliefs and practices which work for many women. "Women who 'adjust' as housewives, who grow up wanting to be 'just a housewife,' are in as much danger as the millions who walked to their own death in the concentration camps… they are suffering a slow death of mind and spirit."[152]

---

151 Vivian Gornick, feminist author, University of Illinois (April 25, 1981). *"Being a housewife is an illegitimate profession… The choice to serve and be protected and plan towards being a family-maker is a choice that shouldn't be. The heart of radical feminism is to change that."* The Daily Illini.

152 Betty Friedan (September 3, 2013). *"The Feminine Mystique."* W. W. Norton & Company; 50th Anniversary edition.

The hard-won freedom of choice has imprisoned women. I just see an exhausted generation trying to do it all.

– ERIN PIZZEY

20 Gender Roles and Expectations

Gender in humans—what is called "sex-role" in other species—is the behavioral manifestation of a person's sex. Although sex and gender have tightly linked qualities, and are predominantly evolutionary, some would say there is a component of choice of one's gender. Sex is binary and gender isn't. Gender roles historically were far closer to being bi-modal than they currently are.

Traditional relationships were largely based on what the other person did, rather than who the other person was. Men's and women's roles were tightly proscribed. Breadwinners and homemakers. Value was determined by how well men and women fulfilled their duties. Regardless of aptitude to the contrary, men were expected to bring home the bacon and women would raise children. The world has shifted to recognize that there are women who like to raise money and men who like to raise a family. In Fortune 500 companies, women without children are promoted more quickly than their male peers. And when fathers are predominantly the go-to parent in an intact family, the children of such a family tend to do better than their cohorts. This suggests that when men and women freely choose a non-traditional gender role with which they feel a particular affinity, they are usually exceptionally good at that role. However, over the last two generations, the rise of women in the workplace has far exceeded the rate at which men have become homemakers. Women used to have a choice whether to work or not. Nowadays they have little choice but to seek employment. So feminism has helped to actually reduce women's opportunity.

When women, in particular, feel pressured to take on non-traditional gender roles, problems occur. There are more and more societal pressures for them to take the lead in becoming more active in politics and business, being at the forefront of societal change, and so on. Studies have shown since the 1950s women becoming progressively unhappier[153] despite entering avenues of life they have been clamoring to walk down. Women's liberation was supposed to help women lead more happy and fulfilling lives. It's actually achieving quite the opposite for those women who think they should be out there pushing and achieving. This is out of integrity for their dominant feminine essence. Women's health and well-being is actually dependent on allowing themselves to connect more fully with aspects of their femininity which have been suppressed by modern workplace and cultural practices.

There are women who can and should lead this sort of life but, because most women don't have a dominant masculine essence, they won't and will never be in the majority of these roles. That's why more men than women are seen in positions of authority. It has nothing to do with women's oppression and patriarchal privilege. It has to do with our respective natures. Many of the gender roles and patterns observed cross-culturally would seem to imply that traditional roles are natural forms of self-organization.

Saying that men and women have different aptitudes isn't sexism—it's actually a statement about reality. If we keep saying that those differences in what men and women choose to do are because of sexism, nobody will end up happy with what they are doing—we're going to keep making laws to "remedy" what is just the result of freedom of choice.

---

153 Betsey Stevenson, Justin Wolfers (2009). *"The Paradox of Declining Female Happiness."* National Bureau Of Economic Research. https://www.nber.org/system/files/working_papers/w14969/w14969.pdf

That's not to say that men have got it all right and that those in authority are exercising their power fairly and judiciously. Neither men nor women are adept, quite frankly. The world is fucked up not because of innate gender differences and their expression but because of class divisions and the wounding of our psyches passed down through the generations. Men, as a majority in authority positions, are ultimately implementing the decisions of the ruling elite, which benefits the full flourishing of neither sex (more in the chapter, *Why You're a Slave*). Men are the protectors and providers who go out into the world and do what needs to be done. So it looks to the world (and women) like men have agency. But this is an illusion. Men are acting at the behest of the corporatocracy, in one way or another, and are largely attempting to do their best at providing for a family or gathering resources to start one.

Masculine attributes (not patriarchy) essentially define the parameters in the world of "doing." Women can certainly perform in roles of authority and agency but would need to be in their masculine essence to do so. Clearly, it's extremely hard to cultivate their divine feminine traits such as softness, passivity, and receptivity when competing in the workplace (see *The Divine Feminine Traits and Qualities*, chapter, *The Divine Feminine*). When women who have a naturally dominant feminine essence try to insert themselves into a paradigm which is essentially masculine, they find themselves becoming dissatisfied with living mostly from their masculine essence for most of the day. The problem with that is that if they introduce their "vortex of confusion" into the world (see *Feelings,* below) then it's certainly not going to make the world any less fucked up. We're certainly a long way down this rabbit hole already because of feminist ideology penetrating the zeitgeist and creating more confusion.

Women do not need to be liberated from restrictive gender roles. Both men and women do, so that they have the option to follow life choices in their best interests.

We have become so preoccupied in clicking, capturing and caging memories that we have forgotten to live them first.[154]

— MITALI MEELAN

21 Narcissism and Entitlement

A narcissist is someone who never successfully individuated as a child. Instead, they see others as an extension of themselves. And as such, these "others" do not have any needs of their own distinct from the narcissist. Narcissists experience themselves as unable to meet their own needs, even as an adult.

As can be seen from the chapter, *Feminist Myths and Narratives,* modern women have been socialized to be antagonistic and feel superior towards men. This has made it acceptable to attack male qualities and achievements in terms of men's leadership, physical prowess, intelligence, practical achievements, inventions, their capacity for protecting, providing, and sacrificing. The world that men have built for the women they love is not enough.

For modern women, especially those who have a high "sexual market value,"[155] there is an incredible amount of stimulation that they receive that was never the case in previous generations. They are better connected,

154 Mitali Meelan (November 28, 2017). *"Coffee and Ordinary Life."* Self-published.

155 Sexual market value is a concept taken from Economics, and refers to how sexually attractive a person is to the opposite sex within the sexual marketplace. Broadly speaking, the higher one's sexual market value, the more sexually attractive they are and the more access they have to sex and partners.

better paid, more sexually free, and have greater societal privileges simply by virtue of their sex.[156]

Modern women understand that they can leverage their appearance for social advantage. Younger women spend an insanely large amount of time dedicated to looking hot, sexy, or cute. It's not just fashion and make-up—many spend hours in front of a mirror perfecting their expressions, especially their smiles. It's said that a man's face is his autobiography; a woman's face being her work of fiction.

In the age of Facebook, Instagram, Snapchat, Tinder, etc, they receive constant validation through clicks, likes, dings, and hearts. They'll even share favorable responses from men with their girlfriends in order to prove to them (and themselves) that they are desirable and relevant. In pre-internet times, pretty women used to get into clubs for free and get free drinks—they still can, and so much more.[157] The trope that women most identify with is "Live, Laugh, and Love." They want to have as much fun and pleasure and stimulation as they can get, and also have the tender, loving, committed, monogamous relationship too (with hot, wall-to-wall sex!) where the boyfriend is just like any of her fashion accessories, so that she can experience the feeling of being/falling in love. They want it all. And why not? So do men. But for most men, aspirational lifestyles are largely a fantasy. For modern women, not so. They even joke about getting Tinder food stamps (i.e. free meals from men).[158]

~

Guys play to win, and women play "not to lose." Losing, for a woman, means not securing a high value mate before her sexual market value

156 College entitlements, child custody favoritism, a gynocentric educational system, women-only programs and classes.

157 There is a recognition that women with a high SMV are so beneficial to pulling in men who desire them (who pay the full entry price) that the loss of revenue deriving from their free admission is simply a small cost of doing business.

158 Brian Collisson, Jennifer L. Howell, Trista Harig (June 20, 2019). *"Foodie Calls: When Women Date Men for a Free Meal (Rather Than a Relationship)."* Sage Journals. https://journals.sagepub.com/doi/10.1177/1948550619856308

has diminished. So for older women, the news is not so great—they are confused and frustrated that they have a sell-by date. The constant validation has reduced to a dribble and, in order to experience relevancy, they engage in group bullying/bossiness to get what they want—a form of hypoagency. Because society listens to women's pain and frustrations more than it does men's, these wounded women can receive the attention they crave at the expense of inflicting considerable social damage.[159] The popular derogatory term for such women (as of 2020) is a "Karen."

More and more, modern women are critical of men who, on the whole, desire young, hot, cute, shapely women. They have largely developed the expectation that they should be considered desirable regardless of how well they keep themselves—men should be attracted to women of any age or body type. I certainly understand the appeal of this narrative because focusing on the packaging irrespective of what it contains is certainly rather shallow. Yet the opposite is not true. There are precious few high status women who would entertain the idea of partnership with a lower-status man. But you don't hear of male janitors demanding the approval of, say, female doctors because they are more than just their job.

Equally, younger modern women are generally too self-centered to be in a relationship. They have never faced demands of emotional maturity from their male peers nor would they seek it in their own terms. It's hard for them to resist the allure of validation that society now offers them and the men who fawn over them and let them get away with shit. In fact, there is no narcissistic or entitled behavior that isn't sanctioned or condoned by 99 men out of a 100. As a result, they remain stuck in a perpetual adolescence. There is little incentive to move from short-term relationships based on instant gratification to more mature, stable relationships where the thrill of the new has moved from passionate to companionate coupling. If she does have a go at something more stable,

---

159 As an example. This woman obstructed a man's car, preventing him leaving, after he realized he'd made a wrong turn. She called the police, claiming he was attempting to run her over. YouTube channel, Chris Hampshire (August 28, 2018). *"Crazy Lady Park Attendant Harassment."* https://www.youtube.com/watch?v=KRkACKpdeIY

it's much easier to "love-bomb" a guy, so that he thinks she's really into him, and then use his ensuing attention to validate her narcissistic needs.

Whereas the male essence is penetrative (both sexually and energetically), the female's is receptive. Entitlement is a toxic aspect of this receiving nature. Women who are mostly in their feminine aspect, and operating from a pure form of "receiving," come not from a sense of entitlement but gratitude for life's blessings.

Narcissism is wounding, and needs our forgiveness. In a world where women (and men) are hurting, choosing to walk around with their pain on display would be unattractive—to themselves, their peers, and potential mates. It's far easier to put on a happy face, fake a good but superficial life, and suck what pleasure there is to be had from it.

There is a certain degree of "natural narcissism" in women owing to their biological programming which men should not shame either. Because for all of human history the priority of men was to ensure the protection and provision of women, women have evolved to expect this from men. When women believe they are not getting what they need from men, they automatically assume one of two things—either men don't care, or that they are intentionally withholding that which she needs. Of course, men as a group positively want women to have what they need—it fills our hearts to be able to contribute to their wellbeing. There's usually a good reason when a man focuses his energy elsewhere, having more to do with his own path, rather than with neglecting womankind. Equally, women have a hard time knowing what they need and often exist in an amorphous state of yearning.[160]

160 This is not my projection. It's something women have told me.

The truth about women is that you can treat them however they want, so long as you don't bore them.[161]

— CORMAC MCCARTHY

22 Feelings

Feelings tell her what she wants, what she needs, and in their absence she feels like a boat without a sail. A woman's feelings are to her what a man's opinions are to him—they are part of her felt identity. They tell her she's alive. It's not that she is incapable of, or indifferent to, abstracting herself from her emotions, it's just that if something feels like it's true then it carries greater weight in her organism. Since women largely favor their subjective feelings as barometers of reality, and feelings are subject to change, bad actors can massage and manipulate these feelings. This is highly problematic in a world where women have gained significantly higher amounts of agency. Programmed, indoctrinated, and fearful women create social conditions which are detrimental to the common good (see chapter, *Feminist Myths and Narratives*).

What men crave is purpose. What women crave is to feel. They desire stimulation and experiential feeling. This is connected to the feminine expression of their life force. It means they need to know they're alive. Do they love to be loved on? Yes! But if they don't *feel* loved on, they will create drama in order to feel *something*. If they're not stimulated they'll

161 Cormac McCarthy (2013). "*The Counselor: A Screenplay.*" Picador.

look for something, even if it feels "bad." For modern women, however, the expression of high-intensity emotions are taken to the next level as a directive for the man to accede to her needs. Feelings are connected to her identity, so any resistance from the man is taken as an attack on her identity, regardless of how those needs are expressed or the demands attached to them.

When a man raises an objection to a woman making a request of him, or when he sets a boundary, the modern woman tends to take it personally. This goes back to how they relate to most of the things men do—they project that the way men behave towards a woman is dependent on how they *feel* about the woman (regardless that he may simply be acting in accordance with an internal value of his own). "If he loved me more, or respected me more, he would do what I want" is a common refrain. They associate a man's actions towards her with his feelings towards her because that is her own operating system.

On the flip side, some woman flaunt their emotionality as "emotional expression," and "don't you dare shame me for being a woman." These woman are trying to mask their own destructive behavior, poor interpersonal communication skills, and intransigence. It's important to be in touch with her feelings (men too) but it's equally important to be in touch, as much as possible, with objective reality. Crucially, this means calling upon her less dominant aspect; her masculine essence. Rational thinking and personal intellect is necessary in transcending faulty beliefs which can lead to dysfunctional, emotion-driven behavior. That's not to say that the realm of feelings and emotions have no place in shaping this world. But it's nuanced. Without reference to one's emotional center, the world would be devoid of color, warmth, and humanity. And without reference to higher-mind attributes, it would be rudderless.

~

If you don't think women are crazy, ask a man.

– COMEDIAN, GEORGE CARLIN.

Crazy...Hysterical...

The use of these terms by men is not particularly compassionate, nor understanding, nor empathetic. But "crazy" is a very real thing (not a misogynistic put-down). Women don't like being called crazy because they believe that men are basically objecting to their normal range of emotions— particularly anger, frustration, sadness, or any other strong emotion "not deemed appropriate." They think it's a phrase men use to put a woman down and control her, but which otherwise isn't true. Crazy could even be the seat of her power! But what a man means by crazy is when a woman gets so wrapped up and captured by her emotions that any efforts by him to connect with her simply produce even more frenzy. This seems like certifiable behavior![162] When a man says a woman is crazy, he's shaking his head in bemusement and disbelief, rather than disapproval and contempt. When heartfelt efforts to be calm and rational are fuel for the fire, it seems like he's no longer dealing with a reasonable human being. Maybe a toddler? But this is simply another example of how men and women are fundamentally different from one another. Women don't understand that men are not judging them, and men don't understand that she doesn't have much of a choice—that she is wired differently. That just seems ridiculous to him. Wouldn't it be better for all concerned if she could just be calm and logical?

Women also refer to this "crazy" aspect of themselves, but they oftentimes publicly use less highly charged terminology, such as a "vortex of confusion." It's like the "N-word." Women can say it about themselves but men are prohibited from doing so. Many women regard this as an embarrassment and something they should hide, especially from other women. We don't understand what it's like to live in that state. So much of the reason that women suffer in this respect is because their beautifully complex hormonal biochemistry is out of whack. Hormonal imbalance problems are a widespread issue owing to stress, diet, lifestyle, teretogens,

---

162 Example:
YouTube channel, Roma Army (December 28, 2020). *"Roma Army Calling Out Toxic Femininity."* https://www.youtube.com/watch?v=C7T6r-hi4Rk

and birth control pills.[163] But mostly, women do not feel safe in this world, whether they are objectively safe or not.

163 Birth control pills effect every single system of a woman's body and how her hormones interact with it. They can alter her ability to form healthy relationships and bonds since it dulls her animal instincts (see *Evolutionary Programming*, chapter, *The Divine Feminine*). Hormonal birth control, 50-plus years since its inception, has never had a formal study to evaluate how it can dysregulate a woman's psycho-physiology.

The big difference between sex for money and sex for free is that sex for money usually costs less.

— BRENDAN FRANCIS

23 Sex and Relationships

The social landscape and how women present themselves has shifted enormously in the last few generations. Typically, a traditional woman was valued for being a key partner as a wife in terms of raising a family and being of service to the community. Highly sought-after feminine qualities were kindness, empathy, sexual fidelity, loyalty to husband and family, caregiving, thriftiness and resourcefulness, and modesty (having socially correct behaviors). Intelligence was not particularly prized but wasn't looked down on.

Since the invention of the pill, and other forms of female contraception, women have become sexually liberated. If a woman is unconscious, she will most likely express her sexuality in ways which either reflect prevailing cultural norms or which are in resistance to those cultural norms. These norms are proscribed to her through magazines, movies, her mother, her peers, her boyfriends, and gender politics.

In much of our culture, sex is objectified. A woman's body is objectified not just by men but also by women.[164] Perhaps moreso. While men

---

164 With women emboldened by a culture which has their back, even they can comfortably objectify male bodies.
Abby Gardner (October 21, 2020). "Bachelorette *Fans Are Mad About That Strip Dodgeball Date.*" Glamour. https://www.glamour.com/story/the-bachelorette-fans-are-mad-about-that-strip-dodgeball-date

may objectify her through, say, watching porn, women do so through passing daily judgment on each other's looks and behavior, usually with back-biting, passive aggression, or astringent asides.[165]

Western women suggest sexual energy in their clothing and appearance (as compared to women in other traditional societies) but are insulted and contemptuous when men of a lower status, than she should would otherwise like to attract and select, are responsive to her "display" (see *Social Status and Hypergamy).* Such low value men are invisible to her until such time as they hit on her. Then, because she perceives him as being low value, it indicates to her (subconsciously) that her value/desirability is potentially lower than she'd imagined, causing her to doubt her capacity to attract higher value suitors. He is an affront to her self-worth, and therefore a "loser" or a "creep."

These modern women simply "wear" their sexuality on the outside. They are force fed ideas about "empowerment" and "liberation" which they equate with "radical self expression" regardless of what other people may think, project, or expect. But does this impulse spring from their true nature? It would be fine if it did. The question they seem to fail to ask themselves is, "Is this how my own divine essence truly moves me?"

Modern women are having unsatisfactory sex because they are mostly in their masculine. The masculine is about being in control. So these women are not able to release and surrender into orgasm, into the experience of being led and ceding control to a man during sex.

~

Women have always given greater consideration to relationships than men. They spend more time thinking about relationships, talking about relationships with their confidantes, and reading about relationships (both fiction and non-fiction). Yet modern women are either unwilling

165 Women also objectify men but nothing is made of this. A dildo could be considered insulting to men since it simply represents a disembodied penis devoid of the need for the full human being. But mostly, women objectify men as "success objects."

or unable to reorganize their internal structure so as to embrace the idea of coupledom. They have emerged from a society that tells them, encourages them, and exhorts them to "have it all." They are the centers of their own universe. You go girl! When it comes to a relationship where another sentient being is part of the mix, they find themselves only able to give half-heartedly. Part of them wants to invest wholeheartedly, the other part doesn't want to deal with the messiness of it all. They just want the fairytale ending.

The fairytale has changed to favor an ending where the woman, instead of sharing her loveliness with a man in his fullness, presents the altar of her loveliness for him to prostrate himself before. He can never hope to possess her, only yearn for her. The modern woman wants to paint a picture (more like a selfie) and place herself in the middle of it in a way that is almost solipsistic. She wants to surround herself with the features which would indicate to others what she values and, thus, how they should treat her. These contain all the trappings of a romantic comedy movie. The cool apartment, the cool job, the clothes, the beach body, the circle of sisters, and the boyfriend. Yet, the work involved in meeting that boyfriend, fully, openly, honestly, and lovingly—meeting him where he is on his own life journey—feels overwhelming to her. Not many modern women (and probably the same could be said for modern men) are equipped for the ride.

This is also true when she has problems of self-esteem. Some consider themselves unworthy of a decent guy so they go for relationships which are likely to end quickly and, when it doesn't pan out, it doesn't feel so crushing. She could see the writing on the wall from the start.

On the one hand, a woman's fantasy ideal is a man who is wild, untamed, and savage, who listens only to himself and doesn't need her to fulfill him. In other words, a bad boy. Which means that the attention he pays her is because he's genuinely interested in her, and maybe she'll get to break this wild horse and tame him enough to ride him at her pleasure. In reality, he just wants to screw, nut, and bolt.

But on the other hand, women are being taught that there are no real differences between the sexes. This makes a man just a more hairy woman. Every woman has an inner mental model of what she thinks a man is, the term for which is the Animus. It's basically every interaction, observation, or experience with a man that gets alchemized into an archetype for her. And this serves as her default for how she interacts with them. Because she believes a man has an identical operating system, when he fails to respond as she might expect, she believes him to be purposefully "misbehaving" or being difficult. She ends up managing him by manipulating, damseling, cajoling, or lambasting him to get him back on track.

In modern times, this Animus has become unrealistic. Rather than it being based on direct experience, her perception of men is colored by numerous unrealistic representations of them, in songs, in movies, magazines, online, etc. For example, chick flicks, like romantic comedies, present the male lover as someone who will sacrifice his wellbeing (his career, his friends, even his life) in order to demonstrate his unconditional love for her. He exists to serve her romantic needs. As she internalizes all of these numerous influences, her perception of what to expect from real-life men shifts in that direction. Men then discover that they are unable to live up to the fairytale expectations, a lengthy shopping list, which these women have been conditioned to believe they are entitled.

With social media reducing face-to-face human interaction to an all-time low, following on from parental rates of divorce at an all-time high,[166] young men and women have neither been taught nor have learned for themselves the key skills of compassionate relating.[167] The overwhelming

166 Even when divorces were harder to come by in generations past, it didn't necessarily mean that people were better at being in a relationship together—they just chose to focus on other metrics. The relationship was not considered a vehicle for personal happiness—it was more likely to be a vehicle for survival, for bringing in the next generation, and for progeny to do better than their parents, bringing the household honor in accomplishment. Marriages were only successful in terms of their longevity, mostly because said longevity was enforced by society, not because they were healthy. With enforced togetherness now easily removed by divorce, what is revealed is that men and women don't possess, and probably never truly possessed, the knowledge of how to live together in harmony.

167 It's fairly common to ghost or send a text to end a relationship rather than sit with the feelings of discomfort of direct communication. This results in a weak individual, never tested in the fires of interpersonal conflict and devoid of the skills needed to sit with pain, to embrace it, grow from it, and integrate it.

majority of modern women regard their relationships with men in transactional terms. Mostly the transaction is sex for favors. Then there are the "queen bees." They are the types of girls who think they are entitled to everything and should be offered life's treasures on a silver platter, like they have a birthright. These women are taught to be "inflated." They are taught that they deserve to have what they want.

Modern women regard men through the perspective of their agenda. They want a man to be the man *they* want him to be, for their own needs. This objectification fails to consider how the masculine energy in each and every man needs to be expressed in its authenticity in terms of those men themselves. They want him to step up and fill a position in her life—to inhabit a particular role she has picked out for him. She believes she has the more important role in the relationship which the man needs to adapt to. The reverse used to be true (with traditional males) and neither attitude serves the best interests of the other unless they happen to be in agreement about what this role looks like. Once they are in a committed relationship, some women start to believe that the man's life is hers and that his time and energy is hers to direct, unless permission is given to do otherwise. This is not so egregious as it sounds. It is simply an aspect of the female operating system that has to be reckoned with—a form of possessiveness.

Modern women say they want their man to be honest. But they also want the man to give them validation at the expense of the honesty they demand ("Does my butt look fat in this dress?"). Conscious men pay close attention to their own subjective truth and are comfortable sharing it, even when it may be hard for others to receive—not to be unkind but to be rooted in what's real. This can be upsetting for modern women who have the idea that if they show how upset they are about something the man has said or done, he would *have* to change—because this is something that *they* would do. If they see that the man is upset about something, they would change whatever that thing is or repress it (until it comes out in a boiling mess, months later). So if a man is being authentic and coming from a place of honesty, and the woman doesn't like his truth, she will get upset and expect him to change what's true for him. Because that's what *she* would do.

When a man is penalized for honesty he learns to lie.[168]

Yet what was true for him never was a problem—problems arose only when he shared his truth, and then painfully learned that it wasn't worth it after witnessing the ensuing hissy fit. The woman is more comfortable punishing him for his honesty than appreciating him for his truth, which was a stated requisite for her originally. Many sincere men have learned the hard way that a woman will not remain in a relationship unless she can police his behavior. She wants the pretense of fairness and honesty while covertly getting her own way.

Gentlemen, when was the last time you heard a woman admitting she was wrong about something? ...When after reflecting on her behavior, she made an unprompted, full and frank apology without equivocation? Followed by taking action to rectify her misstep and setting things up for future harmony? There is a noticeable deficit in moral behavior from modern women where they cannot tolerate admitting to or revealing their own shortcomings. This is why men resonate so much with Jack Nicholson's character in the movie, *As Good As It Gets,* when he states that women, unlike men, lack [reason and] accountability.

Modern women believe men themselves aren't interested in being accountable when those men refuse to acknowledge the accusations/feedback/criticisms placed on them by women. He may state, plainly and simply, that the accusations don't ring true for him. Yet when a man truly feels shame for his actions, a woman often tries to make him feel better. They don't have a sense that a man's honest shame points to how he values himself and his role in the world. When he lets himself and others down, and owns it, it reveals his standards, values, and dedication to his path. They miss out on an opportunity to appreciate how accountable he really is, to celebrate and be inspired by who this man is at his core.

---

168 Criss Jami (2011). *"Salomé: In Every Inch In Every Mile."* CreateSpace Independent Publishing Platform

In a similar vein, modern women express the desire for a man who is in touch with his feelings, who is able to open up and be vulnerable. This gives the man permission to put down his guard. With that, sometimes comes strong emotions and tears. Yet the moment he shows her his vulnerable side, the woman goes into a panic. Women want a rock solid man who will remain emotionally stable during times when she needs an anchor for her own issues/crises/outbursts. And a man's own expression of his feminine aspect can place her in the role of the masculine, which can be very uncomfortable or scary for her. Maybe she can't rely on him to remain steady for her in *her* time of need? Much of the reason women think men are less sensitive than they are is that men rarely show their sensitive side. They fail to see that, from generation to generation, men's pain has been met with resistance rather than acceptance and empathy.

Many modern women have no clue how to add real value to the world or to a relationship. They are constantly on the lookout for men's faults in order to give themselves a feeling of moral superiority. They fear that if a real man would see her for who she really is, he wouldn't want anything to do with her. Tragically, they are right.

I have two brains in my body; but I've never been so dumb.

— GLORIA DELGADO-PRITCHETT

24 Paternity Fraud

Paternity fraud occurs when a woman writes the name of a man, supposedly the biological parent, on an infant's birth certificate, even though she knows otherwise.

Clearly the rate of paternity fraud is exceptionally hard to determine. Some studies indicate that 10% of "fathers" are helping to raise children which they believe to be theirs but are not. It's acknowledged to be widespread, especially with access to cheap and reliable DNA testing to establish the truth, yet men are expected to make nice and suck it up. In the UK, a man cannot get a legally accepted DNA test without the mother's permission—which, clearly, a deceiver would have little incentive to grant. In practice, therefore, a man is not permitted to know if a child is his. I find it amazing that this is not seen as an outrageous violation of his human rights.

There have been many cases of tricked men filing lawsuits in the hope of terminating child support payments, having discovered they were not the biological father. Most decent people consider paternity fraud to be a heinous act. Yet committing paternity fraud is not a punishable offense, in most cases. Lawsuits are often unsuccessful, even after numerous appeals.[169] It is not even recognized as financial fraud, the true extent of which can run into thousands of dollars for the unfortunate male. But perhaps more to the point is the unquantifiable level of emotional suffering these men and their children face by such deception when it becomes known.

Feminist "bioethicist," Heather Draper, has argued that "claims for reimbursement and compensation in cases of misattributed paternity produce the same distorted and thin view of what it means to be a father that paternity testing assumes, and underscores a trend that is not in the interests of children."[170] This suggests that "fathers" have a deficit of character by not placing the needs of the children first—yet mothers get a pass.

There is something sociopathic about modern women in how they would use a man to finance the upbringing of some other man's child. And it's not even a rare occurrence where you can shrug your shoulders and say "well, hey, a few women are like that." I can hardly imagine what the reverse might look like—perhaps if a man raped and impregnated a woman and forced her to care for the child until adulthood? And we think men are the monsters?

A possible solution is for the law to require DNA matching for every man who accepts paternal responsibility and the children he raises. If, as it is currently favored, it is not the state's responsibility to foot the bill for paternity fraud, then there need to be mechanisms in place to prevent unscrupulous women from getting an innocent man to pay for child support.

---

169 IDENTIGENE (08/09/2020). *Paternity Fraud: the Tough Realities Men must Face.* "In 2010, the California Supreme Court refused to review a tough court decision for homeless man Hari Wilburn. Way back in 1991, Wilburn was named as the father of a five-year-old child, even though he was never properly informed by the state. He was subsequently ordered to pay child support. Despite the fact that a 2008 paternity test excluded him as a possible father and that he never acted as father to the child, the court stated that the mother was entitled to back child-support payments in the tens of thousands of dollars (Crouch)" DNA Diagnostics Center. https://dnatesting.com/paternity-fraud-the-tough-realities-men-must-face/?fbclid=IwAR26eE-Ok-82JfiRJHH78errGpllUhRPJlc_b9btMmxr_sUnJV1GktS8OsOs

170 Heather Draper (2007). *"Paternity fraud and compensation for misattributed paternity."* National Library of Medicine. https://pubmed.ncbi.nlm.nih.gov/17664309/

Men know women are powerful, and we don't mind that one bit... Unless, that is, you disempower us in order to feel empowered

—PAUL DOBRANSKY, MD

25 Emasculation

Male emasculation (metaphorically speaking) by women is synonymous with the raping of women by men. It is the energetic equivalent.

When a woman wants to inflict pain and injury on a man and deprive him of his life force energy, she uses various forms of emasculation. At lower levels, she becomes rigid, critical, judgmental, finger-pointing, and is generally bitchy. When she really gets going, she becomes emotionally abusive and "crazy." She "lays claim" to his psyche with no concern or consideration for his wellbeing (just like rape "lays claim" to a woman's body with no concern or consideration for *her* wellbeing). The goal of emasculation is to make the man ineffective and weak, amasculine, so that he becomes compliant.

Emasculated men are not simply a feature of modern times. The sensitive, feminized New Age male was preceded by the "hen-pecked" husband. The foul-tempered, sharp-tonged Katherine from Shakespeare's *The Taming of the Shrew* signals a far longer and more sordid history of enraged females. But whereas those around Katherine were repulsed by her unpleasant outbursts, modern women can expect little social disapproval.

Modern women who emasculate will rationalize their behavior (mostly to themselves) by claiming to help her man become a better person and improve himself. Adopting the role of Kali in her man's life gives her sufficient self-justification for abusive behavior,[171] since her actions have divine roots.

Those women who emasculate also adopt a sexual strategy. The withholding of sex, the false signals sent during sex, consenting to sex then remaining unyielding, faking the orgasm—these are often forms of emasculation.[172] But chief amongst the tools at her disposal are her words. In general, a woman's verbal skills are stronger than a man's. A woman's words have an immense impact on the psychological well-being of a man. They can either be sweet nectar for his soul or they can be poisoned arrows. Contempt, ridicule, degrading him, badmouthing him to her friends, shaming him in public, talking over him and interrupting him mid-sentence, are all verbal mechanisms used to undermine him and submit him to her will.

How she looks at her man and her body language are also both highly effective tools. A woman's eyes are exquisitely expressive in transmitting her intense disapproval of a man's ineffectualness. Tightening the lips, hanging the head in disgust before jerking it back up for another verbal salvo, holding her mouth open in "gaping-disbelief," drumming her fingernails while he is talking, etc, are employed to forestall any hope in the man for a peaceful resolution to the issue at hand.

A woman can emasculate a man not only by what she does but what she doesn't do. Because a man will rejoice in the role of protector and provider, and will bend over backwards to be of assistance, any lack of appreciation and gratitude for his efforts can be a form of emasculation. Because of modern women's entitlement complex, it's almost a given that men should serve women and not expect thanks in return. A simple

171 Kali is a Hindu goddess representing feminine death and destruction, often portrayed squatting on the chest of her dead husband. She has "killed" that in him which does not serve his masculinity, allowing him to be reborn as more of a man, thus reclaiming his masculinity.

172 Note that the lack of attunement a man has to a woman, or her history of sexual trauma, can also determine how she responds to him in bed.

smile, hug, loving look, or acknowledgment of his kindness is enough to fill his tank.

A man needs to earn respect from women and other men. If a woman does not respect a man's conception of himself as a man—how he is doing his best to walk upright through life, his purpose, his thinking, his decision-making, his abilities, his integrity, his mission—she undermines him by her silent or not-so-silent disapproval. The words "I love you" may slip easily from her lips but it's less common to hear her say, "I respect you." It's about knowing him and having a deep, positive regard for him. Even if he tries his best and falls flat on his face, a woman's expression of respect is music to his ears. The lack of it hurts him like hell. Sadly, we live in a culture which increasingly devalues and disrespects men, which makes interpersonal disrespect all the more common.

The penetration of the male heart chakra with malicious intent by a woman is the male equivalent of having been raped. It's effects can have as much of an impact on a man's life as rape does for a woman. A man's heart is his Achilles heel. Perhaps one day it will be considered as socially reprehensible as rape itself. Men may present themselves as strong or macho but under the shell of even the hardest nut is a sensitive soul, which is why emasculation is so effective.

Don't you know that a man being rich is like a girl being pretty?
You wouldn't marry a girl just because she's pretty,
but my goodness, doesn't it help?[173]

— MARILYN MONROE

26 Social Status and Hypergamy

There are many factors which women consider when selecting a mate but a key motivator is a man who can help with her "social advancement." Hypergamy is a theory which points to the female "drive" to feel safe and looked after by choosing a mate of higher status—be it wealth, power, intelligence, confidence, their social rank within their peer groups, and to a lesser extent, looks and physical attractiveness. A competing concept is "social learning theory" which suggests that the preference for higher status men is learned rather than inherited.

Statistics from online dating sites indicate that women are attracted to men with a sense of humor, men who are taller than them, men who specify their profession, men with a higher level of education, etc. The list goes on and on. These qualities suggest a greater ability of the man to access resources which could then be used for her benefit.[174] In no culture, past or present that we know about, have women preferred to mate with low-status, passive men who were unable to access resources.

---

173 Fictional character, Lorelei Lee. *"Gentlemen Prefer Blondes,"* movie, 1953. 20th Century Fox.

174 Lingshan Zhang, et al. (May 30, 2019). *"Are Sex Differences in Preferences for Physical Attractiveness and Good Earning Capacity in Potential Mates Smaller in Countries With Greater Gender Equality?"* Sage Journals. https://journals.sagepub.com/doi/pdf/10.1177/1474704919852921

Women don't desire men they don't admire. No woman harbors sexual fantasies about unemployed, unambitious, or basement-living, rudderless men. They are desirous of men who are socially adept (if not dominant), who exhibit certain traits and behaviors which would allow him to ascend the social hierarchy—those who, by their status, can facilitate her own status aspirations. They are attracted to men who are risk-takers, who are stoic in the face of adversity, who are brave and self-reliant. Men who are intelligent, artistic, adept, or have technical ability. And men who have certain communication skills, like humor or oratory ability. Quite a lot of the behaviors and traits likely to be deemed as deriving from "toxic masculinity" are the same as those that most women find desirable.

It's also claimed that women value intelligent men. It's truer to say that women value the fruits of male intellect which support them in their lifestyle aspirations. Intelligent men are good because they use their smarts to compete for resources a woman can make use of—principally related to wealth and status.

Women, by all accounts, are hard to please! The more desirable traits men as a whole exhibit, the higher the bar is raised. Even then, women are never satisfied—there are always better men to snag! By contrast, men are pretty much happy with a woman who likes sex, is kind-hearted, and who enjoys similar pastimes (the last one being optional).

Because of our different operating systems, those traits by which men judge other men are less interesting to women. A man's character, opinions, values, integrity, his word, and code of honor play less of an important role. Although modern women admire men who perform selfless acts of service to friends and community, this is seen not as a good in and of itself but as an indicator that those men will selflessly give of themselves in a relationship with her.

A woman asks herself the question, "Can I fall in love with this man?" Rarely does she fall in love simply because she just can't help herself, as is almost universally the case for men. Then by some trickery of the mind (unfathomable to me) she really does fall in love with him, complete with all the signs and symptoms that are always present—it's a real and visceral experience for her. In other words, women do not love men unconditionally. They are predisposed to enter into a relationship with a man when such a relationship serves her need for social advancement. The feelings follow as she gets to know him.

When a man has a degree of wealth and power, a woman feels protected. It also elevates her status and, coupled with that, her self-esteem. Additionally, it means she is under less obligation to provide for herself. There is no shame in having these desires. But problems arise when she fails to evaluate whether being in a relationship with this type of provider-male is the right conscious decision for her to make. Is she objectifying him merely as a "success object" (the female version of a man objectifying a woman as a "sex object")? How strong would her commitment and attraction to him be if he were neither wealthy nor powerful? When a man is the breadwinner, he dreams of finding a partner and giving her the fruits of his labor. When she is the breadwinner, she dreams of being independent.

Hypothetically, the quarterback and the cheerleader are a good match for each other, initially, both being young, athletic and ready to take on the world. By the time he is past his athletic prime, and she has advanced in her career, they are mismatched. And this creates an imbalance which may be potentially unresolvable since he is less capable of helping her advance socially.

There are conscious women who feel some discomfort or shame when confronting the hypergamous aspect of their programming, as much as conscious men who *can* see past outer beauty but find attraction elusive (despite wishing to hell they *could* be attracted). Women get frustrated with men who can't get past thinking with their dicks, thinking them superficial, and yet women also have a "second brain" which manifests in a different manner. They objectify men, target them, secure them, then spend their money. In an era of scarcity (and scarcity mentality), this is how women survive.

Women have traditionally chosen men who earn more and have higher status but then find these men to be poor intimacy companions.

Their higher self actually wants men who have high social and emotional intelligence but they've based their choice on their own more base survival instincts (the ability of the man to protect and provide), and then they become churlish and emasculating when their unstated higher needs go unmet. Again, there is some nuance here. For sexual attraction to occur, the masculine traits of confidence, etc, have to be present. A passive man, no matter how connected he is to his feelings and hers, is ultimately unappealing.

A man who thinks negatively of women for being attracted to his social status, while being comfortable with being attracted to physical beauty, fails to appreciate that intimate relations can be more richly complex than our basic drives. Women have preferences for mate selection, just as males do, but we're not ruled by those preferences. The prefrontal cortex plays a greater role in a woman's planning and decision making of her life choices. Once we understand the biological mechanisms we have evolved to have, it becomes easier not to be a slave to them. At this point, we can understand the extent of our personal agency within this "meat suit."

It should be noted that there is a clear divide between conventional hypergamy and gold digging. "Gold diggers" are women who form relationships solely to extract money by feigning attraction. Such women are engaged in fraudulent behavior. If women see a man as a success-object, a utility, an accessory to her wardrobe, then intimacy is impossible. Her love is pragmatic. For she sees him as less than the full man he really is. To an extent, men have brought this on themselves, historically. They demonstrated their ability to provide and women gladly accepted them as a means of survival for themselves and their offspring.

In more modern times, women are less in need of physical protection and can generate their own income. Certain institutional protections and advantages are in place to assist women in these areas—notably the police, courts, educational system, and welfare state. Hypergamy is increasingly redundant for survival but still appears to be a strong motivator in mate selection. As women have gained status through employment, their expectations of men have increased accordingly. They are finding correspondingly fewer men of higher social status as they rise in their own terms. Men who would have previously been candidates for female attention are no longer in the same position. This could explain why women are increasingly less happy with their lives.

The mechanics of hypergamy may operate equally in men as they do in women. Just how hardwired-in hypergamy is to our nature is up for debate. But for our species to progress, we need to create the conditions whereby men and women relate in such a way as to ennoble each other, rather than transact with each other (see chapter, *The Divine Union).*

I've faced blazing guns in the hands of angry men, which is bad; and daggers in the hands of angry women, which is a thousand times worse.[175]

— STEVEN KING

27 Wounded Women

Wounded women are the most dangerous people in a man's world. It's like they are toddlers in a grown up body holding a puppy by its tail. They are unable to practice external consideration meaningfully or skillfully. But those puppies are often conscious men. Wounded women have psychological issues which are relatively unlikely to be solved, even with the loving presence of a compassionate man. While there is nothing inherently wrong with having issues (we all do), a wounded woman is far more likely to cause pain and suffering to the man in her life who loves her the most and bring him low in the long-term—beating him into emotional submission or simply wearing him down. She will provoke a man until it brings out his ugly side, then play the victim in response. She will also have greater expectations of him obliging her to meet her needs, which are extensive and exhausting. He finds himself throwing parts of himself into her insatiable emotional furnace of neediness.

Because of where we are in the socio-evolution of women, most women these days could be considered to be sufficiently wounded to assure an

175 Steven King (October 13, 1993). *"Nightmares & Dreamscapes."* Viking; First Edition/First Printing.

undesirably adverse impact on their significant other. This is the deeply regrettable state of affairs we find ourselves in. In the early stage of a relationship, women want to put their best foot forward (so do men, obviously). Which means problematic behaviors are unlikely to come to light any time soon. Strangely, the good news is that they will most likely tell you almost from the get-go where their wounding lies, if you have ears to hear it. In their experience, most men neither listen nor take evasive action because they are more concerned with scoring (if it is short-term) or rationalizing, empathizing, or downplaying her issues (if they're looking for something more long-term).

Because of the efforts of third (and fourth) wave feminism and the current zeitgeist in general, our society lionizes wounded women. There is strength in the tribe of victimhood, particularly when it is glorified by feminists and the #MeToo movement. With such validation, there is little reason to come to terms with their wounding.

Control and Manipulation

The more famous and powerful I get, the more power I have to hurt men.[176]

— ACTRESS, SHARON STONE

Growing the bonds of intimacy[177] within a relationship requires a state of mind and of heart where tolerance and acceptance are fully present. Any attempt to change, coerce, or shape your partner into what you want them to be is the antithesis of intimacy. Clearly this holds true for men and women alike. Yet the disparity between the two sexes in this respect is so startling wide that this subject, to my mind, clearly has to be applied more to women than to men. There are numerous articles[178]

176 Rabbi Benjamin Blechprint (Ocober 7, 2018). *"Hating Men: The New Racism."* Aish. https://www.aish.com/ci/s/Hating-Men-The-New-Racism.html

177 Intimacy can be defined as a familiarity in union, founded on seeing the other for who they are and accepting them as they are. Both partners trust in the other regarding physical, psychological and emotional safety and concern.

178 Team LovePanky. *"How Can Women Manipulate Men Easily?"* LovePanky. https://www.lovepanky.com/women/understanding-men/women-manipulating-men

and books[179] which dispense advice to women about how to manipulate and control men. It could be claimed that seduction skills are tools of manipulation in men's hands. Yet these tools leave a woman feeling cared for and appreciated (even if, covertly, the manipulator just wants to get between her legs).

Women are attracted to strong men, or those who have a clear purpose, but their reaction to his confidence is to often feel threatened. A happy man is one who feels empowered; who is in his power. He may be focused on his career or passion, or something that is important to him. This makes him attractive because he's living in his truth. But, at the same time, it demonstrates to the woman that she's not his primary focus. She may either subtly or more overtly try to pull his focus towards her and resent him when he resists. For wounded women, if the man is happy the woman must be less happy—a zero sum game, in her mind. He's not "allowed" to be happy because his happiness must be "at her expense." It *feels* unfair.

Women are the primary agents of emotional and psychological abuse in relationships. Many women identify certain behaviors or traits they dislike in men, and then go about the task of fixing them. This is often done under the compassionate pretext of helping men to be better versions of themselves, or some such terminology which has sufficient "plausible deniability"[180] (casting enough doubt over personal culpability that it cannot be ascertained). Being intimate with someone who views you as "less than" is an impossibility since there is little-to-no psychological or emotional safety present. Nor is safety possible from someone who is trying to tie down a man to proscribed behaviors which benefit her at his expense.

A lot of women will get into relationships because they are in a starvation pattern. The love they offer is not based on caring about the man but on caring about what the man can offer to satisfy her needs. So they

---

179 Karen Salmansohn (1994). *"How to Make Your Man Behave in 21 Days or Less Using the Secrets of Professional Dog Trainers."* Workman Publishing Company.

180 A condition in which a subject can safely and believably deny knowledge of any particular truth that may exist because the subject is deliberately made unaware of said truth so as to benefit or shield the subject from any responsibility associated through the knowledge of such truth.

mostly take rather than give and then get into their control drama. And when he is drained, blame their man when their hungry ghost remains famished.

The wounded woman unconsciously places more value on being desired, as opposed to ostensibly wanting to be loved. Being desired feeds the ego. And being desired points to a power imbalance where the woman gains control over the man. As long as he desires her, she can manipulate him to meet her needs.

Men and women generally exhibit different control and manipulation aspects. Whilst men are more blatant, direct, and in-your-face, women have a different sort of power. They are more cunning in that they base their attacks on information they have been collecting about him—ammunition. Intelligence gathering is a woman's currency and where her power to manipulate rests. Manipulative women spend a great deal of energy collecting information about the man so that they can tailor their strategy to him personally.

Gaslighting is one such information mechanism. In order to gain more power, the woman insists that her man question his reality. It's often done subtly and gradually over a period of time, making it hard to detect. The basic message is, "You're the one that's crazy for seeing things that way, because clearly you don't see things clearly! What you feel, you don't feel. What you see, you don't see." Gaslighting can also be non-verbal. By ignoring or failing to recognize, acknowledge, or mirror another person's reality, they are subtly denying its existence. For the conscious man, gaslighting can sometimes be difficult to spot and he may easily get sucked in. Being open to there being possible aspects of himself that he can't see, and being aware of potential trauma patternings conditioned in childhood, he is willing to have his perspectives challenged and is more open to her manipulative suggestions.

Giving him compliments and bragging on him is another one of women's manipulative tactics that can be hidden in plain sight. Encouraging him to keep doing the behavior she wants is what's called positive reinforcement. The clue in its inauthenticity is, when he refuses to be trained, she withdraws her affections.

They also spend the currency of information they have gathered by engaging in high-conflict emotional drama. Throwing a tantrum—the use of non-specific, expansive language. Crying to melt his heart and using mood swings to encourage acquiescence to her demands. Playing dumb. Baiting him. Playing the victim. Playing the little girl to appeal to his protector instinct. These strategies are used to keep the man in the mind-frame to keep sustaining and prioritizing her needs above his. What she may do and say to use him to get what she wants, and have him buy into those things, is her modus operandi. Initially, some men may be unaware of these dynamics and just have a vague yet unsettling feelings of disconcertedness.

We think of women as "the caring ones," "the compassionate ones," etc, by default. Women are neither nicer nor more empathetic, as most believe—they take advantage of their reputations as such because it gives them leverage. They want to be seen to be nice—they are "agreeable." Wounded women understand this and use this to their advantage. They'll often refer to how they care for their man and the number of times they have done caring acts, in order to avoid accountability for behavior. Just like there are instances where professional caregivers (like those in nursing homes) are ostensibly interested in caring for those in their charge, yet later it comes to light that they have been abusing these helpless individuals. To manipulative women, caring is just a job.

Immaturity

JACKIE: *"How do you write women so well?"*
MELVIN UDALL: *"I think of a man. And I take away reason and accountability."*[181]

Society is screwed up in large part because we have a lot of children inhabiting adult bodies. And they pass along their immaturities to their children. "Adulting" means being responsible, accountable, and acquiring

181 *"As Good As It Gets,"* movie (1997). Starring Jack Nicholson and Helen Hunt.

greater and greater amounts of maturity and wisdom. Millennials' use of the term both ironically mocks their delayed mastery of adult responsibilities and tragically points to how foreign it is from their experience.

In terms of modern women, perhaps the most pointed lack of adulting skills is in their psychology. Are modern women capable of "reason and accountability?" Why is it that rather than, from a place of inner calmness, viewing their ego with gentle dispassion and loving acceptance, do they so frequently throw a temper tantrum akin to a two-year-old? Why do many proudly proclaim themselves a bitch? What produces infantilized attitudes and childlike behavior? Irrationality, insecurity, rebelliousness? Being mean, being a bitch, and mouthing off are indeed effective. But these behaviors only work when they can tell that people around them are feeling disempowered by that behavior.

Women didn't get here by themselves—they didn't emerge into the present age from a vacuum—they were enabled by those around them, including men (their fathers and lovers). Women aren't accountable because they are rarely held to account and, as a society, we have insultingly low expectations—insultingly low for women who might otherwise be encouraged to reach their full potential.

When conflict inevitably occurs in a relationship, immature women make little effort to resolve the situation as an adult—giving ground where it is warranted by the facts of the situation and working towards compassionate solutions. Our competition culture is deeply destructive to the fabric of a woman's feminine essence. As the girl emerges into womanhood, she finds little support to develop her psychological, emotional, and sexual maturity. When she was a child, life was about what she could get—energy, attention, resources—with little if any delayed gratification. In fact, most girls are continuously told how special and deserving they are and how they are entitled to what life has to offer. You go, girl! If they don't get what they want, when they want it, they go off the deep end and cry "oppression!" This type of messaging came mostly from the mother. Yet fathers too were culpable in calling her or treating her as a princess. But with fewer and fewer fathers taking an active and evolved role in the lives of their children (owing to loss of custody in divorce), these immature modes of functioning are left unaddressed.

~

Every woman (or, indeed, every person) needs to fully accept her body. A lot of women struggle with body issues for a variety of reasons and it is cruel to demean them about their weight. Even if god hasn't graced them with wonderful genes and their general appearance is less than favorable, I think it's very important to fully accept one's body, whatever size, shape, or configuration it might be in. The problem arises when modern women have an unreasonable expectation that men should appreciate and desire a woman's body, whatever condition it's in. They expect men to find them attractive simply because they find themselves attractive and because there is some sort of patriarchal conspiracy that men have for subordinating their size-group. You could say, they want to have their cake and eat it.

Social constructivism, much loved by feminists, argues that society is the only influencer of sexual attraction. Yet our biology also programs most people to reject certain physical characteristics which indicate that others would make poor mates. There are evolutionary explanations for male attraction related to fertility. "Men tend to seek relatively young women with full lips, breasts, and hips, and a smaller waist, because these indicate sufficient estrogen levels to successfully birth a child. Men also look for facial symmetry, shiny hair, clear skin, and white sclera."[182]

As previously described, women have several criteria for mate selection on dating sites. So why are so many overweight women surprised when men apply their own standards?

With 39.8% of adult Americans being obese[183] comes a growing political voice to normalize what is an abnormal condition. The media also

182 Jennifer S. Denisiuk. *"Evolutionary Versus Social Structural Explanations for Sex Differences in Mate Preferences, Jealousy, and Aggression."* Rochester Institute of Technology. http://www.personalityresearch.org/papers/denisiuk.html

183 Craig M. Hales, et al. *"Prevalence of Obesity Among Adults and Youth: United States, 2015–2016."* Centers For Disease Control. https://www.cdc.gov/nchs/data/databriefs/db288.pdf

panders to the fat-acceptance model rather than reflecting the serious health concerns that can arise from obesity. It's natural for a woman to have a healthy, shapely body. It's natural because heart disease and the myriad of ailments that stem from being overweight are not meant to be attractive. There is nothing beautiful about heart disease or that it kills more people than cancer. And there's nothing empowering about a society which reframes self-destructive behavior as beautiful.

In the end, again, it comes down to accountability. Apparently it's easier to lie to yourself that you're attractive and can maintain good health, and also demand others change their thinking, rather than gather evidence, face facts, and develop self-discipline. Whatever the problem is, the answer is not in the refrigerator.

Lions and tigers, and bears, oh my![184]

— DOROTHY

28 The Fear-based Operating System

Both men and women experience similar physiological responses to fear and analogous fight/flight/freeze reactions. Yet women seem to be more predisposed to fears and phobias (fear of flying, agoraphobia, fear of the dark, etc) than men when not directed by the autonomic nervous system.[185] It's been found that women experience higher fear arousal than men for all objects (mice, spiders, snakes, bugs, etc) and situations.

The world as seen through the eyes of wounded women is binary—all women are vulnerable and all men are a risk to them.

Feminists would have women believe that, through their toxic masculinity and social conditioning, men have a certain malevolence towards women—men who need to be defanged, declawed, and made safe. For modern women, there is definitely a level of distrust and malevolence towards men. The malevolence derives from the conditioning women have had, to believe that men are one or two steps away from physically or sexually abusing them. The everyday reality just does not bear this out, even in this fucked up world. Men take value in helping, not hurting,

184 Dorothy in *"Wizard of Oz"* movie (1939). Starring Judy Garland. MGM.

185 Fredrikson, M., et al. (1996). *"Gender and age differences in the prevalence of specific fears and phobias."* Behaviour Research and Therapy. https://pubmed.ncbi.nlm.nih.gov/8561762/

women. There is a strong male urge to provide and protect. It's no longer considered that our physical strength is there to prevent harm to those we love (at the expense of our own lives if necessary) but to be used to dominate and subjugate. Do men dominate and subjugate? Of course! But not as often as is depicted. It's a very small percentage of men who are a threat to women, and to other men.

Women fear for their physical safety more than men (though men are significantly more likely to become victims of violent crime). They believe their feelings are a clear representation of reality, never mind the chances of them being physically or sexually harmed by men are slim. Therefore if they *feel* that they are in fear for their safety, in their minds they must indeed be in danger, whether it's immediately present or close at hand.

I'm learning to be careful with what I feed the mind and keep in the heart.

— NHUNG HOANG

29 Conclusion

The ego-driven me-me-me culture has degenerated into a form of narcissism where the modern woman's notion of individualism is that of accessorizing objects and people in her life. The boyfriend, child, career, plant medicine retreat, or yoga class are seen as how good they make her look. Feminist boosterism has been her key ally in making her feel empowered, giving the message that she is special and powerful. And even more special and powerful that men, owing to her goddess within.

So, as a conscious man aware of the feminist paradigm and modern women, what should you do? If you're to be an authentic male, how can you play nice with women who don't play nice with you? Maybe your hopes rest on finding a good woman who doesn't buy into the victim narrative of male oppression and who never will. The unfortunate conclusion is that most modern women are mostly unsuitable for intimate partnerships. It's just the nature of our times and it's not their fault. It's owing to generational layers of inhumane treatment of the weaker by the more powerful, resulting in dysfunctional ways men relate to women and women relate to men, and the layers of subtle and not-so-subtle indoctrination that perpetuate this "separation-culture."

Every man wants to be approved of and loved by women and this makes love a resource that can be given or withheld. This is how women have shaped the world, either through loving freely yet wisely, or by using (conditional) love as a tool of manipulation.

Human societies have always been gynocentric. Determining paternal parentage in hunter-gatherer societies was virtually impossible yet everyone knew who the mother was (see *Sex and Relationships*, chapter, *The Divine Feminine*). From the moment they are born, men are conditioned to love female love and attention, with those beautiful orbs smooshed into our faces (that we never fail to take pleasure in) giving us literal sustenance, and so much more. We care about women's safety, pleasure, and wellbeing above other men's needs.

Yet modern women are out of alignment. A woman can only truly give that which is overflowing from within her—a gift, in some sense. It doesn't matter what or how big those gifts are—it only matters how loving she can be in delivering them. If she is always looking to "get," then she will always experience lack. That which she believes she is giving is actually just a manipulation or a transaction "to get." This means that few modern women look at their internal agendas, their programming, and how they manipulate themselves to fit their expectations. They are unlikely to be accountable to themselves, for themselves. No matter how fine she is, no matter how many good qualities she possesses (and there are many such women), without a growth mindset, or with too much wounding, she cannot stay the course with a conscious man. She will try to dominate him, in some sense. She will want to win, or blame, or emasculate, or manipulate.

So it's unwise to go near a relationship with a modern woman until it's clear that she presents little danger to a man's sanity, his career and reputation, future offspring, and his financial assets. Women are openly fucking with, and fucking over men in droves, pre- and post-divorce, and men are convincing themselves that this is not happening (until it does). There are many men who have reluctantly stopped dating. They very much enjoy the company of women and spending time to develop intimacy. But the harsh truth is that many men are aware that the juice is not worth the squeeze. For all the promise of sweetness, so many modern women come with bitterness and the destructive behaviors to back them up. Your mission (should you choose to accept it) is to encounter and work with women who are exceptions to the rule. If you are looking to pair up, always be screening for red flags, and be very, very careful.

Part Four

Modern Men

You are a man, not just *a man; don't be diminished.*
Live up to your grand potential.

– RICHELLE E. GOODRICH

Modern men are having a hard time finding a way to be in this world that makes sense to them. They are grappling with social, financial, academic, sexual and spiritual issues, many without having the maturational ability to resolve them. Like modern women, they have emerged from conditions unfavorable to their true expression as men. Whether they had an absent father, a distracted father, or a tyrannical father, whether they had an invasive or manipulative or emotionally distant mother, many are left feeling predisposed to distrust both sexes.

I had a romance novel inside me, but I paid three sailors to beat it out of me with steel pipes.

– PATTON OSWALT

30 Traditional Masculinity

Most of the contemporary conversation about traditional masculinity focuses almost exclusively on how certain masculine norms, traits, and values were harmful, violent, or toxic to those around them and society as a whole. Yet in the circumstances of their times, such men were often an asset to society. Unlike our present age, wars were more common and common men were expected to fight and die in great numbers. The problem lies in villainizing them in retrospect, mostly at the behest of modern women. Expendability and disposability have long been "a given" but both traditional and modern men are now actually despised by society. They are sent the message that even their sacrifices carry no weight and that men can never purge their toxic masculinity. This is after decades of anti-male propaganda.

Traditional men exemplified such qualities as sacrifice, duty, and industriousness—all in the service of women, children, and country. These men were the linchpins of society. They worked mines where few woman cared to go. They worked on construction sites in the sweltering heat, dripping with sweat, dirty, and without complaint. They tirelessly gave and gave, cutting through the dangers of their labor with quips and jokes. In the past, these men were so busy surviving, protecting, and providing that they left part of themselves behind in order to "get the job done"—they left behind their feminine essence. They left behind their hearts. Their heart was too busy to be a heart. Give a traditional man a void and he'll fill it. Give him a problem to solve and he'll fix it. A man's gotta do what a man's gotta do. Today, we're still grappling with this legacy. Traditional masculinity favored doing over being. Success at all costs. The biggest insult a traditional man could receive was to be called a "loser." They may have brought home the bacon but they were poor husbands and emotionally distant fathers. They carried addictions, like alcoholism, to help stuff down the painful emotions arising from a life of conformity and duty.

Traditional men and their women have co-created this world. As men have been the drivers of change, so too have women been the back seat drivers of change. "It may be a man's world, but men are easily controlled by women."[186] A man chooses the route, it's his bus, and she chooses whether or not to get on the bus and let the man drive. She only gets on the bus if she believes in his competency to get them to a desirable destination which will end up meeting her needs. Or, quite often, because women are more relational, they may use their tools of feminine influence to alter his direction (hence how men and women have co-created the world). "There are two questions a man must ask himself: The first is 'Where am I going?' and the second is 'Who will go with me?' If you ever get these questions in the wrong order you are in trouble."[187] Problems occur when the woman doesn't know what she needs and when the man has no consideration for other road users.

When it comes to well-being, everything that is bad for women is generally worse for men—both traditional and modern. If women sometimes feel the despair of loneliness and isolation, it's worse for men because they're supposed to be strong and self-sufficient and to not even have the need for connection. Men are less able to turn to other men because they are, generally speaking, in competition with each other for women and

186 Ashly Lorenzana.

187 Sam Keen.

resources. Men are wary of showing their vulnerability. Stereotypically, they'll punch walls, climb mountains, drink beer, watch MMA, play video games, and admire fast and powerful cars. But speaking to their fragility, uncertainty, feelings of anxiety and overwhelm and showing the world their emotions is taken as a sign of weakness. Many men grapple with their pain in isolation. A woman who is facing inner turmoil can turn to her female friends and family without being judged deficient and will likely be met with compassion and empathy because her femininity is not challenged by doing so. Without a support network, a man is more likely to take his own life in despair.

Even though their organisms craved it, traditional men were too disconnected from themselves to feel the emotional deficit of intimacy, depth, and quality of relationships with either men or women. Men "talked past" men to the human doing opposite them, rather than the human being. His woman was there to perform the role of wife, mother, and homemaker. Success was measured in material achievement and social advancement. The glue which held them together was their sense of duty—they were committed to each other in ways which diminished them.

Traditional men may attract women by their money and their social status but they will never experience the kindness and devotion of a woman who really cares about him. This is what men hungered for and what was mostly missing. The intimacy that men's hearts craved was assuaged by extra-marital affairs or hookers, if they had the time and money. If they didn't, they might go to strip clubs because, whether they knew it or not, they were starving for female energy—to encounter the essence of a woman; to encounter her inner beauty. They did so because they just couldn't find it "in the real world." The woman that their organism craved didn't exist. Yet what the women in strip clubs offered him was merely a particular delicious illusion, for the price of admission.

We've all been raised on television to believe that one day we'd all be millionaires, and movie gods, and rock stars. But we won't. And we're slowly learning that fact. And we're very, very pissed off.

– TYLER DURDEN, *FIGHT CLUB* MOVIE

31 Gender Roles and Expectations

Men tend to value their own competence and utility because society has placed those aspects of being a man far ahead of anything else. Their historical role has been to provide and protect—in the workplace and the home. For their efforts, there had been an understanding that if they worked hard and smart and played by the rules (or subverted them intelligently), they would be graced with the rewards of power, money, sex, and relevance.

We've now reached a point in time when men have, to all intents and purposes, worked themselves out of a job. Men have almost exclusively been the builders of civilizational prosperity (putting aside that the planet has been raped to achieve that). And baring the glaring disparities in wealth distribution, all the "stuff" in the world has been brought into existence through the muscle-power or brain-power of men, overwhelmingly. Men have dug coal out of the ground, designed and built factories and skyscrapers, invented and produced gadgets galore, and developed complex systems to manage it all. With the advent of automation, robotics, computers, and A.I, pretty soon there won't be a need for man's traditional role. That is unless we don't destroy the planet or suffer from a global economic collapse in the meantime.

Compared to the Boomer generation, and taken as a whole, men's ability to contribute their energies to the world has been in decline for decades. They have a diminished ability to generate a productive income and have greater levels of debt. Given that men seek to express their masculinity through their work or their passionate endeavors, being chronically under-resourced by an anemic economy and high cost of living has left many adrift and aimless, scrabbling around for low-wage/gig/part-time employment. There is a crisis of confidence amongst them as to what value they have—what do they want to do with their lives, what the hell *can* they do with their lives? They end up spending countless hours on the internet, playing video games, and "chilling."

Historically, there had been a strong social expectation to decide on a career, a 9-5 job, get married, have 2.4 children, and 1.3 dogs. For better or worse, this gender role has vanished. Instead, young men have complete freedom in how they pursue their interests but with little knowledge of their own unique strengths and abilities, little opportunity to invest in themselves without incurring unsustainable debt loads, and little motivation to overcome either. While women's options have expanded into traditionally male roles, society still largely views with suspicion men who are nurses, early years/elementary school teachers, stay at home dads, etc.

So many men are suffering both in terms of their options for well-paid, meaningful work and also for the lifestyles they no longer have access to because of their reduced capacity to generate an income. This includes the opportunity/onus of being the breadwinner and financing a home and a family. Many women seem to be more interested in breaking away from men (through easier divorce laws, state-support for single motherhood, alimony and child support settlements which disproportionately favor the mother, etc) than either stepping into the role of breadwinner or of sharing the financial burden with men equally. Generally speaking, the difference is that, in a relationship, men have an expectation to provide financially while women can choose to.

The older generation of Vikings no doubt complained that the younger generation were getting soft and did not rape and pillage with the same dedication as in years gone by.[188]

— C. PETER HERMAN

32 How Modern Men have changed: Good and Bad

Men have begun to internalize the idea that their very maleness, their masculinity itself, is something that is unhelpful to the world, if not harmful. It's becoming part of the identity of modern men. They've taken on board the notion of "toxic masculinity" whereby they see themselves almost as a toxic substance with a warning label on the side which women ought to read before letting it anywhere near their own bodies. They are at the point where hearing any conversation involving a declarative statement about the harmfulness of men automatically goes unchallenged, either by silent disagreement or shame-felt agreement. They just take it on the chin because at some level they think they deserve to be diminished. They feel themselves as lesser human beings and they see other men as lesser men. Because modern women are so vocal and so vehement about toxic masculinity, the thought is that they must have a point—because where there's smoke there's fire. Modern men find themselves swimming in a

188 C. Peter Herman, et al. (May 1, 1986). *"Physical Appearance, Stigma, and Social Behavior."* Psychology Press; 1st edition.

cultural soup of generalized male distrust and this grinds away at their self esteem. They become pale versions of themselves.

Modern men's masculine qualities are underdeveloped owing to a deficit in guidance from male elders and from an overly feminized society. Modern men largely derive their sense of being a good man or "real" man from the consensus of women, not from an inner alignment with their true nature as a male-human-spirit-animal. They feel they need to be selected by a woman, not the other way round.

They don't, nowadays, derive their sense of manhood from other men because many have never encountered a male role model, father figure, or mentor in their childhood who took a direct and positive interest in their development. More and more boys are being brought up by single mothers, encounter mostly female teachers,[189] and are left at sea when it comes to being brought into touch with their masculinity. They're left with an interesting mix of video games, porn, and serve-the-woman messaging, all the while being shamed as an inherently bad male, having a certain skin color, and having the wrong political beliefs. Men have nowhere to learn how to be men and are struggling to understand their lives and their purpose, their dent in the universe, and are looking for answers.

Men have become softer in nature over time—more compliant and accommodating. Partly this is due to a changing world. To a large extent, we no longer need to hunt, to process game, do hard manual labor, push a plow, fight hand-to-hand in a foreign land. We can jump in a car and travel miles with little physical exertion, flip up the thermostat for more heat, send a drone to bomb an enemy. The downside is that modern men tend to lack the strength qualities of traditional men. In today's world, femininity is the ideal standard. Modern men believe they have to prove to women that they are different from those traditional men. They become ever more soft-spoken, more apathetic, more uncertain of

189 "Why aren't boys more engaged in school? According to Sommers, 'schools today tend to be run by women for girls. Classrooms can be hostile environments for boys. They like action, competition and adventure stories. Those are not in favor. Games like tag and dodge-ball are out; tug of war has become tug of peace, and male heroes have been replaced by Girl Power." Dr. Helen Smith (2014). *"Men on Strike: Why Men Are Boycotting Marriage, Fatherhood, and the American Dream - and Why It Matters."* Encounter Books.

themselves, less overtly confident, more apologetic, etc, because of their supposed male privilege. Men are learning how to empathize, actively listen, show their vulnerability, know their love language, etc. These traits are actually well-worth learning but by themselves are sadly incomplete. Men are still, in a certain way, like boys—lacking in grit and unable to stay the course of life's inevitable setbacks. They carry a certain aversion to male energy and, confusingly for them, find that women aren't much attracted to what they had thought women wanted to see in a man.

Professor Eric Anderson suggests that, because men have less antipathy towards homosexual males than they did historically, they have no need to signal their heterosexuality to other males by hyper-masculine posturing (through misogyny, homophobia, or hyper-objectification of women).[190] This now allows them to exhibit behaviors that would otherwise have resulted in ostracism by straight men—like cuddling and kissing other men on the cheek (and even the lips, when drunk). I would agree but would suggest that men are becoming more fluid because the standard of "good" behavior has shifted towards the feminine.

The world is far more limited in opportunities for men than it used to be. With automation, robotics, A.I., jobs shipped off to China, an anemic global economy, etc, the means to generate a living wage are becoming harder and harder. Coupled with the anti-male bias in society, men are becoming more and more passive, whether they want to or not. They are still living at home despite being in their late twenties/thirties. This is due to a combination of unaffordable housing costs and a lack of confidence in their own spirit of independence.

Modern men are more lonely than they've ever been. They find it hard to develop close, intimate friendships into adulthood. Yet there is also evidence that the next generation of men is transitioning into "increasingly intimate, emotive, and trusting nature of bromances [which] offers young men a new social space for emotional disclosure, outside of

---

190 Mark McCormack and Eric Anderson ((October 19, 2010). *"'It's Just Not Acceptable Any More': The Erosion of Homophobia and the Softening of Masculinity at an English Sixth Form."* Sage Journals. https://journals.sagepub.com/doi/10.1177/0038038510375734

traditional heterosexual relationships."[191] As relations with women become more problematic, younger men are increasingly looking to their male friends to meet the emotional needs once fulfilled by intimate female partners…"because if I get into a fight with my bromance, he forgives me five minutes later. And if I get into a fight with my girlfriend, she brings it up again five months later!"[192]

Some men need to learn how to cry. Others need to learn how to stop crying. Traditional men were told that "boys don't cry" and were encouraged to stuff down their emotions to "get the job done" or be considered a pussy. Many modern men have learned the value of connecting with their pain and expressing their emotions; of owning up to themselves and showing their vulnerability. And many are stuck in this modality and don't know when to stop aimlessly emoting and start taking action, *despite* the way they are feeling. A man in his power is someone who knows how to master his emotions rather than being a slave to them—not through suppression but by wise management.

Men have been culturally-conditioned either one way or the other—too much in their masculine or too much in their feminine. Both men and women have been hurt in many ways which have adversely affected their energy bodies into a state of imbalance. Primarily, a man needs to feel his own masculine essence and fully inhabit it.

---

191 Sefan Robinson, Adam White, Eric Anderson ((October 12, 2017). *"Privileging the Bromance: A Critical Appraisal of Romantic and Bromantic Relationships."* Sage Journals. https://journals.sagepub.com/doi/full/10.1177/1097184X17730386

192 YouTube channel, Male Psychology Network (August 3, 2019). *"A Generational Perspective on Softening Masculinities. Prof Eric Anderson, Uni of Winchester, UK."* https://www.youtube.com/watch?v=YDRn7Ee3y-Y

He who sacrifices his respect for love basically burns his body to obtain the light.

— AMIT KALANTRI

33 Sex and Relationships

With all the problems men face in the post-#MeToo era, the atomization of human intimacy, and men's reliance on cyberspace for a semblance of connection (as a substitute for messy relationships in "meat space"), many men are struggling to connect with women. Where traditional males would frequent strip clubs, modern men are turning to sites like OnlyFans. Better than porn sites (which only satisfy their needs for sexual arousal and release), OnlyFans offers mystery and anticipation, a sense of community through "friend groups," validation, high-level responsiveness from content creators, and no harsh judgment—guaranteed. Men can experience all the best features of a long-distance relationship with a dream-girl who will do most of the heavy lifting for the "relationship"—for money. Real-life relationships can blow up in your face when a woman may choose to reject a man harshly. For the cost of a subscription, modern men can guarantee themselves loving connection without the gut-wrenching frustrations and rejections all too common with modern women.[193]

---

193 "The problem is that games and porn are entertaining, inexpensive, easily accessible, and reliable. Women can be entertaining, but they're expensive, inaccessible for most men, and from the male perspective, shockingly unreliable."
Dr. Helen Smith (2014). *"Men on Strike: Why Men Are Boycotting Marriage, Fatherhood, and the American Dream - and Why It Matters."* Encounter Books.

What's not to like? On the face of it, this choice meets the harsh reality of the modern dating scene with cold, clear logic—shop elsewhere! Add to the list, hook up apps, sex dolls, dating simulation apps, realistic VR sex, etc. Modern men are becoming "digisexual." Yet what's left behind is the opportunity to build themselves into better men. They never have to develop the skills to relate better nor find resilience in the face of life's vicissitudes. With legalized marijuana in one hand and a gamepad controller in the other, life is sweet.

So how about "real women?" Being in a relationship means allowing love to flow through our organisms. How we go about doing that, how to both have strong boundaries yet also surrender to another's influence, makes relationships difficult. We have layers of crap which serve to inhibit true intimacy.

When a guy starts a relationship with a woman, he appreciates her novelty and all the different facets of her mind, body, and soul which wait to be discovered, like a foreign land. But he very quickly returns to an automated way of thinking, based on prior relationships, and pushes her into that frame—rather than being with her, in the moment, seeing her for who she is, as a discrete and completely unique individual. There's no judgment in this—it just reflects how the mind works. We carry within us certain energy-conservation adaptations which have allowed our survival as a species by allocating limited mental processes more efficiently. There is only so much sensory information that the brain can process so it creates useful shortcuts. It creates recognizable patterns, archetypes, and schemas that can be applied to different situations to achieve something workable. We secure the storm of sensory stimuli onto these fixed points and shortcuts. In other words, it's a hack. It's like turning on a light switch. As a toddler, you spent quite a lot of mental energy figuring out how to turn on a light switch. As an adult, there is no need to replicate that energy every time—your brain has created a "light switch schema" that works without using much energy to figure it out. This can get you into trouble when applied to more complex things, like relationships.

Many people have something they love passionately. It could be collecting old farm implements, cross country skiing, foraging for mushrooms, or playing the harmonium. They devote themselves to their interests—obsessively practicing, learning, researching, and talking with those who share their passion. But when it comes to the person we love most in our lives, we don't do any of this. And then wonder how it all went wrong.

~

The opening phase of a relationship is the seduction. Women want to be seduced. They want the man to approach her and lead her through the initial stages in a way that leaves her feeling both safe and stimulated, and wanting more. Much has been learned by the "seduction community" in the last 15 years. Many men have been learning the art of seduction basically from scratch. There have been many "black hat" techniques employed by pick up artists who perform, as an actor might, in a way that women find appealing. Although out of his integrity, he presents himself as her ideal romantic partner (even if he has never authentically internalized any of those qualities). It's a game with the prize being he gets to lay between her legs (if she falls for his persona). The woman may enjoy the attention and the sex but can only connect with a ghost. Mostly though, the "white hat" techniques employed nowadays arise from a guy presenting himself authentically, unashamedly owning his sexual/romantic intent without being creepy or obnoxious, and conducting himself skillfully through the interaction. He brings the highest version of himself through the practice of self mastery and she is the lucky recipient of his attention.[194]

Beyond the seduction stage, the main problem for most men in relationships with their woman is that they are largely unskillful. This should come as no surprise. We are neither taught compassionate communication nor female psychology, let alone how to "fuck her open to God," to borrow

---

194 Recommended are:
James Marshal, thenaturallifestyles.com
Dan Bacon, themodernman.com
I don't vouch for everything they say as being white hat but they are definitely at that end of the spectrum.

a phrase from David Deida.[195] We're not even taught how to relate to ourselves. On top of this is the shame that is projected onto masculine sexuality. Sometimes we're lucky enough to stumble into a relationship and try to make it work. We have to learn about relationships by *being* in relationships. But there is also much that can be learned either beforehand or between relationships. There are plenty of relationship manuals out there, mostly read by women. This needs to change. You wouldn't get behind the wheel of a car without first having received some instruction and you also need to read up on the rules of the road.

The number one thing a man needs to look for when considering pair-bonding is a very simple observation—is the woman actually capable of being in a relationship? Before weighing up her looks, her character, her personality, her life circumstances, or the way she giggles and wiggles—this is the preeminent question which must be answered. Many women have many fine traits and qualities but are incapable of "behaving" themselves in a relationship. A man who starts a relationship with a woman, where the relationship is doomed from the start, has only himself to blame for not screening her out to begin with. Where women have too many expectations and requirements for a potential mate (their shopping lists of desirable attributes), men have too few. There's no shame in loving a woman. Sometimes men make the mistake of a giving a chance to a woman who is never going to arrive at the fullness of her being any time soon. They place more faith in her ability to evolve and grow, and less faith in their own capacity to search for someone better suited to their aspirations.

Just because there are several indications of compatibility doesn't yet mean that the relationship stands a chance. Modern men need to undertake the serious work of screening out women who fail to make the grade. And that means most of them, regrettably. If you're nice to your dog, it'll love you for life. If you're nice to a woman, who the hell knows? Modern women, as wounded as they are, as indoctrinated as they are, as lost as they are, and as entitled as they are, neither understand nor appreciate

195 David Deida (2017). *The Way of the Superior Man: A Spiritual Guide to Mastering the Challenges of Women, Work, and Sexual Desire.* Sounds True; Reprint edition.

what it takes to successfully live with a man. They have little conception of the necessary skills and qualities that they need to embody in order to conduct themselves well to ensure a healthy relationship.

Just because there is sexual polarity between men and women does not signify that there is genuine affection, fondness, and respect for men in general. Because of their narcissism, there doesn't exist a bond of female approval which extends beyond their biological imperative to feel satisfied from positive male attention. Modern women tend to rant and rave about deficiencies in men and demand a litany of conditions for pair bonding that any modern man worth his salt would do well to run screaming from. Instead, the question men pose themselves is, "what sort of pretzel-like configuration do I have to twist myself into to be an acceptable mate for a female?" "His self-esteem and self-image depend upon her smile, her approval."[196]

Getting to know someone really well is not such an easy task when the other is either lying to you or lying to themselves. Finding a "good woman" is like trying to find a needle in a needlestack.[197] Unlike finding a needle in a haystack, which is impossible to see, there are plenty of observable women who are potentially dateable. The trouble is finding the right needle among all the other needles without getting stuck all the time. A friend of mine, who thought he had found an evolved woman, also succumbed to his own mind games. In the early stage of a new relationship, the woman brought up for discussion the conditions under which he or she might leave the relationship. He considered this subject an incredibly healthy and mature thing to discuss, even while the rest of the relationship was exceptionally positive and passionate and no roadblocks had yet been encountered. He understood that building a strong foundation for growth required this level of healthy honesty. Indeed, this would have been healthy coming from a healthy person. But it was coming from an unhealthy person. He gave her more credit than was merited and she

196 Rollo May (May 1, 1991). *"The Cry for Myth."* W. W. Norton & Company.

197 A tip of the hat to YouTube channel, Better Bachelor. https://www.youtube.com/channel/UC9ctsJZ2aD1nCexfqj342NQ

became a "fucking made-up thing" in his head (see below). He admitted it had been his job to perform due diligence in selecting a partner and his desire to believe her at face value had trumped reality.

Almost all relationships have anger, judgments, expectations, personal criticisms, etc. Many men put up with bad behavior mostly because they don't know how to hold their ground or have poor boundaries. Such relationships are commonly a "battle for his soul." In the face of a woman who is in the throes of her own drama, they will constantly capitulate to her "needs." Men will say almost anything just to stay out of the doghouse, pretending to agree with her point of view. She may be appeased for a while but over time will lose respect for her man.

Where women play mind games with men, men play mind games on themselves. They paint for themselves a picture of the relationship, and the woman's qualities, before either of which has been revealed. They are lost in their unmet needs and project on her the ability to meet those needs. In the words of Johnny Depp, speaking of his alleged domestic abuser, Amber Heard,[198] "I've loved you for so many years. But you know what? You didn't exist. You don't exist. You're not there. You're a fucking made-up thing in my head."[199] Nice guys, especially, do favors for their woman in the hope that later they will get something from her in return. They create an expectation in themselves and an implicit obligation from their partner that was never actually articulated. When she doesn't deliver, they get reactive and bitter.

---

198 Ben Ashford (February, 2020). *'See how many people believe you.'*...Daily Mail. Amber Heard had mocked actor, Johnny Depp, for claiming he was the victim of domestic violence daring him to "tell the world and see how many people believe you". https://www.thisismoney.co.uk/news/article-7966723/Amber-Heard-ridicules-Johnny-Depp-claiming-hes-domestic-violence-victim.html

199 "She was beautiful, seemingly incredibly interested in me and my work, and I fell for it. She bombed me with what appeared to be love. It was not until much later that I understood that she had an agenda, namely to get married to me in order to progress her own career and to benefit financially, and she knew how to bring it about. She knew what she wanted, and I was an easy target .
She presented herself as a carbon copy of me, with precisely the same interests, thoughts, favorite writers, taste in music and art as me! Rather than see this as calculated, sociopathic and emotionally dishonest, I convinced myself that it was endearing and sweet.
She came into my life to take from me anything worth taking, and then destroy what remained of it."
- Johnny Depp's testimonies about his ex-wife Amber Heard.

~

Just like sex is more of a woman's thing than a man's thing (see *Sex*, chapter, *The Divine Feminine*), intimacy is more of a man's thing. A man's feminine aspect is to receive and be penetrated by intimacy experienced with a woman. Just as a woman experiences sex as double-edged (it can be overwhelming or even abusive), allowing a woman to penetrate him to his emotional core is both necessary for a man's health and potentially devastating when she misuses that power.

Men, in general, recover more quickly from physical abuse than emotional abuse, either because nature designed them to be physically resilient or because being able to "take a beating" is an aspect of manhood that is socially normalized. Possibly, it's part of the warrior aspect of masculinity to take physical injury, hold it, carry it, and move forward with it. Men have no shame in displaying their physical scars—quite the contrary. But no one sees his emotional scars and there is no pride in displaying them in the same way as those physical scars.

This is so little understood that it is assumed that when men protect themselves, largely unconsciously, from women, it is because they are deficient in emotional intelligence. Nothing could be further from the truth. The man has simply locked off his vulnerable heart because he knows instinctively that the emotional environment is unsafe, and perhaps he has had many salutary lessons already. In order for men to be vulnerable, there needs to be a reasonable expectation of safety (for a woman to surrender to a man sexually, she needs the same expectation). He needs to be confident that his vulnerability won't be used as ammunition with which to attack him. Modern women, consciously or unconsciously, are playing a dissonant game with men. They want men to open up and be softer and more vulnerable yet have little to no expectation of themselves as having a sacred obligation to hold his vulnerability with delicacy.[200]

---

200 Staff reporter (6 March, 2012). *"Women gain happiness from seeing their partner upset - because it 'shows their relationship is strong.'"* Daily Mail. https://www.dailymail.co.uk/health/article-2111203/Seeing-man-upset-makes-women-happy--shows-relationship-strong.html

Just as a woman can feel the pain of sexual misencounters and struggle to overcome her pain to trust again, so too do men with their broken hearts. It's of the same order of magnitude. Men would be wise to practice "emotional chastity," which is being studiously careful with whom they choose to be vulnerable. Women are more agreeable[201] than men at a population level, but that doesn't mean they are less harmful.

The first lesson may have been received in his childhood from his mother. If she carried her own wounding in the form of negativity towards men (like, "all men are bastards," "all men are emotional midgets," etc), whether she expressed it or not, spoken or unspoken, this would have an impact on the boy's undefended psychology. He might go on to develop a self-loathing of his own masculine essence. Or he might feel that he could never trust a woman because they were inherently contemptuous of the masculine in him. Because his mother is essential to his nourishment, because of his need to receive her intimacy, he might reconstruct himself, so as not to jeopardize the relationship, by becoming amasculine. He can't allow himself to become the thing she dislikes even if it means rejecting his true nature. The mother gets to mold her boy into the ideal version of the kind of man she craves, and he never evolves into the man he was "destined" to be.[202]

This dynamic is also encountered in adult relationships. Because of emotional wounding (as well as narcissism and entitlement), wounded women demand that his attention be focused on her and her issues. She may not openly do so, but she will have unspoken expectations that he magically fix her. But the wounding that some women carry is such a "bottomless pit," it will either leave him exhausted or distracted from his own life purpose, or both. Such women feel that he should prioritize her needs above his own long-term goals and the true expression of his life force. She becomes a succubus—a woman who will suck a man's energy and pull him down.

201 Agreeableness. Psychology Today. https://www.psychologytoday.com/us/basics/agreeableness

202 YouTube channel, HuffPost (November 30, 2015). *"I'm Raising My Son As A Feminist."* https://www.youtube.com/watch?v=AeF6IGwDkl4

Men's taciturn nature is an adaptive strategy for dealing with manipulative and controlling women. Women who wheedle and nag and poke and prod cannot be engaged at the verbal level, as even mild resistance is sufficient encouragement for her to keep chipping away at his will. A far better strategy for dealing with manipulators has been to simply not engage with them.[203]

Conscious men are particularly susceptible to wounded women because they are generally heart-centered, decent, good men who are not afraid of a challenging situation. A compassionate man will be empathetic and drawn to helping her heal. And this is part of being a noble man who cares and is protective towards those he loves. But there is a point where he cannot "save" the wounded woman. If he's lucky she'll just weigh him down for years and years. At worst, she can drag him down with her. The challenge is to be ruthless by setting aside feelings of love and care for her, and leaving her in order to honor his love for himself.

Because most modern women are dysregulated, most modern men will have to choose how to relate in moments where the crazy hits the fan. It takes a strong, centered, confident man to let it all roll off him. He needs to be reasonable, rational, logical, non-threatening, and non-threatened.[204] This may be helpful when dealing with some modern women who chronically behave like children. When an interaction with her does not fulfill her drama needs, her mind is re-trained to expect boredom.

Some, however, can be more than challenging to stay present with. If that's what you want (because "she's worth it") then go ahead. You have a lot of growth opportunities ahead of you! Can you offer compassion and kindness while she attempts to emasculate you? Will you draw a line in the sand around acceptable behavior? Can you defuse the situation by teasing her gently and making light of her words/eye-rolling? And should

203 Although the work of marital stability expert, John Gottman, has been methodical and insightful in understanding poor relationship dynamics, Stonewalling (one of his Four Horsemen of the Apocalypse) is characterized as a negative reaction, rather than a contextually appropriate response.

204 Dr.O.Vijayasree. *"Transactional Analysis."* Pp. 9-10. http://www.mcrhrdi.gov.in/splfc/week3/M-Transactional%20Analysis.pdf

you? Yes, you may be an unfuckwithable, 360-degree,[205] spiritual, warrior-magician-lover-king but why would you choose a partner who looks for chinks in your armor in which to stick her little knife?

Just as women have to take a chance on a man and do their best to screen out potential partners who might turn out to be sexually or physically abusive, a man has to have the same level of due diligence when screening out women who might break his heart. They don't, because they are not aware of the potential for catastrophic damage or they proudly believe they are man enough to take it.

Now, personally, I'd advise any man to take a zero-tolerance position to the most egregious behaviors like, physical abuse, coercion, manipulation, and poor self-control. But even so, the wary will be conscious of how she conducts herself, and to those little signs of character defects that she shows him early on in the relationship. They're signposts to what he can expect in larger doses later down the line. At best, she may be someone he can never fully trust because her wounding might cause her to behave unpredictably in times of stress or crisis—he may not be able to count on her when he needs her the most.

For some however, maybe this path could make him a more well-rounded man as he develops insights and skills in the face of adversity. Maybe it could align him with his higher purpose. Maybe he sees contentment and happiness as illusory and impermanent, and prefers something more concrete, like awareness itself, regardless of circumstance—being aware in the moment, whatever the moment has to offer? In the words of Bruce Lee, "Do not pray for an easy life, pray for the strength to endure a difficult one." Or perhaps he'd rather seek a more evolved woman who can go places the less evolved can't? There's actually no right and wrong—he just has to know what he's letting into his space and allow himself to be expanded. If being in such a relationship closes his heart, then he would be wise to either readjust his outlook or readjust his choice in women.

All being said and done, it's a man's relationship to his own values

205 The 360 degree personality is a term coined by the American poet, Robert Bly. It refers to the full expression of our true nature without internal resistance or censorship.

which sets the stage for a relationship with a woman. Modern men need to reflect upon and recognize basic standards of acceptable behavior from the women they select. If he's never willing to say "No," and will readily compromise or dump his values, never draw a line in the sand, then he merely becomes a supplicant.

Learning how to break up with a girl is as important as knowing how to say hello to her when he first sees her. When men and women's fundamental reasons for being in that relationship permanently go out of alignment, it's time to consciously uncouple. If a man is unaware of the tipping point in a relationship when it's time to exit, nor is decisive enough to end it, the consequences are that he allows the relationship to drift inevitably towards distant rocks, picking up baggage and trauma along the way, when he could be more aligned with what he *does* want. It's a waste of life force energy to be with the wrong person, an intimate or not.

In order to have good mental health, men need to be loved and respected. All sorts of pathologies arise if these needs in men are not met. It's no good verbally appealing to men to open their hearts when their hearts have been broken since infanthood. The parenting many boys experience is conditional love, or pseudo-love. Narcissistic mothering, single mothers, absent fathers, no respectful male guidance, and wounded masculinity all contribute to his demise. For many, the message has been, "If you bring glory to the household (good grades, a degree, a respectable career, etc), I will show you love." Clearly then, a strong, centered, present, conscious man is, in part, the product of a mother who knows how to love and respect the boy (and his father). This is a love that the man takes into him from his mother, which then flows through him to the future women in his life, creating a virtuous circle and so benefiting women through the generations.

If only our eyes saw souls instead of bodies. How different our ideals of beauty would be.

— UNATTRIBUTED

34 Evolutionary Programming

There is a hierarchy of instincts for men, consisting of three key components to their evolutionary make-up in the following order of priority: Procreation, Protection, and Provision. Unless we become aware of our evolutionary programming, our choices will be unconscious and limited.

Procreation. Top of the list is procreation. Mother Nature has it so that, not just the human species, but any species places procreation at the top of the list. Procreation trumps protection with almost every species risking its life to have sex.

The way men are constructed by nature is to scan for signs of fertility in a woman. Curvaceous body, beautiful and symmetrical face, etc. "Attracted mostly by pleasing appearance, they look for their soul mate in a graveyard of beautiful, nicely dressed forms, unmindful that a devil may be housed within."[206] We have a tough time seeing past outer beauty and then compound the problem by projecting inner beauty—how can someone so beautiful on the outside be anything less on the inside? Her outer beauty is

206 Paramahansa Yogananda (1995). *"How to Cultivate Divine Love."* Self Realization Fellowship.

simply a reflection and manifestation of her nature, we surmise. Her thought shapes her form. And it's just not true. This is called the Halo Effect—a tendency for a good impression in one area to translate automatically to good impressions in other areas. This is a big, big problem for men to transcend. How do we get past that? How much are we a slave to our biology? How can we find desirable an unattractive woman whose beauty is internal? There are so many women out there who are gorgeous and beautiful on the inside, and yet who look like a horse! Tragically, there is no attraction. Women have their own struggle with hypergamy, although there are doubts whether this is evolutionary programming (see *Social Status and Hypergamy*, chapter, *Modern Women*).

There are very big differences in what attracts a man to a woman, and a woman to a man. While men may celebrate women's increasing achievements in the workplace, this, though admirable, is not a turn-on and doesn't serve as a mechanism of attraction for men. Men are more attracted to youth, beauty, and the way she moves and talks, and to desirable female qualities. It's how men are constructed and it's not something that can be rationalized out of existence. Men don't go for wrinkly, old crones nor fat, shapeless, blotchy-skinned women, unless that's all we are capable of bagging. Given the choice, we would basically go for shapely, curvy, full-breasted, fertile, clear-eyed, pretty, cute, or hot women.[207]

There is a myth that female beauty is ever-changing and culturally determined. The reason models are skinny is not to project desirability as potential mates—it's to sell clothes. Attractiveness based on waist-to-hip ratio is a far better metric and is universal across all cultures. Appreciation for the preferred "hourglass figure" is programmed in the male mind because it provides him important biological clues about a woman's youthfulness and fertility. Does

207 Devendra Singh (2016). *"An Evolutionary Theory of Female Physical Attractiveness."* University of Texas at Austin. https://pdfs.semanticscholar.org/00dd/e6b664c882410fa5e4ed1d7e17f994636793.pdf

she have wide enough hips to squeeze out a baby and large enough breasts to feed it? As far as the chemistry of physical attraction is concerned, it's very hard for a man to disregard a woman's physical appearance. Finding and focusing on one physical element that he does find appealing, can sometimes be a way of circumventing some of this programming but it's an uphill struggle which women need to realize and accept. To a large extent, both men and women are proscribed in their behaviors and actions because of inherent biological proclivities.

Unlike men, who almost instantaneously and unconsciously assess every woman's desirability—hot or not?—women mostly see just a sea of men. Whereas men may initially objectify a woman by her appearance, a woman will objectify a man by his invisibility. She waits for a man to emerge from and distinguish himself from the herd—to approach her with confidence and presence before paying him attention. Women have their attraction to a man activated more by what he's doing, how he communicates, how he holds himself, how present and grounded he is, and how he makes her feel—not by his hotness (unless he is a prime specimen). If she wants him to approach, she may send him indications of interest through body language but will be unlikely to make the first move.

Of the hundreds of species of primates in the world, only a handful are monogamous.[208] Yet monogamy, the prevailing narrative of social arrangements in the human primate species, is thought to be natural and normal. The claim is that, ever since there were anatomically modern humans, women traded sex and fidelity to men in return for protection and resources. It would make sense if we'd always lived in nuclear families where resources were only shared within the family unit. But for 95% of human history we've lived in hunter-gatherer societies which had been arranged in a form of primitive communism with very little sense

208 Titi monkeys, night monkeys, callitrichids, langur/mentawi island leaf monkeys, gibbons, and prosimians.

of private property. These societies were characterized by a "fierce egalitarianism," meaning that an individual who had access to additional resources was required to share them with the tribe (an idea today which many would find abhorrent).[209] The individual was the smallest component of the greater whole and self-concerned behavior was seen as senseless. Resources were shared, sex was shared, children were raised communally, and women went and gathered the much-needed calories for the tribe (hunting provided less). The transactional nature of modern relationships is derived from scarcity where women trade sex and conditional love for resources, power, and status from those men who can provide it.

Protection. Men's natural predisposition is to protect anyone "within reach." We don't even have to know or like the person, particularly. When we hear women crying out in pain, regardless of whether it's physical or emotional, we have a visceral reaction and tune in so as to see if we can help—whether we want to fuck her or not. This may be an unconscious driving force to demonstrate our desirability as a sex partner but I think it goes beyond that.

Protect trumps provide. If a woman asks a man for something and the man says, "no," then he is coming from a place of protection. He is protecting any number of things; his resources, his energy, his honor, his time, etc.

Provision. Provide is the state women want men to be in. Men also feel great, ample, and generous where they have the resources to provide what they have to those they love (not just, but especially women). This provision doesn't have to be material—it can be a service, some humor, some playfulness, some wisdom, their presence, their time, etc. In modern relationships, the more men demonstrate to prospective partners that they can provide for them (materially

209 Christopher Ryan and Cacilda Jethá (2014). *"Sex at Dawn."* Harper.

and socially), the more they demonstrate that they have control over resources and their social environment, the more likely they can attract the favors of more desirable women. Women in turn recognize their utility and estimate how their own needs could be met by his use-function and productivity.

Our evolutionary roots suggest that provisioning was not done at the individual level, at least in terms of the hunt. Man's nature was cooperative rather than competitive. It's simply not the case that the alpha hunter would leave camp alone at dusk and return in the morning with a slain deer across his mighty shoulders. Game was hunted in groups, as a group effort, and the spoils returned to the tribe to be shared equally.

Disposability. We've all heard of the phrase "women and children first," as it relates to prioritizing safety and well-being. This relates to the concept of "male disposability" which describes the tendency to be less concerned about men than women where harm is anticipated. In a recent study,[210] given the choice, participants were more willing to inflict harm on men than women. In one experiment, the participants were asked to sacrifice one hypothetical individual to save a greater number of people (aka the Trolley Experiment). In another, they were permitted to keep a sum of money but by doing so the researchers' "confederates" would receive an electric shock. In both, women were harmed less often than men and, in particular, women were even more averse to inflicting harm on other women.

The psychology of male disposability is millennia in the making. Men have not paid attention to themselves. The most important thing has been to get the job done, often at any cost, or by any means. But leaving themselves behind in the process. They've put

210 Tim Dalgleish, Davy Evans, Lauren Navrady, and Ellen Tedeschi. Chivalry is Not Dead When it Comes to Morality, Cambridge University's Brain Sciences Unit and Columbia University, June 8 2016.

their backs into their work and neglected their hearts (to be rather romantic about it). Men have turned away from their sense of being in order to focus on their sense of doing, in turn creating a kind of cultural dissociation. Showing up for our obligations but being absent from our selves.

Part Five

Wounding and Trauma

Wake up, be aware of who you are, what you're doing and what you can do to prevent yourself from becoming ill.

– MAYA ANGELOU

It is not only the ratio of pleasure to pain that determines the quality of a life, but also the sheer quantity of pain. Once a certain threshold of pain is passed, no amount of pleasure can compensate for it.[211]

— DAVID BENATAR

35 Suffering from a Historical Perspective

The biggest problem in most people's lives is, and has always been, psychological trauma (which is simultaneously neurophysiological trauma). Trauma is what creates a maladjusted ability to connect with others. My contention is that our last few millennia on this planet have led to civilization as we know it developing unfavorably as a response to, or as a consequence of, accumulated and unintegrated stress and trauma. Essentially, this is the study of suffering from a historical perspective. Not only is it at the level of the individual, but all of humanity is locked into a cycle of trauma patternings. Trauma is "anything that's too much, too soon, or too fast for our nervous system to handle, especially if we can't reach successful resolution."[212] I would also add that trauma is anything that should have happened which didn't, especially in early childhood, where non-consideration of a child's needs can be life-threatening or

211 David Benatar (September 15, 2008). *"Better Never to Have Been: The Harm of Coming into Existence."* Oxford University Press; Illustrated edition

212 Mark Banschick M.D. (March 26, 2015). *"Somatic Experiencing. How trauma can be overcome."* Psychology Today. https://www.psychologytoday.com/intl/blog/the-intelligent-divorce/201503/somatic-experiencing

life-damaging. With trauma comes a loss of feeling, a loss of resilience in engaging with life's inevitable painfulness. Trauma can stunt growth and development because it can capture a person's energy and agency and cause them to react from pain and fear.

My view is that the problems we face today have nothing to do with the true nature of men and women or any inherently flawed biological programming. Neither masculinity nor femininity are toxic. It has to do with the wounding and trauma stored at the level of our nervous system, a cancer which grows from generation to generation, compounding suffering, until we now find ourselves in our present-day sorry state of affairs. What we see are human beings programmed and regulated by pain and fear which they're trying to cope with in dysfunctional ways. It's been a long time coming—and now it's here.

This hypothesis is an extension of the idea of generational trauma.[213] We are coming to understand more about epigenetics, where we have an additional set of genes which respond to experiences as we move through daily life. The epigenome switches on (or off) the gene pool so that various genetic traits are expressed based on the prior actions of the epigenome.[214] Several studies have been conducted on survivors of the Holocaust and their offspring. For example, incidences of suicide and PTSD in the children of survivors far exceed the rate found in the general population.

This has led me to consider the human nervous system as a central aspect in respect to the development of civilization. Psychological trauma is and has been thrusting our civilization toward ubiquitous/large-scale states

---

213 As an example:
Tori DeAngelis (February 2019). *"The legacy of trauma."* American Psychological Association. https://www.apa.org/monitor/2019/02/legacy-trauma
Also:
Latria Graham (May 1, 2018). *"We're Here. You Just Don't See Us."* Outside magazine. https://www.outsideonline.com/2296351/were-here-you-just-dont-see-us
Despite nothing bad ever happening to her (in her story), the generational trauma experienced by the author causes her to reflect poorly on her social environment (logical fallacy - appeal to emotion). She prefers to call for institutional change and special privileges rather than acknowledge and resolve her inner pain.

214 Nagy A. Youssef, et al. (May, 2018). *"The Effects of Trauma, with or without PTSD, on the Transgenerational DNA Methylation Alterations in Human Offsprings."* Brain Sciences, MDPI. https://www.ncbi.nlm.nih.gov/pmc/articles/PMC5977074/#:~:text=Our%20review%20found%20an%20accumulating,of%20genes%20and%20the%20metabolome.

of fight/flight "normalcy"—a population which is evermore chronically traumatized. And so it's necessary to see the world through the spectrum of trauma, if we wish to calm ourselves the-fuck down. Whether someone is suffering from a mental, emotional or physical dysfunction, it all has its roots in unresolved trauma. Trauma is distress without resolution. We are normalized to trauma. But because it is normalized, we don't recognize it as such.

The smoking gun can be found in the way we react to traumatic events. Or, rather, how we don't react.

Neurobiologist, Robert Sapolsky, authored the book, *Why Zebras Don't Get Ulcers*, in which he explained that zebras and other wild animals have a way of dissipating stress from their bodies after a traumatic event—they simply shake it off. These are known as neurogenic tremors. If a gazelle narrowly escapes being eaten by a cheetah, it then finds a safe place, hidden from view, and spends up to a half hour rhythmically shaking to recalibrate its nervous system. It is shaking with fear and shaking off fear by dumping off adrenaline and allowing the nervous system to down-regulate. These spontaneous shakes and tremors allow the body to release any muscular bracing and return the animal to normal movement.[215]

The only animals which don't go through this shaking experience are domestic animals, zoo animals, laboratory animals, and human animals. What correlates them is that they are all "caged." Human beings are caged by society (see chapter, *Why you are a Slave*). Shaking is an automatic way of dealing with stress stored in the body—something that can only be short-circuited by taking animals out of their natural environment, away from their true nature, and imposing an unnatural, alienated existence upon them. Their emotions become frozen at the cellular level.

In our western model of medicine, shaking is pathologized and seen as a symptom of panic attacks, PTSD, anxiety and social phobias, not as

215 Two examples:
YouTube channel, Jim Hopper (September 21, 2017). *"Impala in and slowly out of collapsed immobility."* https://www.youtube.com/watch?v=Ox7Uj2pw-8o
YouTube channel, Danny Vikander (October 22, 2012). *"Trauma bear."* https://www.youtube.com/watch?v=eT406oGeodI

a healthy response to those conditions. If we catch ourselves shaking, we try to stop them by force of will because of the shame we feel at being judged for being weak and out of control.

Unhealthy people have shaped civilizations, and civilizations have shaped people in unhealthy ways—a vicious cycle. This began when we started to see ourselves as separate and disconnected from people and planet (see *Disconnection,* chapter, *Why you are a Slave).* We started to see our best interests as being distinctly separate from the needs of others. We started to cage human beings, physically or mentally. Over time, other people's thoughts, feelings, desires, and needs have steadily grown of lesser importance to our own. Even our children only exist to serve a role in our lives.

True human enlightenment will happen when all human beings on this planet have regulated their nervous systems.

— PETER LEVINE

36 The Central Nervous System

Essentially, by now, as a conscious man, you've most likely encountered the concept of the conditioned ego and the importance of transcending its limitations to realize your true nature. This is eminently true but it's not the whole story. We also have within us trauma patternings contained at the cellular level. Understanding this is not a question of transcending ego—it's about somatic release. When you find yourself triggered by a certain circumstance, its not necessarily the conditioned ego which is responding; it could be your conditioned nervous system.

From all the possible things that might be considered a priority to heal for our future as a species, the most critical right now is nervous system regulation. Few people understand its importance. The level of dysregulation in the general population is endemic. And this dysregulation takes an enormous amount of time and knowledge to embrace, integrate, and ultimately transcend—knowledge which really isn't mainstream. And, at the personal level, it's not an easy process—it requires courage and a lifetime's practice. Ideally, the nervous system has an inherent "intelligence" whereby it helps the human organism self-regulate or feel well-balanced. But it can only do so once certain conditions have been met.

The nervous system has the responsibility of perceiving and assessing how much safety or danger is present in the moment and then regulating the human organism to deal with any threats so as to return to a state of ease as soon as possible. It not only perceives and assesses but also instantly chooses whether to "fight, flight, or freeze" its way back to safety and what immediate behaviors are necessary. That's the plan, so to speak.

Say a soccer ball is speeding towards your head. You perceive it within milliseconds of impact. You either deflect it with your hand (fight), duck its path (flee), or brace for impact (freeze). You could say, your nervous system is obsessed with your safety by being obsessed with possible threats. As a survival mechanism through human and pre-human history, being "overly concerned" with danger meant greater chances of survival. The more indifferent to danger an organism is, the less likely it is to survive long enough to pass on its genes. The rustling in the bush most likely isn't a hungry predator but your nervous system will always serve up to you that possibility because not to do so might be to ignore that outside chance at your peril. Anything we've lived through is supposed to make us more resilient and more capable at assessing threats—our nervous system essentially grows itself and responds more and more appropriately to environmental threats.

When practicing new skills, we store procedural memories in a way so that we can replicate them (procedural memory allows you to ride a bicycle even if you haven't ridden one in years). Having become aroused at the possible threats to your safety, and taken any action necessary to meet those threats, the nervous system ideally goes through a process of extinguishing any residual "instructions." When the previously mentioned gazelle shakes and trembles, it is completing the act of escape. It is extinguishing all of its procedural memories related to the traumatic event. If did not do so, these would be stored as unconscious memories sending a false message to freeze every time the gazelle experienced something similar to the original traumatic event, whether life- threatening or not. In so doing, it extinguishes the feeling of threat so as to maintain its mental health and not live on edge 24/7.

Procedural memory, implicit memory, emotional memory, somatic memory, perceptual memory are the building blocks of mental models, or schemas. And these can lead to a priming of the organism for action or reaction. When procedural memories are locked into their trauma origins, they can short-circuit the organism and hijack higher-level functioning. But if the environment continues to signal threats, then the nervous system becomes conditioned to perceiving threats, even after possible threats are in reality no longer present. As perceived danger increases or persists, we become progressively less able to override our impulses and progressively less able to control our behavior because the nervous system was never able to resolve itself back to a condition of feeling safe.

One analogy is a traffic jam caused by people up ahead rubber-necking at an accident on the other side of the freeway. The traffic won't flow freely because of an incident that bears no relevant information for the direction it is heading. When the nervous system gets into a traffic jam it leaves us out of flow, rigid and reactive, and with impaired agency, much like individual drivers in each car.

Human beings acquire resiliency to traumatic events by how they experienced life in their early childhood—they had a nervous system that was built from the ground up. They were not born with it. It had to be co-created with their caregivers. This means that early childhood experiences, if not handled well, can produce nasty repercussions in adulthood.

Adverse childhood experiences are the single greatest unaddressed public health threat facing our nation today.[216]

— DR. ROBERT BLOCK

37 Adverse Childhood Experiences

The first three years of a human being's life are the most critical in terms of his future wellbeing.

When we're born, we're fundamentally helpless. All we could do was send out signals for our needs to be met—by crying, writhing, or wriggling. We could only express our suffering; we couldn't manage it. We had no ability to take control of the environment other than by hopefully attracting our caregivers to cuddle us, feed us, or relieve us from physical discomfort. Whereas in utero our needs were met through direct connection with the mother's body, it suddenly starts to dawn on us at a primal level that we are separate and there are now no guarantees.

Some cultures foster a deep and loving connection with infants, toddlers, children and young adults where their needs are attuned to by their carers as they pass through various stages of development. These children usually make a good transition into adulthood. In civilized societies, we are born into this world whole yet by the time we reach maturity many do not perceive themselves that way. Self-help books have proliferated in the last couple of generations as people have recognized their self-worth issues. They are grappling with problems of self-worth without realizing

216 Dr. Robert Block, former President of the American Academy of pediatrics.

that they have a problem with self-hate. Yet no human is born into this world lacking in self-worth. They are conditioned to self-hate.

Children are not born embodying maladaptive, inhumane, or anti-social behaviors. They are not born "bad." But things can go terribly wrong when the needed ingredients for their full flourishing are not in place. A toddler or an infant, and certainly the fetus, is at its most helpless and vulnerable at this stage of life as a human. Its ability to cope with adversity has not even begun to be developed. If a mother drinks, she shares alcohol with her unborn child. If she smokes, she shares 4000 different compounds, many of which are toxic. These things are relatively well-known. But the chemicals of rage, of fear, of stress, are also shared with the baby and we don't have social policies to protect these babies from them.

Once born, a baby needs its mother (or caregiver) to teach it how to self-sooth and regulate its emotions. It needs to feel connected and attuned to by her as she gives it verbal, physical, and emotional signals that it is not alone and everything is going to be alright. Cooing, rocking, singing, eye-gazing, cradling, smiling, etc. This attunement is critical for helping the baby build a healthy nervous system (the baby cannot do so by itself). If the infant never receives this attention, or the attention that it does receive is harmful, it will develop a dysregulated nervous system (and potentially future mental illnesses and personality disorders). "As the ACE (Adverse Childhood Experiences) study[217] has shown, child abuse and neglect is the single most preventable cause of mental illness, the single most common cause of drug and alcohol abuse, and a significant contributor to leading causes of death such as diabetes, heart disease, cancer, stroke, and suicide."[218] While abuse and neglect are extremes, other "survival stressors" can also do substantial harm.

Childhood trauma is developmental trauma, and can have repercussions into adult life. If they don't get what they need as a child, if the natural unfolding of their development was adversely impeded, certain aspects of their humanity will either be missing or maladaptive. They will not have

217 *"About the CDC-Kaiser ACE Study."* Centers for Disease Control and Prevention. https://www.cdc.gov/violenceprevention/aces/about.html?CDC_AA_refVal=https%3A%2F%2Fwww.cdc.gov%2Fviolenceprevention%2Facestudy%2Fabout.html

218 Bessel van der Kolk (2014). *"The Body Keeps the Score: Brain, Mind, and Body in the Healing of Trauma."* Viking.

done the work of healthy individuation. Some children grow up unable to empathize. Some develop personality disorders.[219] We're bringing into this world human beings who we raise to hurt other human beings. Who will then, in *their* pain, hurt other human beings.

My contention is that this is now the norm.

~

Women and children are treasured by society. But not *all* children. When a boy transitions to manhood, he finds that his only value was his latent ability to be a useful male. One whose value would only be recognized once he demonstrated that utility to others. If he was lucky, he was loved and cared for simply for being a kid. He was worth something—or at least that was the message he received from society more broadly. Once he stopped being a kid, that all fell away and he experienced a generalized sense of worthlessness. Modern childhood for boys is a con—it gives him the illusion of love. Yet real love doesn't suddenly vanish or be withdrawn at the onset of maturity.

Separation from the mother—away from being loved, fed, and bonded—is an aspect of humanity that never truly leaves men. All of us can at some point feel the pain of separation—where our needs are ignored, rejected, or reviled—where we feel helpless. In those moments, we become like an infant. We look to other women to give us what we need. If they can't provide it, we try to provide it to ourselves. If we can't provide it to ourselves, we fill the gap with stuff to distract us from the pain—PCP, pastries, pilsner, porn, poker, priests, or politicians.

> *Either we spend time meeting children's emotional needs by filling their cup with love or we spend time dealing with the behaviors caused from their unmet needs. Either way we spend the time.*[220]
>
> — PAM LEO

---

219 Example. Borderline Personality Disorder – a state of severe emotional dysregulation with periods of rage, terror, profound depression, and mostly negative emotional instability. Individuals may exhibit a manipulative aspect and also a self-preservation aspect. They often develop certain somatic and chronic pain complaints.

220 Pam Leo (2007). *"Connection Parenting: Parenting Through Connection Instead of Coercion, Through Love Instead of Fear."* Wyatt-MacKenzie Publishing; 2nd edition

We have to break the cycle of hurting children and sending them into adulthood as hurting humans who believe that children must be hurt to grow into healthy humans. A hurting human is not a healthy human, and a hurting humanity cannot create a healthy, peaceful world.

– L.R. KNOST.

38 Childhood and Parenting

Childhood is the most crucial time in the life of a human being. It is the bedrock of our creative, conscious, logical, and ethical experiences as adults. We spend an enormous amount of time being children compared to other animals. So why is that? Simply stated, it's to learn the task of becoming a complex organism—an adult. So if the child is prevented from learning—either by having their thinking and learning done for them or by restricting their perceptual experiences (too much screen time, helicopter parenting, etc)—they become adults who are unable solve their own problems and who either don't care or don't know how they harm others and themselves. They become children walking around in adult bodies having not learned how to be fully adulted. Children who are coddled in childhood grow up to be ineffective adults because they've been shielded from insult and injury. Too much of either is a bad thing but if they're never exposed to them they never learn how to deal with the slings and arrows of misfortune.

Historically, and in terms of "original sin," children were regarded as being born with a built-in predisposition to be immoral. Although central to the Catholic church, this perspective seems to have pervaded the social fabric through the Middle Ages. Consequently, it was the parents' responsibility to harshly correct their offspring's evil tendencies, to remove sin, and bring them salvation. This was later mitigated by the thoughts of philosopher, John Locke (1632 – 1704), who believed that children were born neither good nor bad, and were essentially a blank slate (a tabula rasa). They were predisposed neither to goodness nor badness but had to be shaped to become morally true. Punishment and rewards were considered appropriate (and still are to this day). He preferred "disgracing" a child when they transgressed and positively reinforcing approved behavior with affection. Swiss philosopher, Jean-Jacques Rousseau (1712 – 1778) later proposed that children were born inherently good and would unfold into inherently good adults if allowed to follow their own inner guidance. None of these three approaches to child-rearing differentiated between adults and children in any substantive way—children were viewed mostly as "immature adults." Currently, we believe that children, regardless of their culture, pass through similar stages of development unique to being a child.[221] Threads from all of these approaches still exist to this day, corporal punishment being an example of a method of correction that has stood the test of time (although less commonplace), and "time outs" are instead used as a form of "disgrace".

In this day and age, more and more people are becoming aware that it was the relationship with our parents/caregivers—the intensely focused troublesome aspects of it—which created the most significant levels of dysfunction in our adult lives. So it can be said that if you experience dysfunctional relationships as an adult, no matter how healthy or caring you perceived your parenting to have been, in actuality you were programmed to behave dysfunctionally by them. It's not your fault and it's also not theirs; because where did they receive *their* programming from?

All too often people believe that their childhood was unexceptional,

221 With contributions from Maria Montessori, Lev Vygotsky, Erik Erikson, John Bowlby, and Jean Piaget.

pretty good on the whole, and devoid of major traumatic events. Yet there are many common experiences that can be traumatic but are often not perceived as such. Later in life, these same people start developing mysterious ailments. Their anxiety, stress, seemingly random panic attacks, difficulties bonding with their newborn son or daughter, unhealthy relationships, digestive and immune system problems and a host of other things are all linked to adverse childhood experiences. What we are beginning to understand is that trauma is not necessarily those big jarring events like an auto accident, surviving sexual abuse, or being abandoned emotionally.

Of course, no parents are perfectly wise and loving. At some level, their style of parenting will adversely impact their children's development. This is inevitable, in human form. The question is, at what point do parents make poor parents?

Dysfunctional families in our culture are sadly the norm. It is the reason we have so much hate mixed with love in our relationships. They exist on a spectrum but most are either at the worse, or much worse, end of the scale. The unhealthy emotional environments in which children are being raised contribute enormously to personal and social wounding and dysfunctional behavior. You don't have to hit to hurt and children don't have to be terrorized by their parents to suffer enduring harm. Sticks and stones are rarely as damaging as harsh words.

Childhood trauma occurs through lack of attunement to the child's cues for care and attention. Most parents do not understand how to place their child's best interests foremost. There is a broad spectrum of interpersonal antagonism between parent and child where, at worst, the self of the child gets denied its right to exist and is ultimately buried. As an adult, we can conceive the difference in valency between a stressor which is "mild" and one which is harmful. But to the growing child, they are experienced as the same kind of threat and stress. An amazing reality to accept, but true. Childhood trauma teaches us how to dissociate from our lived experience at many subtle and gross levels. Which brings me to my point (and thank you for sticking with me!)—a man choosing to live consciously has to contend with how he has been conditioned to live unconsciously. His level of consciousness is negatively correlated with the unresolved exigencies of childhood.

How many of us were punished for "bad behavior," or rewarded for "good behavior?" How many of us had "helicopter parents?" How many were expected to achieve some performance threshold to win parental approval?

Direct and active punishment is the most obvious form of controlling a child in order to enforce compliancy. It's such a normal part of childhood (and adulthood!) that we never question its place in sound parenting. The parent comes from the perspective of being superior to the child and uses physical and verbal aggression to enforce behavioral standards. Being labeled "naughty" or "bad" can basically mean any behavior the parent disagrees with. Often, children are conditioned to see themselves as bad even though they did nothing wrong. Since the child is helpless and dependent on the parent for their material well-being, they have little to no choice but to suck it up. As a result, they may internalize such treatment and learn to blame themselves rather than the parent. This eventually turns into toxic shame, and a perspective of being unworthy or undeserving of the blessings in life. Rejection, or conditional "love," is also a form of punishment. Here, in order for the parent or teacher to accept the child and meet their needs, the child has to comply. I once heard a mother tell her daughter, "If you don't stop crying, I won't be your friend." To the girl's ears, her mother was threatening to withdraw her primary source of emotional support which at that age would have been catastrophic. The girl learns how to erase her own identity.

Rewards and praise are simply the flip side of punishment.[222] They are mechanisms to reinforce behavior desirable to the adult, the motivations for which are largely self-serving. From the preschool setting forwards, rewards are given out like confetti, even for the smallest of achievements. After almost any effort by a child, no matter how minor or insignificant, the teacher comes back with a "Good job!!" And how kids love to collect

222 Alfie Kohn (2018). *"Punished by Rewards—The Trouble with Gold Stars, Incentive Plans, A's, Praise, and Other Bribes."* Boston: Houghton Mifflin.

stars! They believe that by showering the child with positivity they will develop self-worth. In fact it achieves quite the opposite. It conditions the child towards narcissism and entitlement where they come to believe that no matter what they do in life, regardless of merit, they deserve only the very best rewards and recognitions. It also produces a listlessness because, no matter what effort they devote to life, they're always going to be extrinsically "rewarded"—so why do anything that requires a lot of self-discipline?

In the space of two or three generations, we have conducted a huge, global science experiment on our children. Whereas kids used to roam freely in the neighborhood to play, as their parents before them were able to,[223] they are now closely monitored. Concerns about pedophilia and child safety in general have fragmented children's lives. Helicopter parents[224] (and teachers) treat children as being less capable, competent, and self-sufficient than they actually are. It's exacerbated by impatience or time-deficient lifestyles where the child's slow pace of learning is just not quick enough. If there's five minutes to get the kids out of the door to school and one is still learning how to tie their laces, the parent will often jump in and do it for the child, short-circuiting their learning process. All of this encourages the child to remain dependent, passive, and unmotivated. Clearly, it's mostly with good intentions but the result is the infantilization of a generation—a learned helplessness. The result over time is co-dependency, manipulation, and controlling behaviors in adult relationships. They have become completely dysfunctional. Having helicopter parents conditioned them to appeal to authority for their safety (see chapter, *Why You are a Slave*).

Lastly, there is the child who is expected to prove or provide something to the family—to perform for love and attention. So many parents are not able to be honest with themselves about why they chose to have kids. Their children are coerced into roles and expectations which are unfair and

223 Children used to exit the home to play tag football, climb trees, explore nature, etc, with the message to come home when the street lights go on. They were free-range children.

224 A style of child rearing in which an overprotective adult caregiver discourages a child's independence by being too involved in the child's life

age-inappropriate. One example is to caretake an alcoholic mother—the mother is incapable so the child looks after her with the expectation of bringing the mother back into the land of the living so that the mother then becomes capable of doing her job as a parent. Or the father who wants a golden child to reflect family honor—who may push his son to achieve high grades and in order to become a doctor.

On the face of it, all the above could be claimed to be examples of responsible parenting. They are so enmeshed in our culture that we hardly notice them happening. In actuality, they fail to recognize the child as a discrete and unique individual whose life path needs to unfold organically.

~

Pain can be a sacred gift. Feeling the pain that cracks the shell which encloses your understanding is a crucial component on the path to integrating and transcending childhood suffering. Understanding eventually leads to forgiveness, with no lingering resentment. For those who cannot move through the pain and grief, they will experience some level of self-hate, lack of wellbeing, and suffering throughout their adult lives. They might go on to recreate the judgments and condemnations they received as a child in their relationship with the world they walk through.

Single parenthood and even the nuclear family are completely anomalous to human history. For 95% of our history, human beings lived in hunter-gatherer societies. The whole tribe would bring up children with the roles of parents being more diffuse. The child itself would have the option of seeking out those peers and adults with whom it felt the greatest affinity. Having proximate access to aunts, uncles, and grandparents afforded the child a greater propensity to develop practical and social skills than in today's world. These societies were egalitarian, meaning that everyone was as important as everyone else. We thrived because we were cooperative and intelligent. This missing aspect of true community can be considered a path of healing for the current human condition of dysfunctional human beings.

Today's boys and young men are learning bad habits in the absence of powerful, positive male role models. There is a relative absence of masculinity in both home and school life. Most teachers are women and public school programs are largely framed around styles of learning which are more favorable for girls. Boys mostly feel constrained, imprisoned, and suffocated by the experience. Their natural rambunctiousness is redefined as disorderly and disruptive and for which Ritalin provides the solution. But I would say we need more masculinity, not less.

It's very understandable why we are inauthentic. It's understandable why we lie to each other and ourselves. In childhood, our entire existence was completely dependent upon people who, essentially, had the power of life or death over us. There were huge consequences for speaking our truth to their power. So many of us chose to abandon or hide our personal truth to preserve our wellbeing as best we could. It was too terrifying to stand up for ourselves.

Ultimately, parents need to be skillful in their parenting. There is no blame here. The behavior of parents is determined by their own life experiences. Most learn from their own parents who were themselves unskillful. And their own nervous systems were largely built upon the fight/flight/freeze response, making it hard to attune to the needs of their child. Parents once understood that their purpose was to produce a "good" and compliant child. Today, the challenge is to raise an adult who is capable of unfolding his fully-realized, god-given powers and capacities with compassion for others who are also realizing their own true nature. To do so means being attuned to the emotional life of their children and offering them mature guidance in an age-appropriate way.

A scar is what happens when the word is made flesh.

— LEONARD COHEN

39 Physical Trauma

There are a number of things outside of relational trauma patternings that could also be present. Near-death experiences, bad accidents, and serious illnesses can also leave their mark. As an adult we know that surgery and anesthesia may be necessary in dire situations but, to a child who has not developed the ability to take in the big picture, they can be disorienting and terrifying.[225]

Pregnancy and childbirth can also be traumatizing. Complications can arise while the fetus is developing. Mothers who are in stressful situations, who smoke or drink or do drugs, who are not getting enough nutrients, pass chemical information to the baby which informs it that all is not right and to prepare to enter a world with certain deficiencies. The babies are then fundamentally wired for stress and health complications.[226]

225 I remember waking up in hospital when I was about three years old with my arm tied by a bandage to the bars of a crib. Unable to wrest myself free I panicked, screamed, and cried for help. I had no idea that I'd just had a blood transfusion after having swallowed a whole bottle of kiddie-aspirin.

226 Female holocaust survivors who experienced extreme malnutrition and related stress during their internment later resulted in their offspring being primed for obesity, since the message babies received in utero was to expect a nutrient-deficient world. Hazani, Elizur & Shasha, Shaul. (2008). *"Effects of the Holocaust on the physical health of the offspring of survivors."* The Israel Medical Association journal : IMAJ. 10. 251-5. https://www.researchgate.net/publication/5308139_Effects_of_the_Holocaust_on_the_physical_health_of_the_offspring_of_survivors

Because of how normalized society has become to medicalizing childbirth, the percent of c-sections being performed has skyrocketed to about 50% of births. This not only deprives the baby of the inoculum it receives from the mother by vaginal delivery but also means that the all-important bonding time between mother and child is delayed while the mother is anesthetized and sewn back up. The mother is also more likely to suffer from neonatal depression which impedes her ability to connect and bond.[227]

Giving birth to a baby is hard on women, if not traumatic. Between 40-50% of women will experience shaking and tremoring and are "made comfortable" by medical professionals to minify her experience, rather than encouraging her to allow her body to naturally dissipate unresolved stress.

In addition, unborn babies will launch a significant hormonal stress response when delivered a jab from an invasive medical procedure (which may be determined to be medically essential). This strongly suggests that they can feel pain even at 18 weeks of pregnancy. Since they do not have a regulated nervous system with which to mitigate the effects, it may well be that traumas of this nature will be stored and carried in the body (producing unwanted outcomes as they develop and grow).[228] Premature birth or complications during delivery can be highly stressful to newly forming human beings who have no mechanisms for grasping what is happening to them.

A sensory stimulant, perhaps even more important than post-birth maternal attunement, is movement (the vestibulocerebellar system).The infants of all other primate species are constantly being picked up and carried by their mothers. Only in human primates do we set the baby down for long periods. This is effectively "sensory deprivation" and is a type of physical trauma. In utero, the dominant sensory input for the

227 Josef Neu, MD and Jona Rushing, MD (2012). *"Cesarean versus Vaginal Delivery: Long term infant outcomes and the Hygiene Hypothesis."* NCBI. https://www.ncbi.nlm.nih.gov/pmc/articles/PMC3110651/

228 Rachel Gitau, et al. (January 1, 2001). *"Fetal Hypothalamic-Pituitary-Adrenal Stress Responses to Invasive Procedures Are Independent of Maternal Responses."* Journal of Clinical Endocrinology and Metabolism.
https://academic.oup.com/jcem/article-pdf/86/1/104/9130745/jcem0104.pdf

developing fetus is motion—its other senses are effectively non-functional. "I believe that the deprivation of body touch, contact, and movement are the basic causes of a number of emotional disturbances which include depressive and autistic behaviors, hyperactivity, sexual aberration, drug abuse, violence, and aggression."[229]

To the conscious man, it's therefore also necessary to look past the conditioned ego and consider the level of preverbal trauma he may be carrying—his developmental programming. This type of conditioning is held at the nervous system level, and talk therapy, internal inquiry, or meditation will be unlikely to have much impact on mitigating its effects. Somatic release therapies, like breathwork, TRE or Somatic Experiencing, are far more beneficial.

229 James W. Prescott (November 1975). *"Body Pleasure and the origins of Violence."* The Bulletin of The Atomic Scientists. http://www.deconnection.org/site/images/publicaties/body%20pleasure%20and%20the%20origins%20of%20violence%20-%20j.w.%20prescott.pdf

There are wounds that never show on the body that are deeper and more hurtful than anything that bleeds.[230]

— LAURELL K. HAMILTON

40 Emotional Abuse

Of all the traumas a human organism can experience, emotional trauma is the least appreciated and most damaging. Unlike physical abuse and its intentional infliction, and because it leaves no outer scars, emotional abuse has virtually *no social sanctions against those who would maliciously use it against others.* Feelings and emotions are at the center of our daily experiences, especially when it comes to relationships. Because of this, close relationships are where any emotional damage is at its most pronounced.

Emotional abuse is at its most keenly felt in childhood and is the hardest abuse to heal from. Although some forms of physical punishment have fallen out of favor (e.g. corporal punishment), emotional punishment is still going strong. The damage parents do on an emotional level is staggering, even when they are doing it "for the good of the child."

Feelings and emotions matter because our psychology and emotional health are hugely impacted by them. To be healthy, human beings need to have their feelings and emotions valued and respected with as much consideration as any other human right.

230 Laurell K. Hamilton (December 30, 2006). *"Mistral's Kiss."* Ballantine Books.

It will generally be found that as soon as the terrors of life reach the point where they outweigh the terrors of death, a man will put an end to his life.

— ARTHUR SCHOPENHAUER

41 Suicide

A fundamental biological imperative for the human organism is to survive. In order to tip the balance, a certain type of world has to be a created. An inhumane world where the callous abuses and indifferences to a man's sufferings reaches a certain level. A world which demonizes him and terrorizes him beyond even his ability to comprehend. At that point, he will put an end to his life. Suicide is virtually unheard of in hunter-gatherer societies and is a marker of just how dysfunctional our civilized world is and has been for thousands of years (see *The Cultural Paradigm,* chapter *Why you are a Slave).*

After unintentional injuries, suicide is the leading cause of death for men between the ages of 20-34 (and third leading cause for ages 35-44).[231] Men who are from lower socio-economic groups or lower occupational categories are more likely to commit suicide, as are men who have been divorce-raped. Traditionally, men have lived lives stoically. Stoicism has its good points and bad. On the down side, men have felt less able to understand and express their feelings and emotions, partly because society is largely indifferent to male suffering. Two-thirds of the homeless

231 2015, Centers for Disease Control.

are male,[232] most alcoholics are men,[233] most inmates,[234] most gamblers, and most victims of homicide.[235] There is not much cognitive dissonance when regarding such problems through the lens of race—we recognize minority groups are more likely to struggle when facing systemic problems because of their relative powerlessness—yet, when men as a group are chiefly impacted by these problems, we are blind to *their* powerlessness.

The principle catalyst for male suicide is not mental ill-health but the breakdown in intimate partner relations.[236] Men with broken hearts struggle to integrate their pain in an environment which pays little mind to their misery. When a man is divorce raped—when he loses his kids in a custody trial, when he is dealt with contemptuously by the woman he used to love, who also slanders him to her friends, and a myriad of other insults he doesn't see coming just for being a man—he sometimes finds no solace other than in the sweet embrace of "not feeling pain."

232 U.S. Conference of Mayors, 2007.

233 Men consistently have higher rates of alcohol-related deaths and hospitalizations than women. Minino AM, Heron MP, Murphy SL, Kochanek KD. Deaths: final data for 2004. National Vital Statistics Report, Volume 55, No. 19, August 21, 2007. Hyattsville, MD: CDC National Center for Health Statistics.

234 92 percent of the approximately 176,974 federal inmates are men. Federal Bureau of Prisons, Aug, 2019.

235 90.3 percent of 12,996 homicides are men. US Department of Justice, FBI, 20010.

236 Glen Poole. *"Research confirms 5 uncomfortable facts about young male suicide."* Australian Men's Health Forum. https://www.amhf.org.au/research_confirms_5_uncomfortable_facts_about_young_male_suicide
Christopher Mackney (July 8, 2014). *"I am Chris Mackney and I Have Something to Say from the Grave."* A Voice for Men. https://avoiceformen.com/featured/i-am-chris-mackney-and-i-have-something-to-say-from-the-grave/

Resisting yourself is like refusing to swallow
the cure to your own misery.

— CHRIS BALE

42 Shadow Work and The Process of Integration

Shadow work refers to a term first coined by Swiss psychologist, Carl Jung. The shadow aspects are those amorphous yet ever-present parts of our psyche that lay hidden in dark corners. Down where it's dark and dirty. The stuff we would rather disown, repress, suppress, and ignore, and that, if seen, would make us look bad, to ourselves or others. These are the deep-seated, powerful habits contained in the body/mind which sends up signals for us to behave in unconscious ways.

A conscious man is ever on the lookout to shine a light on this hidden player and integrate what he finds by purifying it—the psychological equivalent of kidneys filtering toxins from the blood. This is work that separates itself from the "positive thinking" focus of much New Age spirituality.

The first thing to become aware of is that something needs to be integrated and dealt with. Because, number one, it expands us and, number two, if we don't heal what initially hurt us, we'll bleed on those who didn't cut us. The work is necessary in order to support our personal evolution and to not add to the world's pain by our behavior. "He who steps upon his misery stands higher."[237]

237 Friedrich Hölderlin.

Conscious men use any number of approaches which may include various therapies, journaling, meditation, somatic practices (like yoga), self-reflection and solitude, participating in men's groups, plant medicines, etc, in order to cultivate self-compassion and radical authenticity.

But because our society is hugely individualistic, integrating our shadow aspects is for the most part considered a personal process. If you want help, you can pay for it by seeing a therapist. It seems the only type of human being deserving (hopefully) of receiving nurturing and validation is a young human being—a child. And the sole emotional care providers for the child being his/her own immediate family. Once an adult, you're on your own and you're the only one responsible for your happiness, is the messaging. We seem to fail to realize that an adult needs the same thing a child does. Like the child, the adult's emotions yearn for unconditional love and acceptance. If these emotions had their own voice, they would express pain for being told that they shouldn't be the way they are—that their presence was unacceptable. Emotions want to be loved exactly for what they are, by others and by ourselves. That's not to say that they may not be based in delusion, it's just to say that they need to be seen, recognized and welcomed into existence, just like a baby. Emotions don't affect facts. But facts should affect emotions, which is where integrating our shadow aspects comes in. It requires a spiritual warrior to both honor his emotions and challenge them with love by parenting them—a Shadow Master. It takes a Divine Woman to stand by him while he does so, tending to him where it serves his unfolding (See *The Practice of Love*, chapter, *The Divine Union*).

~

Because our window of tolerance for the stresses the world delivers to our doorstep has become so small (a world unfit for human consumption), when we experience something adverse we can easily spike into a state of overwhelm. So it's of vital importance not to allow trauma to get stored up and to build one's capacity for resilience. This is a process of cultivating "cellular safety." You can't trick your mind into thinking it's safe, because the body keeps the score at the cellular level. So this involves consciously putting safety into the nervous system through a somatic practice. The first thing is to become aware that something needs to be integrated and metabolized, and to then process procedural memories. This involves slowly and systematically deactivating unhelpful procedural memories and fight, flight, and freeze responses to make a more resilient, spacious, and recalibrated nervous system.[238]

---

238 Recommended reading:
Peter Levine (2010). *"In an Unspoken Voice: How the Body Releases Trauma and Restores Goodness."* North Atlantic Books.
Bessel van der Kolk (2015). *"The Body Keeps the Score: Brain, Mind, and Body in the Healing of Trauma."* Penguin Books.
Stephen W. Porges (2017). *"The Pocket Guide to the Polyvagal Theory: The Transformative Power of Feeling Safe (Norton Series on Interpersonal Neurobiology)."* W. W. Norton & Company.
Teal Swan (2016). *"The Completion Process: The Practice of Putting Yourself Back Together Again."* Hay House Inc.
Robert A. Johnson (1994). *"Owning Your Own Shadow: Understanding the Dark Side of the Psyche."* HarperSanFrancisco
Recommended viewing:
YouTube channel, Irene Lyon.
https://www.youtube.com/channel/UCBkXgroE9ZWUg4iSDEUKqVA

Part Six

Why You are a Slave

None are more hopelessly enslaved than those who falsely believe they are free.[239]

– JOHANN WOLFGANG VON GOETHE

Realizing and questioning unhelpful thought patterns, belief structures, and programs in oneself which had previously been subconsciously operating on autopilot is just half of the work of the conscious male. Becoming conscious to your interior workings brings insights and clarity to your programs and patternings in exactly the same way that becoming conscious of the external world brings insights and clarity to how the world works.

239 Johann Wolfgang von Goethem(1978). *"Elective Affinities."* Penguin Classics; Reprint edition.

In both cases, you become more and more able to see things as they really are. Expanding one's consciousness inwardly better improves one's ability to the engage in the task of expanding consciousness outwardly. Once the grip of one's psychological narrative has been sufficiently loosened, it then becomes much more difficult to pull the wool over your eyes. And at that point, you begin to see the Matrix.

Most spiritually minded people focus on the inward expansions of their consciousness. Yet the outward expansion exists on the same continuum. Both are of equal importance and both are vital in one's journey. A lot of people have an unbalanced approach. There are those who are slavishly interested in government and politics yet regard personal exploration of their inner realms as an exercise in New-Agey bullshit. Then there are those people who are more interested in spirituality and enlightenment for whom the outer world is more like a dream, and for whom big-stage politics is "totally three-dimensional, man." Yet, objectively speaking, they share the same ideals. Someone engaged in relentlessly honest self-exploration and shadow-work is doing something that is just as valuable as the person engaged in undercover reporting of a corrupt agency. Going to shamanic retreats, taking plant medicine, practicing meditation, or seeing a therapist with the aim of having transformative personal breakthroughs is as worthwhile as a citizen journalist filming police to show the world their thuggish brutality. Consciousness is expanded in both instances. They are the left leg and the right leg, standing on ever-shifting ground.

It's therefore necessary for conscious men to realize how civilization is shaped to enslave their minds and their productive capacities—how the powerful have rigged our lives to predispose us to mental confusion/illness at a personal level and tyranny at a societal level.

Slavery, it's believed, is something in our past. We've recognized the enslavement of African Americans as a social injustice and now can give a nod to history with the passage of the 13th Amendment after the end of the Civil War in 1865. This overt form of slavery can also be recognized in other civilizations (like Ancient Egypt) and in contemporary forced labor (estimated to be around 40 million people).[240]

Yet the people of the world are slaves through covert mechanisms which hide this fact from their view. And it is as real and as pernicious as the chattel slavery they believe they left in their past.

240 *"Forced labour, modern slavery and human trafficking."* International Labour Organization. https://www.ilo.org/global/topics/forced-labour/lang--en/index.htm

We may have democracy or we may have great wealth concentrated in the hands of a few, but we can't have both.

– LOUIS BRANDEIS, SUPREME COURT JUSTICE

43 The Ruling Elite

The ruling class, also known as the ruling elite, are essentially few in number but whose power extends to dominate the rest of humanity. Essentially, they are greedy, fucking psychopaths (to use the technical term) who rule from the shadows. Their accumulated actions, based on their desire for power and domination, have led to the world we now know. A world stripped to the bone of its natural resources and a global populace in despair. They arose to form kingdoms, monarchies, empires, and dynasties, and whose power today rests in corporations, governments, and financial institutions. They are the rich "one percenters."

The wealth, power, and influence of the ruling class extends and embraces the entire globe, generating obscene profits from its activities. To quote Matt Taibbi, by extension, it is "a great vampire squid wrapped around the face of humanity, relentlessly jamming its blood funnel into anything that smells like money."[241] This transnational elite sets the international agenda.[242] It exercises control through interlocking boards

241 The original quote referred specifically to Goldman Sachs.
Matt Taibbi (April 5, 2010). *"The Great American Bubble Machine."* Rolling Stone Magazine. https://www.rollingstone.com/politics/politics-news/the-great-american-bubble-machine-195229/

242 David Rothkopf (2008). *Superclass: The Global Power Elite and the World They Are Making.* Farrar, Straus and Giroux; 1st Edition

of directors and stock ownership, acting through private clubs, societies (like the Skull and Bones)[243] and institutions (like the Federal Reserve, IMF, World Economic Forum, etc), dominating national governments, both democratic and authoritarian, in order to move ever closer to global governance solely in their best interests. They have a coordinated agenda, at a global level, to essentially rule the world. They put your regular Bond villain to shame.

The rich seek to get richer at the expense of both regular people and other rich people (like bands of warring brothers). This produces a scarcity mentality. There is abundance that is around us but it's controlled, limited, and policed at the behest of this tiny ruling elite, not by and for the benefit of all people. This ruling elite consciously and continually seek to perpetuate this misery in order to suppress the full realization of humanity's powers and potentials. They sow the seeds of dysfunction as best they can and nurture disharmony and confusion. They care little for left-politics or right-politics but find this limited choice useful since it gives the people the illusion of choice and agency.

They don't even need to come up with ways to confuse and distract the populace—all they need do is recognize emergent dysfunctional behavior, foster its development, and harness it for their own political agenda. The point is to make people crazy. The actual narrative is unimportant just as long as everyone is confused and oppositional and fighting among themselves. In the Bush era, it was right-wing Christian fundamentalists. That was the craziest thing around and that was what was nurtured. Now it's politicized medical science, left-authoritarianism, social justice activism, BLM, and third-wave feminism. This is what sows the seeds of "crazy" in our world and distracts us from the real culprits. "I want this country to realize that we stand on the edge of oblivion. I want every man, woman and child to understand how close we are to chaos. I want everyone to remember why they need us!"[244] Fortunately, people are waking up.

243 https://www.bibliotecapleyades.net/esp_sociopol_skullbones.htm#menu

244 John Hurt, as the character, Adam Sutler. *"V for Vendetta"* movie (2005). Warner Bros.

They are becoming more aware both of themselves and how the world works—certainly not everybody; not even a majority.

In *Why Can't We Hate Men?*[245] the writer describes the "millennia of woe" women have suffered at the hands of men. The reason this resonates with so many women is because there is a grain of truth in this. The story of human history has been one of enormous repression, oppression, and suffering. And, on the face of it, it looks like men have been the driving force. Wars have largely been comprised of men fighting and killing other men. Think of the millions and millions of ordinary people who have been killed by genocide, war, and structural poverty over millennia. There have been more male rulers than female, more generals, more "mad scientists." But the millennia of woe can actually be demonstrated to have been the power struggle by the ruling elites either amongst themselves, using ordinary men (or talented men) as pawns in their wars, or directly/indirectly with, let's call them, the 99% who historically have sought to unshackle themselves.[246] Women were never particularly singled out for oppression. Life was a shit-show for both men and women, other than for an elite few. But to a feminist, seeing only through the lens of gender power dynamics, subtleties are lost. Worse still, their anger, sense of resentment, and desire to punish means that the demonization of modern men is perfectly justifiable as payback. In truth, it has nothing to do with patriarchal oppression. It has to do with the damaged and wounded expression of men trying to survive in a hostile environment (men have also experienced millennia of woe but this is ignored).

The cultural norms and social institutions presented to mankind are designed to produce obedient workers who lack the critical thinking skills necessary to piece together the truth about the nature of reality—who lack the will to even care. And they go on to have children of their own when they have not even fully matured, mentally or spiritually

245 Suzanna Danuta Walters (June 8, 2018). *Why can't we hate men?* The Washington Post. https://www.washingtonpost.com/opinions/why-cant-we-hate-men/2018/06/08/f1a3a8e0-6451-11e8-a69c-b944de66d9e7_story.html

246 From the Spartacus revolt, to Shay's Rebellion, to the Tiannamen Square protests, and countless others.

themselves. Doing so maintains the corrupt control systems set in place that are designed to maximize profits for the ruling elite. Thankfully for them, an ignorant population doesn't care about things that truly matter. And they certainly seem not care about the crimes committed by their own governments. Despite our potential to be a peaceful, harmonious species, we have come to a point where we, as a people, have passively allowed multinational billion dollar corporations to come to the verge of destroying the planet. "Since World War II, we economic hit men have managed to create the world's first truly global empire, and we've done it primarily without the military, unlike other empires in history."[247] This form of predatory capitalism is the logical result of "normal" capitalism and was predicted by Karl Marx in capitalism's infancy.

247 Story (June 5, 2007). *"John Perkins on "The Secret History of the American Empire: Economic Hit Men, Jackals, and the Truth About Global Corruption"."* Democracy Now!. https://www.democracynow.org/2007/6/5/john_perkins_on_the_secret_history

We'll know our disinformation program is complete when everything the American public believes is false.

– EX-CIA DIRECTOR, WILLIAM CASEY[248]

44 The Control System

The control system is in place to keep a population ignorant, submissive, confused, fearful, desperate, and distracted. Without it, people might start to see themselves as free and sovereign human beings. Without it, they might collaborate for their collective wellbeing. And without it, the curtain of deception crumples to the floor.

---

248 Barbara Honegger, "I am the source for this quote, which was indeed said by CIA Director William Casey at an early February 1981 meeting of the newly elected President Reagan with his new cabinet secretaries to report to him on what they had learned about their agencies in the first couple of weeks of the administration.
The meeting was in the Roosevelt Room in the West Wing of the White House, not far from the Cabinet Room. I was present at the meeting as Assistant to the chief domestic policy adviser to the President. Casey first told Reagan that he had been astonished to discover that over 80 percent of the 'intelligence' that the analysis side of the CIA produced was based on open public sources like newspapers and magazines.
As he did to all the other secretaries of their departments and agencies, Reagan asked what he saw as his goal as director for the CIA, to which he replied with this quote, which I recorded in my notes of the meeting as he said it. Shortly thereafter I told Senior White House correspondent Sarah McClendon, who was a close friend and colleague, who in turn made it public." https://amallulla.org/casey/

Free-range Slavery

You've got so many days to live and you sell them one after another. Hey? Who can pay me enough for my life? Ah! But they throw at you your week's money and expect you to say, "thank you" before you pick it up.[249]

– JOSEPH CONRAD

Human beings avoid the reality of their enslavement because to see it directly is to be in existential anguish.

A chattel slave is someone who is forced to work for another, either where it is deemed lawful to appropriate the labor of another or where it is sanctioned by cultural norms. The chattel slave is totally subject to another person's will, from the time they were acquired up until their sale or death.

Global capitalism, the dominant economic paradigm we find ourselves with, means that we are dependent on earning an income in order to have access to the resources we need to survive. It's a pay-to-play system. Generally speaking, we are free to choose and leave employment (which makes us "free-range") but we can only "choose" to trade our labor for currency with a capitalist framework (ranging from mom and pop businesses to big corporations). Capitalism is non-consensual. This is a more profitable form of slave ownership than labor-by-the-whip. Traditional slaves were compelled to give their labor in return for minimal room and board but there was never any incentive to give more than they could get away with. Why would a slave offer a creative solution to a problem for the benefit of a landowner?

Just as chickens become more productive and happier when allowed to free range, so too are humans. Instead of being owned by a slave owner and driven into the ground, they are instead allowed to freely float between "slave owners" (and be driven into the ground by stress and the daily grind). Employers are *de facto* slave owners because the

249 Joseph Conrad (2016). "*Victory: An Island Tale.*" Penguin Classics.

majority of humans, after receiving wages and paying bills, barely have enough for the room and board provided for them by their wages, with little actual distinction from a chattel-based model. They are "wage-slaves." But for those who provide additional value, higher wages are paid—a middle class (and a dying breed). Unlike chattel slaves, in other aspects of their lives, they are free to exercise a limited choice as a consumer, a voter, a vacationer, a hobbyist, etc. In comparison with other wage slaves, they enjoy certain measures of relative freedom, respect, and social equality.

But inherent in this model is also an "arms race to the bottom." One group of workers can compete with another group by accepting lower wages and conditions at work. Rather than face unemployment, the first group drops their wages below the second. And so the cycle repeats. This only serves to enrich the owners of capital. The goods and services that are produced and sold to consumers may become somewhat cheaper in price but the consumers (who are also the workers) find themselves progressively less able to afford them because of this race to the bottom.

The problems inherent in economic stratification are the primary cause of human misery. There are many other motivations that drive human beings but economics is literally the foundation of survival. Without access to basic resources (and today that means purchasing power) people's lives are severely constrained. So many times, every day, unethical practices by employers go unchallenged because to do so would be to risk losing one's job. The relationship between labor and capitalism is inherently censorial. When people cannot speak their truth without jeopardizing their means of survival, the majority will remain silent. Collectively they are compelled to enable bad behavior and so the world they inhabit becomes progressively worse.

Just as businesses manufacture goods from raw materials, so too is human labor a commodity. It has value to the employer who uses it to create more value. An employer is able to make his profit by the work of his employees adding value to raw materials. If a factory worker is required to work a nine-hour day canning tomatoes, a small proportion of that time is spent covering the cost of his wage. The remainder of that time is work which is unpaid, or "surplus labor," and it is from this that the owner extracts surplus value. To be a little simplistic, if the owner paid a worker $100 a day for canning tomatoes and sold those cans for $100, he couldn't make a profit. He's unable to pay the worker his true value without going out of business.

In order to extract as much value as they can, owners may fire workers who want a better wage, decrease wages up to the point where they are unable to retain workers, demand that other workers increase their productivity; set workers in competition with one another to drive down their wages, or any number of methods which inevitably reduce the quality of life but increase the quantity of profit. There is automatically an antagonistic relationship between two parties looking to maximize their wellbeing but with employers having more power (especially if there is a pool of unemployed workers waiting for the opportunity to fill the shoes of those who might be fired).

Mainstream Media

The ruling class in every age have tried to impose a false view of the world upon their followers.

— GEORGE ORWELL

History is written by the victors, the saying goes. And in order to control the people, the ruling elite controls their frame of reference, making them easier to control. It does this by conscious manipulation and exploitation of people's sense-making faculties, playing on their cognitive biases, in order to get them to behave in ways which serve their agendas.

The Mass Media exists to tell Mass Man what to think and believe. It seeks to control his reality. It feeds the public a carefully crafted mixture of truth and falsehood so as to appear to be trustworthy while at the same time creating the narrative (and hence thought-conditioning) that will suit the agenda of the ruling elite.[250] Even after politicians and authority figures have been caught in lies, and have even sometimes admitted to lying, the majority of the public's default position is that the rest of what they hear is the truth. They are less likely to have the default position that they are generally lying to manipulate the public and that facts and assertions should be met with skepticism.

Eighty percent of the television news reports are scripted and prepared by public relations companies working for the government or big corporations.[251] They decide what is watched, listened to, read, and shared. Disinformation is weaponized to spread false narratives to advance the agenda of the ruling elite and manufacture consent of the general populace. By filling their minds with false information, people no longer know what's real, no longer know who's pulling their strings and, ultimately, no longer know themselves. For decades (moreso before the advent of the internet) print and broadcast media, owned by the rich, generally trumpeted narratives which were in the interests of the ruling elite. Since most Americans declare themselves to be "patriotic" (those that support the State), the ruling elites have found it profitable to provide them with an enemy/enemies (a boogie man)[252] in order to scare them into supporting policies which were not in their best interests, in the name of "defending their freedoms." The spreading of fear, hatred, and suspicion of "others" has operated as tool more powerful (thus far) than love itself. Giving the people the idea that they are at a constant existential risk is useful in keeping the mass of humanity shaking in its boots and desperate for "protections" offered by their rulers. By setting us against one another,

---

250 To elaborate:
Chris Kanthan (April 30, 2018). *"Syria – A Case Study in Propaganda."* Activist Post. https://www.thedailysheeple.com/syria-a-case-study-in-propaganda/
And:
Liam K. (March 9, 2014). *"Is Everything in the Mainstream Media Fake? 6 Examples Of Mainstream Media Manipulation."* Waking Times. https://www.wakingtimes.com/everything-mainstream-media-fake-6-examples-media-manipulation/

251 YouTube channel, Team Coco (January 29, 2014). *"Newscasters Agree: Don't Worry, Be Happy Edition."* https://www.youtube.com/watch?v=KZ1mA1NeUmU&feature=emb_logo

252 From the Red Scare communists, to Negroes, to Middle East rulers, to terrorists, to CoVid-19, etc.

dividing us, and distracting us from the realization that we have more in common with those "others" than we do with our rulers, they win.

Nowadays, if there is something that is in the public interest that has come to light that would adversely affect the dominant political narrative, the media don't even have to attempt to discredit it. With just a handful of companies controlling what information people are exposed to, they can simply ignore it.

Case in point, the Institute of Northern Engineering issued the results of a study,[253] concluding that the collapse of the 47-story World Trade Center building (WTC7) on September 11, 2001, far from being the result of fire (subsequent to the "terrorist attacks" of that day), was a result of "a global failure involving the near-simultaneous failure of every column in the building." In other words, a controlled demolition. The broadcast and digital mainstream media have been completely silent about this and other copious evidence which pointed to a false flag attack conducted on the American people by its own government in order to conduct a so-called "war on terror."[254] This war on terror was then relentlessly sold to the public by the corporate media for the unexpressed purpose of attacking civil liberties and garnering support for wars of imperialism. At the time of writing, the war on terror has cost the US approximately $6 trillion (plus $8 trillion in interest payments).

There are many, many, many examples of mainstream media avoiding newsworthy stories. The vast majority of people will never be presented with anything remotely challenging the official narratives. What *is* reported is a social construct to program their minds and "manufacture consent."[255]

253 J. Leroy Hulsey, Ph.D., P.E., S.E., University of Alaska Fairbanks, Zhili Quan, Ph.D., Bridge Engineer South Carolina Department of Transportation, and Feng Xiao, Ph.D., Associate Professor Nanjing (2019). *"A Structural Reevaluation of the Collapse of World Trade Center 7."* University of Science and Technology Department of Civil Engineering. Institute of Northern Engineering. http://ine.uaf.edu/media/92216/wtc7-structural-reevaluation_progress-report_2017-9-7.pdf

254 Two notable documentaries include, *"Hypothesis - Steven E. Jones"* (2010), and for a broader perspective *"JFK to 911 - Everything Is A Rich Man's Trick"* (2014). There are now many resources online including 911Truth.org and Architects & Engineers for 9/11 Truth.

255 Noam Chomsky (2002). *"Manufacturing Consent: The Political Economy of the Mass Media."* Pantheon.

Human beings are the subject of an everyday war crime. They face an indiscriminate attack on their sensemaking abilities through lies and propaganda, psychologically more damaging than a hot war. Censorship operates like a forcefield which protects the powerful from the "peasants" being able to access information which could provide to them untold benefits.

The Cultural Paradigm

> *We seldom realize…that our most private thoughts and emotions are not actually our own. For we think in terms of languages and images which we did not invent, but which were given to us by our society.*
>
> – ALAN WATTS

Human beings have been around for many thousands of years. For only a relatively short period (essentially since the dawn of agriculture), we have existed in civilizations whose dominant characteristic is/was the sequestration of the surplus produced by workers—something that was never previously possible. For the first time in human history, not everything was held in common. And most of what we consider we know about human beings is divined from this "recent" experience. My contention is that most of what we believe about our nature is inaccurate, since cultures derived from civilizations distort our perceptions through cultural narratives. The lives of humans before civilization has often been characterized as being sub par. Thomas Hobbes regarded the natural state of mankind at that time as being "solitary, poor, nasty, brutish, and short…war of every man against every man."[256] As noted in *Suffering from a Historical Perspective* (chapter, *Wounding and Trauma*), accumulated and unintegrated stress and trauma are key components of our so-called civilized world. Therefore the study of modern humans is the study of atypical humans and cannot be relied on as a meaningful guide to human nature.

256 Thomas Hobbes (1651). *Leviathan or The Matter, Forme, & Power of a Common-Wealth Ecclesiastical and Civill.* Printed for Andrew Crooke, at the Green Dragon in St. Paul's Churchyard.

All cultures are distorted—from our urban environments to gamer culture to family dynamics, and all the other social systems of which we are a part. All cultures arose and were created from a struggle for access to and ownership of resources—between universal human needs and the needs of those who wished to control other humans (whom they considered an obstacle to their selfish desires). It is this class struggle which gave rise to societal paradigms, economic systems, and orthodoxies. The ruling class's greatest success has been in the molding of each individual's perceptual frame of reference. The Mass Media, and other mechanisms by which the ruling class transfers narratives to the human mind, gives us a cultural paradigm which is accepted by Mass Man—giving him a blueprint which he believes is his own creation. Where once he wore outer chains, now he wears cognitive chains, the existence of which remain oblivious to him. Cold steel on flesh is eminently obvious but men are unaware of the inner chains they carry, all the while bearing the illusion that they are free.

At greatest risk are the young, since they enter the world knowing nothing of its make-up, taking what they perceive mostly at face value. The single most important evolutionary trait that human beings have is their ability to adapt to their environment and its parameters (for example, a child born in one country but brought up in another will have no difficulty in learning the language). The human mind is incredibly "plastic." In this environment, from their earliest years, children receive distorted societal programming through the educational system, their parents in the form of generational indoctrination, and media received through their devices. Their fresh minds and spirits progressively become corrupted. As they move through the school system and on to university, they find themselves presented with ideas which fall within a thought spectrum of approved concepts, ideologies, and cultural norms. "...given the external power structure of the society in which they function, the institutional role of the schools for the most part is just to train people for obedience and conformity, and to make them controllable and indoctrinated."[257] They fail to develop the necessary critical thinking skills to do anything more than parse the ideas contained within of a proscribed set of state-sanctioned text-books. Free-thinking individuals do not fit the agenda of the control systems meant to repress the full realization of their humanity. The paradigm we live under depends on us not thinking too hard about the control mechanisms. All that is needed is functional, obedient students or workers with only as much intelligence as required to perform their tasks. Bricks in a wall.

Life is full contact with no pads. By design. A byproduct of concentrating wealth into the hands of a few is that it keeps the rest of us busy with the basics of survival. We're appeased by superficial consumerism, alcohol, video games, and streaming services. We're too exhausted to contemplate how the system actually works, and too bemused to create better conditions for our lives even if we did.

Capitalist, communist ("state capitalist") and "mixed" economies, laissez-faire or planned economies, social democracies, neocolonialism, etc, are disguised forms of tyrannies where the wealth produced by the people eventually trickles up to the upper echelons. Some societies are more humane than others (where people have stood up to power in the past and been granted concessions) but all of these systems are erroneously considered the products of the collective actions of all human beings acting in their human nature. For all of recorded history, it's been considered normal and natural that human beings accept the "natural order" that they be the subjects of rulers. People knew their place because they were birthed from parents who held a certain social position (for example, a farmer's son was expected to become a farmer). Owing to movements for emancipation more recently, most rulers now hide behind proxy institutions, like governments or NGOs, which give the people the illusion of self-determination but which they themselves largely control. But because humans in their natural habitat are not "subjects," and because

---

257 Noam Chomsky (2002). "*Understanding Power: The Indispensable Chomsky.* The New Press.

all civilizations have not lived within their means, they all collapsed. They weren't part of Mother Earth's natural order. They were not subject to the natural balance of life found in nature, which is self-sustaining. They had neither included nor integrated the Laws of Life (in relation to holistic human development) nor the Laws of Nature.

The Money System

Give me control of a nation's money and I care not who makes it's laws.

— MAYER AMSCHEL BAUER ROTHSCHILD

Money is a construct. It is not real wealth. People need resources to survive. They need things like clean water, nutritious food, good farming land, homes, transportation, the natural resources Mother Earth provides, people who have skills to add value to products and services, etc. In other words, tangible, real wealth. What they don't need is money. Money simply allows them to access those resources—it's a claim on real wealth.

Money was introduced several thousands of years ago, not as a step up from barter economies as many suppose, but in its own right as a tool of enslavement. Money, in fact, predates barter. The ruling class of the time, the Sumerian priest kings,[258] issued the earliest forms of money (clay tablets), using their temples as proto-banks. They enslaved people by limiting access to resources based on their ability to pay. Money also enabled the creation of debt, which is a claim on the future labor of the debtor (or their children) who must sell their labor to pay back the debt.

Today, the richest 1% own more than twice as much wealth as 6.9 billion people,[259] and half of the world's population lives on less than $2 a day. Today's ruling class has had a long time to perfect the money system since the days of the priest kings. They control the banks[260] and also

258 There may have been earlier priest kings for whom we have no written records.

259 Oxfam (January 20, 2020). "*Time To Care.*" https://www.oxfam.org/en/research/time-care

260 The combined assets of the seven largest banks on Wall Street exceed the GDP of every nation on Earth other than the USA.

control the creation of money or, more accurately, currency. They snap their fingers and suddenly there is this magic paper which then gives an authority to those who want to exchange it for stuff that is real—assets which are immorally, but legally, bought.

When banks, central banks, or governments create currency out of thin air, it heads downstream to their billionaire base who use it to purchase real-world goods and services (or government bonds), slipping through the fingers of regular people who must exchange a third of their lives working for bits of paper (or ones and zeros in a bank account) to have access to a fraction of the resources available to the richest few. Whether it is wise or not to do so, they can create unlimited amounts of currency. Because they want to control as many global resources as possible, they establish economic systems (capitalism being the latest) to make sure humanity has as little claim on wealth as possible, or is even in debt to them. Currency is returned to them via bills, fines, loan repayments, directed taxation, bonds, interest payments, profits derived from the exploitation of people's labor, or foreclosures/seizures—and then safely secured in their tax havens.

We have an economic system which regularly decimates peoples lives, homes, and livelihoods about once every four to seven years, through "recessions." The richest do not generally see a reduction in their wealth, as they are at the front of the queue when governments are handing out bail-out money. At these times economists, essentially, throw their hands up and say, "Well, what are you going to do?" As if recessions are immutable natural systems and the market system is the best and only way of organizing societies.

The working class essentially has had no choice but to borrow and go into debt in order to participate in the economy. Wage growth has failed to keep pace with the escalating costs of basic goods and services, such as affordable housing, healthcare and higher education.[261] The more people become desperate and reliant on currency/credit to access the means of

261 Contorted metrics are used to calculate the rate of inflation, such as hedonics, which fudge the rate much lower than it should be. See http://www.shadowstats.com/

survival, the better the banksters can control the behavior of these modern-day indentured servants. This is financial feudalism.

~

In the USA, a key turning point was the creation of the Federal Reserve. In 1913, Congress gave this private cartel of bankers the right to issue money for the nation. The supposedly sovereign government of the people, which had had the right to issue the nation's money, *transferred* that right by law (The Federal Reserve Act) to a group of private bankers. Once it's understood that the Federal Reserve is not a government agency, and is in fact a cartel, it follows that only a few wealthy individuals are in charge of the economy, not the American public. You could say that it was an act of treason because the purpose of a cartel is to promote the interests of the members of the cartel. You could also surmise that the American experiment failed long ago and that it never truly represented the will of the people.

> *I believe that banking institutions are more dangerous to our liberties than standing armies. If the American people ever allow private banks to control the issue of their currency, first by inflation, then by deflation, the banks and corporations that will grow up around them will deprive the people of all property until their children wake-up homeless on the continent their fathers conquered.*
>
> — U.S. PRESIDENT, THOMAS JEFFERSON

By creating new currency, the Fed can decrease the value of the existing currency in circulation, thereby lowering the buying power of those holding it. By inflating the currency supply, the Fed has been slowly stealing the wealth from the people without them directly noticing it. The Fed prints new currency out of thin air, delivers it to Wall Street (via the federal government), which then purchases the hard assets of the nation. This allows them to claim ownership of something without providing an equivalent energetic exchange of their own. Money for nothing. It is much easier to just create new currency than to raise taxes since people are well-aware of tax increases, and tax revolts were once common. Inflation is currently regarded by the populace as an economic inevitability and, although noticeable (they may wish their elected representatives would address the issue), they rarely consider it a direct function of government separate from the economic system.

When people exchange their labor for currency, the powers-that-be can steal back that currency more quickly (and hence keep the labor for free) by engineering a currency collapse (via hyperinflation). The currency is watered down to such an extent that it is completely devalued. Since slavery is a claim on people's labor without recompense, the people become *de facto* slaves. If someone works for 40 years and has saved his money for retirement—and then the currency collapses—he has given 40 years of his life for nothing. He has nothing to show for it; just like a chattel slave.

The Fed has been looting the people for the last hundred years through progressive dollar devaluation, reducing the purchasing power of every hard-earned dollar. When the Fed can electronically "print" dollars instantly, it makes the exchange of our labor for currency (working for money) a scam. We are trading our time and life force energy for a reward which has no intrinsic value—something they can essentially print for free. Currency only has value in that it can be traded for real wealth—hard assets and the energy and talent of people. So with infinite printing at the Fed's disposal, currency they pass over to their billionaire buddies, they can effectively buy and "own" anything they want with no energetic exchange of their own.

They are now looting us as rapidly as they can by printing trillions of dollars and buying up real stuff with this "monopoly money."[262] Probably very soon, we will see a global market crash that pales in comparison to the Great Depression—as a deliberate act. The hyperinflation of the debt bubble, and its ensuing collapse, will ensure the multi-decade plan

262 Saloni Sardana (Sep. 17, 2020). "*US billionaires' wealth grew by $845 billion during the first six months of the pandemic.*" Insider. https://markets.businessinsider.com/news/stocks/us-billionaires-wealth-net-worth-pandemic-covid-billion-2020-9-1029599756?utm_source=reddit.com

of the Federal Reserve to be the buyer and lender of last resort—creating a two-tier society with a handful of rich people at the top, everyone else impoverished, and nothing in between. Nobility and peasants. That makes the Fed (and other central banks) the most powerful organization on Earth. They control the national currency which people need in order to access resources to survive. And because of the petrodollar, they have at their disposal, by proxy, the entire US military which they may use as they see fit, even against American citizenry, if needed (regardless of the Posse Comitatus Act.[263] I can't imagine they would choose to be lawful in just this one respect).

Banking cartels exist in every region of the globe, generating obscene profits from their activities, including weapons manufacturing, funding wars (both sides), and controlling the global trade in drugs. The major US and international banks intentionally launder trillions of dollars in dirty money from criminal organizations.[264] And, as they accumulate more and more wealth and power, they undermine democracy, exploit the weak and vulnerable, ruin lives, and kill hope for millions. But even in the absence of central banks, governments which issue currency are also playing a long con by claiming to represent the best interests of the people (since they were "democratically elected"). The human species, even if they collectively wanted to, could not pay back the full amount of debt owed to the bankers since there is not enough currency in circulation to do so.[265]

Banks create currency in other ways too—through gambling with depositors' currency in the stock market and through the Fractional Reserve Banking system.[266] In this type of banking system, banks make

---

263 The Posse Comitatus Act and the Insurrection Act define and limit circumstances under which U.S. military forces can be deployed on American soil. However, since corruption exists at the highest level in all our social institutions, there are unlikely to be any serious repercussions for the government of the day ignoring these Acts.

264 Jason Leopold, et al. (September 20, 2020). "*Secret Documents Show How Criminals Use Famous Banks To Finance Terror And Death.*" Buzzfeed News. https://www.buzzfeednews.com/article/jasonleopold/fincen-files-financial-scandal-criminal-networks

265 $220 trillion in debt compared to $85 trillion in currency.

266 Federal Reserve Bank of Chicago (1961). "*Modern Money Mechanics.*" https://upload.wikimedia.org/wikipedia/commons/4/4a/Modern_Money_Mechanics.pdf

currency by loaning out depositors' currency (i.e. not their own) and charging borrowers interest for the privilege.[267] This is where the vast majority of currency has historically come from. The currency that is loaned out is invariably deposited in another bank account and that currency is once again loaned out at interest. And so the cycle repeats.[268] As long as banks are willing to loan and there is demand for those loans, new currency is created. Up until recently, the banks were required to keep 10% of depositors' currency in reserve to stop runs on the banks in the eventuality that depositors lose faith in the banks ability to store their currency safely. Yet, despite the Federal Reserve removing the reserve requirement in 2020, I believe that bank loans will play an increasingly less important role in currency creation going forward since the risk of default is too great both for the banks and their potential borrowers. "Money printing" is now the biggest game in town.

At least with cash, currency can be physically stored for future use. But government-issued digital currency (not block chain-based) will soon complete the web of social control. At the moment, they are slow-playing the transition but, once all cash economies have been abolished and local currencies criminalized, they will have absolute control over the world's population because they will be able to automatically monitor and tax every transaction and enforce compliance of their rules through confiscation of people's bank balances, in part or in whole. People are increasingly choosing alternative methods of storing value, including precious metals (bullion, not ETFs),[269] cryptocurrencies, local currencies, and time banks. But there are no guarantees. Developing skills that are useful to others can also be a store of value (and these can't be taken away from you).

---

267 The money to repay interest does not actually exist in the money supply, overall. Banks never create additional money for the purpose of meeting interest repayments, making defaults an inevitable part of the system.

268 Recommended reading: TZM Lecture Team (January, 2014). *"The Zeitgeist Movement Defined: Realizing a New Train of Thought."* (1st Edition). p152. https://www.thezeitgeistmovement.com/wp-content/uploads/2017/10/The_Zeitgeist_Movement_Defined_PDF_Final.pdf

269 In this crazy system, precious metals derive their supposed value from a derivative (ETFs like "paper gold") rather than the other way around. ETF gold represents a claim on physical gold. Since there are more ETFs in the system than physical, should a reset occur and the market correct to fair value, investors in ETFs would lose big time.

"When everything is subject to money, then the scarcity of money makes everything scarce, including the basis of human life and happiness. Such is the life of the slave—one whose actions are compelled by threat to survival."[270] We are now at a such a level of unrestricted, unfettered pillage by the richest human beings in the world that it makes you wonder why we take it. This money system paradigm is increasingly resulting in a neofeudal economy, where inequality robs $2.5 trillion from U.S. workers each year.[271] Billionaires are only billionaires because we legitimize the existence of currency. What if we didn't? Suddenly the rich and powerful would no longer be rich. And if they weren't rich, could they be powerful?

The Police and National Guard (and petty bureaucrats)

Theirs not to reason why,
Theirs but to do and die.

—ALFRED LORD TENNYSON

Human beings have free will and this is a problem for those who wish to control them. You can never remove free will from a human being—you can only present him with less and less favorable choices. Choice of action can never be taken away. All that those who have power can do is put increasing amounts of pressure on people's ability to choose a course of action for themselves. Sometimes the choice is between death, and not dying.

Unlike other species, human beings can be made acutely aware that their lives can be taken away from them, either by force or by denying them access to resources (usually by denying them the ability to work for currency to purchase the means of survival, or by punitive fines and seizures). You cannot threaten an animal with death—they simply have no concept of their mortality. The police, national guard, military, contractors,

270 Charles Eisenstein (2011). *"Sacred Economics: Money, Gift, and Society in the Age of Transition."* North Atlantic Books.

271 Carter C. Price, Kathryn A. Edwards. *"Trends in Income From 1975 to 2018."* WR-A516-1. Rand Corporation. September 2020. https://www.rand.org/content/dam/rand/pubs/working_papers/WRA500/WRA516-1/RAND_WRA516-1.pdf

and petty bureaucrats play a vital role in ensuring that, if people do not comply with authority, they can face painful sanctions.

The individuals who make up the ruling elite—those who control a disproportionate amount of property, money, and political power—hire state-sponsored thugs to do their dirty work and enforce their wishes. More and more, these thugs are selected for their antisocial qualities by recruiters who then program them for further mindless obedience. They have the responsibility of protecting the system from those who would challenge it. The laws of a nation (the judicial system) are backed up by force should the populace fail to comply with them, either through financial pain (in the form of fines), physical pain or death (in the form of clubs, tasers, guns, tear gas, rubber bullets, the electric chair, etc), or loss of freedom (prison). Because people recognize this coercion at some level, they remain scared and compliant, or "law-abiding," for most of the time. Robber baron, Jay Gould, was reputed to have said, "I can hire one half of the working class to kill the other half," and this is not so far from the truth.

In recent times, there has been a move to use private security forces and mercenaries, both at the national level and by wealthy individuals/groups. In a presentation to Wall Street banksters, media theorist, Douglas Rushkoff, was asked, ""How do I maintain authority over my security force after the Event?"[272] (the Event being some sort of societal collapse). These people have their own private armies.

Being a member of the "stormtrooper class" (the police/military/national guard) is to receive the embrace of a brotherhood and is an escape from the annoying task of complex thought in preference of unconscious, simplistic thinking. It fulfills the primary human need to belong. They experience unity consciousness (the dark side of it). The fundamental rule is simple to understand and execute—you obey the person in authority. At this point, their minds can rest easy—you just follow orders. There

272 YouTube channel, Neurohacker (January 14, 2021). *"HomeGrown Humans - Douglas Rushkoff - Team Human - Hosted by Jamie Wheal."* https://www.youtube.com/watch?v=oXYWy2f5wsI&feature=emb_logo

may be established rules but they are secondary to direct orders. And, generally, what rules there are simply codify abusive practices that place a wall between them and others who oppose their behavior—those outside the brotherhood. There is nothing else that has to be considered by the stormtrooper. It makes day-to-day living very easy.

> *"War is a racket. It always has been. It is possibly the oldest, easily the most profitable, surely the most vicious. It is the only one international in scope. It is the only one in which the profits are reckoned in dollars and the losses in lives."*[273]
>
> – MAJOR GENERAL SMEDLEY BUTLER

We're a social species, and this is to be celebrated. The downside is that we can be "herded." The window dressing presented by "the dark side," to belong to a brotherhood and be able to protect the country they love, often has greater force than actually seeing the truth of things. By "honoring" those military men who have sacrificed themselves in service of State and Family, an illusion of care is created. Men need to feel loved, acknowledged, and cared for, and will trade battle scars to get it. This is how Mass Man is made. He fails to realize he's giving up his life to defend, not democracy, but the interests of corporations which use the veil of a "people's government" as cover for their agenda.

Only by a society having as its goal the fully expressed consciousness of each individual, can the stormtrooper class be eradicated. It is virtually impossible to reason them out of their unconsciousness.[274] They do not have the mental software to process complex information. Because conscious men and women do not have this deficit, they suppose it to be inherent in others. They believe that all human beings can grow to be conscious,

273 Major General Smedley Darlington Butler (July 30, 1881 – June 21, 1940). "By the end of his career, Butler had received 16 medals, five for heroism. He is one of 19 men to receive the Medal of Honor twice, one of three to be awarded both the Marine Corps Brevet Medal (along with Wendell Neville and David Porter) and the Medal of Honor, and the only Marine to be awarded the Brevet Medal and two Medals of Honor, all for separate actions." https://en.wikipedia.org/wiki/Smedley_Butler

274 Sadly, the transformation of the character, Marine Jake Sully, in the movie, Avatar, was just fictional.

given enough time, energy, opportunity, and love. This is true, on the face of it. However the scale of the stormtrooper's obedience to the masters of the matrix is so great that putting flowers down the ends of their guns[275] or blowing bubbles at them[276] at them will not bring them any closer to unity consciousness (the light side of it). Acts of love and kindness in the face of abusers is beautiful, in a sense. There's a beauty in the hope that simple acts of humanness can touch another's heart. Tragically, this is exceptionally unlikely to happen. Stormtroopers have to be capable of challenging their own level of consciousness—something that was never selected for in the first place by their masters. Their commitment to their commanders and their brotherhood extends only to the edge of their own circle, not to the Brotherhood of Man. "The members do not feel that they are alone with their own smallness and helplessness, as they have the powers of the hero-leader with whom they are identified."[277] You're either on the inside or the outside. Protesters screaming abuses in their face merely assure them they're on the right team.

We could add to that list petty bureaucrats, who are the white collar stormtroopers of the ruling elite. Banks and mortgage companies employ ordinary people who would themselves never evict a family plus their possessions onto the sidewalk outside the house they'd resided in for 30 years. But they would never hesitate to push through the paperwork which sets those wheels in motion. As long as they don't have to pull the trigger themselves, they can point to "policies" which justify their actions. They can account for themselves as morally blameless by compartmentalizing their thinking, rather than synthesizing it. The stormtroopers we call sheriffs get to do the actual dirty work. Both are just "doing their jobs" and "following orders."

Compartmentalization and fragmentation of thought keeps the

---

275 Putting flowers in guns was captured in an iconic image by photographer, Bernie Boston, taken on October 21,1967, during the Vietnam war protests.

276 YouTube channel, The Real News Network (July 2010). *"Officer Bubbles"- From Bubbles to Bookings?"* A Toronto police officer threatened then arrested a G20 activist for blowing bubbles during a mass detention in Toronto's Parkdale community. https://www.youtube.com/watch?v=PGMTm3QRwEc

277 Ernest Becker (1997). *"The Denial of Death."* Free Press; 1st edition.

stormtrooper class sane, for to see the harm they do to others and to feel their pain would be to become all too human.

If the machine of government is of such a nature that it requires you to be the agent of injustice to another, then I say, break the law.[278]

– HENRY DAVID THOREAU

The Prison Industrial Complex

If you are to punish a man retributively you must injure him. If you are to reform him you must improve him. And men are not improved by injuries.

– GEORGE BERNARD SHAW

It's difficult to extract value from an underclass. A poor, young man (often of color) doesn't represent an opportunity for exploitation since his productive capacities have been stunted by his lack of education and lack of opportunity to add value in the workplace. But if you can lock him up and get taxpayers to foot the bill, then, hey presto, you can make a lot of money.

Before the 1980s, there were no private prisons in the US. Since then, prison privatization in the USA has become big business (generating more than $80 billion/year) and men are disproportionately paying the price in both time spent behind bars and in their pocket books. "Fascism should more appropriately be called Corporatism because it is a merger of state and corporate power."[279] Nowhere is this more apparent than in the alliance between the State and private prison corporations. Of course, the more people are incarcerated the more profit can be extracted from tax payers who pay their state/federal government to contract with these companies. They profit from housing, feeding, transporting, and selling necessities

278 Henry David Thoreau (2014). *"Civil Disobedience."* Libertas. *https://libertasutah.org/books/civildisobedience.pdf*

279 Italian fascist dictator, Benito Mussolini (1883-1945).

to prisoners. It's in their interest to make sure that crime pays—not for convicts but for *them*. In 1983, the prison population was 648,000. It's now 2.3 million people (20% of the global prison population).

The Prison Industry Enhancement Certification Program in 1979 also granted US companies the opportunity to use prisoners as cheap labor (they receive less than $1/hour). Male prisoners are a massive labor force in the US and slavery is functionally alive and well. Federal Prison Industry sales to federal agencies were $531 million in 2019.[280]

Welcome to the modern chain gang.

Controlling the Control System

To learn who rules over you, simply find out who you are not allowed to criticize.

– VOLTAIRE

The natural order of human beings is to evolve their consciousness; to become more and more conscious—more wise, more intelligent, more aware, more knowing, more loving. In doing so, they must meet the control system which fights back, sometimes subtly, sometimes forcefully.

"The most important real estate on the planet is the space between your ears…Your thoughts, your ideas, your opinions, and your perceptions are incredibly important to those who wish to seek to control society."[281]

There are countervailing forces which want to control you and do not want you to become more conscious; to see things with more clarity, to see reality as it really is, and to potentially do something not in their best interests. There are elements within society which are consciously coordinated to enslave you, as much as there are certain self-deceptions and cultural/social zeitgeists which perpetuate this enslavement. These can reinforce each other either by conscious coordination or by happenstance.

280 FAR & Beyond (August 7, 2020). *"Federal Prison Industries: Where is the Data on Program Effectiveness?"* The Coalition for Government Procurement. https://thecgp.org/federal-prison-industries-where-is-the-data-on-program-effectiveness.html

281 YouTube channel, James Corbett (November 18, 2020). *"How to Spot a Propaganda Trial Balloon."* https://www.youtube.com/watch?v=qDop7jQMURk

Cui bono? Who benefits from gaining at your expense by suppressing your full expression as a human being?

~

With social media, there is a race to the bottom of the brain stem. This is how social media is constructed. Tech engineers determine what goes to the top of your social feed by several metrics which have nothing to do with your best interests as a fully functioning human being. It also doesn't help that social media is a place where people go to be the shittiest version of themselves. Whatever gets the most clicks, likes, comments, etc, or is driven by outrage at what the other side is doing invariably shows up first. Whether by design or accident, your mind is being shaped by what's being presented to you by social media algorithms. Information which is more thoughtful and grounded and which takes time and attention to process, and where the reader does their own inner work of appraising, evaluating, and considering it's merits is less likely to win out over "information in a nutshell" memes and click bait articles. It's why modern-day humans compared to the past have an attention span shorter than a goldfish.[282] We are behaving as if we are in the service of technology on *its* journey to evolve into newer, cooler stuff. We're just the batteries of the Matrix rather than technology assisting human beings on *their* journey to evolve their consciousness.

The internet has been the key instrument in terms of consciousness-raising of the workings of the external world. This does not serve the interests of the ruling elite, hence the efforts to control, corrupt, surveil, regulate, and censor social platforms like YouTube, Twitter, and Facebook and go after net neutrality. Peer-to-peer sharing of information has long been targeted. A minority of people are attracted to higher truths. The majority are comfortable resting in their own well-established mental ruts. The term "conspiracy theorist," a term invented by the CIA to discredit

282 A 2015 study by Microsoft which observed the impact of modern digital technology devices on attention spans (the study is no longer accessible on the internet).

numerous challengers to establishment narratives, is helpful in misdirecting unconscious men and women to see an enemy amongst their own ranks.

Social media is the latest information war zone. But what we're seeing is the "boiling frog" plan of attack—it's not the heavy-handed policing of yesteryear (although we are almost at that level of blatant control, anyway).[283] Every group or institution with nefarious intent is aggressively fighting for control of your mind and the result is mass insanity. Unfortunately, I see many people regressing at the moment, and I see the media as an intentional force in trying to get people to lower their consciousness. A perfect way to tell if someone is operating at a low level of consciousness is if they're constantly placing tens of millions of their fellow citizens into an outside group they subsequently demonize. It's perfectly fine and healthy to harshly criticize the system itself and the many powerful individuals doing awful things within it, but once you start dehumanizing large swaths of the population as a matter of your worldview, you are most certainly on a very counterproductive path that will lead to merely a black hole of nothingness for society.

Pieces of freedom are gradually being peeled away. For example, in 2019 YouTube put out a statement "specifically prohibiting videos alleging that a [hate] group is superior in order to justify discrimination, segregation or exclusion based on qualities like age, gender, caste, religion, sexual orientation or veteran status" and "denying that well-documented violent events, like the Holocaust or the shooting at Sandy Hook Elementary, took place." More simply, employees/A.I. at YouTube are ill-equipped to know the difference between content providers exploring issues of racism and hatred, and those who promote it (given the indiscriminate nature of channels being removed).

But this is just the window-dressing to appear "admirably concerned." Because in reality any channel which challenges any aspect of the official narrative is being demonetized. Many of these channels rely on advertising

283 As an example:
Dr. Joseph Mercola (November 15, 2020). *"Operation Warp Speed — A Technocratic Chess Piece?"* Organic Consumers Association. https://www.organicconsumers.org/news/operation-warp-speeds-a-technocratic-chess-piece

income to generate revenue so, by demonetizing them, YouTube can effectively kill them off by starving them out. Some have been completely removed—deleted—those whose message was just too strong (even if questionable).[284] Silicon Valley has the power to control thought—and they're using it.

The process of keeping thought channeled in a particular direction extends to YouTube's home page, which is personally tailored to the user. The algorithm selects video recommendations based on viewing history and then gradually recommends other videos which are socially/politically anemic (music, popular culture, kids doing cute things, mainstream news, etc). Users who tend to watch content from a certain personal perspective are fed these related videos and are shepherded towards a narrative which makes them docile. There will never be an occasion where their information bubble will be pierced. This didn't use to be the case—much of the counter-narrative information I accessed years ago came prior to these changes. Back then, trending videos used to be on the home page, some having gone viral with mind-blowing information (like 9/11 Truth and other false flag attacks). Now, with users stuck in their bubble, new information never materializes unless they specifically search for it. But even then, when a user searches on a subject for which a counter-narrative exists, they will be presented with search results which favor preserving the mainstream narrative. For example, "Federal Reserve" will return not one result which seriously calls into question the machinations of this cartel of private bankers.[285] If you know a thing or two about the Federal Reserve, you can dig deeper and find relevant content with more specified searches. But for the average user who is coming to this fresh, they don't know what they don't know and YouTube/Google wants to keep it that

284 Examples include the infamous Alex Jones, The RapeOfJustice, the Richie Allen Show, APlainTruth, TruthmediaRevolution, CustomGrow420 (cannabis channel), Natural News, Highwire News, Red Pill 78, Fake News Report, Press For Truth, World Alternative Media, Last American Vagabond, The Dollar Vigilante, The Conscious Resistance Network, Jay Myers (quality conspiracy analysis), and others. https://transparency.tube/

285 Allum Bokhari (January 2019) "THE SMOKING GUN': Google Manipulated YouTube Search Results for Abortion, Maxine Waters, David Hogg." Breitbart. https://www.breitbart.com/tech/2019/01/16/google-youtube-search-blacklist-smoking-gun/

way. Information is chosen for them, not by them. But most people are not looking, nor even knowing that they would be well-advised to look.

The larger society is being programmed to believe that these subjects do not actually exist, let alone how to access them. And more and more, with digital media, our censors can literally control the perception of the world around them (a monopoly over the public mind they long ago achieved with legacy media). The social media behemoths are the mass media of the 21st century, coming into daily contact with millions of people. Yet, the window of accessible information, brought about by the unintended consequences of the invention of the internet, is now rapidly closing.

Without open access to information, we cannot make good decisions. Good information is often available behind paywalls but can be expensive to access, especially if you're just interested in a particular article or paper. So restrictions are economic rather than technological. Even this book comes with a price tag because I need currency to access resources—I can't simply give the book away for free, much as I'd like to. We have a world swamped with "free" information which is mostly bullshit. How we screen out bad information from good is the challenge ahead of us.

~

There is a belief that science is impartial, apolitical, and ultimately interested in unraveling the truth of the matter. It used to be that studies emerging from the scientific community would challenge the status quo. These studies would perhaps be sidelined or misrepresented by the powers-that-be but, because they challenged authority narratives, they were considered by most people to closely comport with reality and were subject to peer review which met faulty science with good science. Or if a study had industry backing behind it (like Big Pharma), its findings would be taken with a very large grain of salt.

Now, at the highest levels, "scientific" institutions and journals have largely been captured and are under control of the ruling elite to peddle scientific-like propaganda. Or "truthiness."[286] In this post-truth society, individual scientists who step forward to tell the truth face losing their jobs and their reputations. Public faith in science is still almost universally favorable which makes the manipulation of purportedly scientific findings to shape a narrative a mouth-watering opportunity for those in power. If a scientific message derived from a "study" can be invoked to support a position (an appeal to authority) without the need for the scientific method having been correctly applied to derive an understanding, then it becomes more of a religion to control the masses. Such was the case when the most prestigious medical journal of the day, The Lancet, published a study claiming that the use of Hydroxychloroquine to treat covid-19 patients actually increased their risk of death.[287] The study was a complete fabrication. The journal had historically been scrupulous in its efforts to practice due diligence to ensure that false, inaccurate, or misleading information never made its way into print. The fact that the fraudulent study was so easily revealed when challenged, demonstrated an irredeemable lack of integrity on the part of the publisher.

~

The exodus from Tibet following Chinese persecution of Buddhist monks, and the aspects of Buddhist mentality that have now spread worldwide, has given us an appreciation of our fundamental nature. But even mindfulness practices are being co-opted to make us pliable! They are being marketed as a healthy way of coping with daily stresses (i.e, the ravages of capitalism). By keeping people focused on their inward processes, mindful meditation directs people away from critically appraising their outer world. It offers an internal sanctuary in an unjust world. It's just a "more evolved" way of

286 The quality of stating concepts one wishes or believes to be true, rather than the facts. It is used to describe something that feels truthful. Facts and logic have nothing to do with truthiness. The truthiness of something is only measured by it instinctively feeling correct.

287 Prof Mandeep R Mehra, MD. Sapan S Desai, MD, Prof Frank Ruschitzka, MD. Amit N Patel, MD.(May 22, 2020) *"Hydroxychloroquine or chloroquine with or without a macrolide for treatment of COVID-19: a multinational registry analysis."* The Lancet.

coping. Mindfulness, and many eastern religions, suggest that the causes of our suffering are largely self-generated—it's our attitudes which cause us pain. The focus is deflected from the political and economic systems which shape the way we live. Instead of being a liberating force, it helps its adherents adapt to the very conditions that caused them to have these unbearable stress loads. By withdrawing to an internal realm, the public realm is relegated to lesser importance. "Mindfulness, like positive psychology and the broader happiness industry, has depoliticized stress. If we are unhappy about being unemployed, losing our health insurance, and seeing our children incur massive debt through college loans, it is our responsibility to learn to be more mindful."[288] Facebook and Google use mindfulness meditation as a tool to extract greater productivity and profits from its workers.[289]

Modern-day stresses are almost unbearable, what with trying to find work/keep a career, having less and less disposable income, managing debt, keeping skills and studies up-to-date to leverage in the workplace, raising children without alienating them, being a great lover without getting #MeToo-ed, being a great partner without attracting a succubus, trying to find clean and healthy things to eat and drink, ingesting the messages of the fear-mongering media, dealing with a more and more authoritarian state and polarized society. On and on. Human beings were never designed to deal with this level of stress as part of their natural environment and the so-called mindfulness phenomenon passively accepts the dictates of the marketplace as consumers pay for their mental and emotional relief. Is mindfulness simply a way to make us feel okay with the madness that surrounds us?

~

At a younger age, we are often confused by the fact that each person we

288 Ronald Purser (June 14, 2019). *"The Mindfulness Conspiracy."* The Guardian. https://www.theguardian.com/lifeandstyle/2019/jun/14/the-mindfulness-conspiracy-capitalist-spirituality

289 Roanald Purser (December 6, 2019). *"How Mindfulness Morphed from Ancient Spiritual Practice to Big Business."* Jacobin Magazine. https://jacobinmag.com/2019/12/corporate-mindfulness-ron-purser-interview

admire seems to have a different version of what life ought to be—what a good man is, how to live, and so on. We then follow one persons' and then another's way of being, depending on whomever is most luminous at the time—the one with a voice like James Earl Jones, or the body of Dwaine Johnson, or the authority and success of Richard Branson, or the presence of Adyashanti. We looked up to them and tried to pattern our ideals after them.

Nowhere is this more problematic than with spiritual teachers. Much of the messaging of self-help or spiritual gurus is that your greatest enemy is your self. This idea has become a dogma which fails to take account of "other enemies." It leaves people feeling that they are entirely responsible for the circumstances in which they find themselves, and they have only themselves to blame. They didn't have the right mindset—because, you know, our mind manifests and creates our reality. And they even chose this life for themselves before they entered this earthly realm. It's true that many people fail to see how their own mind is contributing to their situation (those who are unconscious at some level), but many of these gurus are wolves in sheep's clothing. They claim to be about personal liberation but end up herding their followers into a narrow ideology which ignores broader social forces which oppress and suppress the common man. The very label of "spiritual" gives them a force which can blind those who wish to see things as they really are. If a mechanic does a poor job on your auto, you can get your money back. Yet there is such breathless acceptance and deification of spiritual leaders that their effectiveness is not measured in the same way as other professional walks of life. This is a very useful tool in the hands of those who are confused, incompetent, or downright unscrupulous. Their followers become polarized and entrenched in their own tribal positions and have a level of moral disgust with others who question or challenge the messaging.

No man is great enough or wise enough for any of us to surrender our destiny to. The only way in which anyone can lead us is to restore to us the belief in our own guidance.

— HENRY MILLER

45 Authority

Authority is power. It represents the ability to determine and implement a course of action. Experts, thought leaders, popular pundits, scientists, etc, in today's world, are people with a purported expertise in a particular field. They are the supposedly authoritative source we are asked to believe on a particular issue but whose stature has, in actuality, been illegitimately created by the power elite to give credibility to a particular narrative. They are the political appointees at the head of all major institutions, and many lower level experts, that have been bought and paid for by vested interests. Even the supposedly "benign authorities" of the past (the Dan Rathers, the Walter Cronkites, even your personal doctor, etc) were molded by establishment narratives. Ordinary people have long been programmed to turn over their critical thinking capacities to people they've been asked to trust.

Obviously there has been a lot of wounding over millennia surrounding the use and misuse of authority, embedded in dominance-hierarchy. A lot of people are so sick to their stomachs of authority that they just want to do away with it completely. They are "anti-authoritarian" and this is to be mostly welcomed. Most humans have an "obedience problem" (in contrast to a disobedience problem). Consenting to authority only works where that consent can easily be withdrawn, with no punishment for so doing. Equally, there is no requirement to stop critical thinking while consenting.

The conscious man realizes that the world, as presented, doesn't make sense and that there are shady establishment salesmen trying to sell him snake oil. The danger for him is that, in the absence of good information from those in authority, he may swing towards compelling explanations from alternative authorities which are, nevertheless, also based in falsehoods (whole or partial). Perhaps it's David Icke, QAnon, The Scamdemic, Critical Theory, Red Pill psychology, or other seemingly coherent grand narratives.

The problem with most of the people who have been entrusted with positions of authority is that they have neither been competent nor caring nor conscious. But authority itself is not the problem. Vertical meritocratic hierarchy is not the problem. Power is not the problem. The problem lies in the lack of its judicious implementation (for power without abuse has no appeal to those who would otherwise wield it). Yet refusing to accept authority, or superior competence, simply because you yearn to be equal (or superior) to others is to unconsciously exist in a state of unintegrated powerlessness. In its purest form (and authority is considered a divine masculine trait), authority is a mechanism for progress. A better mechanism for progress than absolute equality.

You follow directives when the person who is giving them has more competence than you—when they've done the work that you are either not capable of doing yourself or because you've devoted your time and energy to other concerns. Your obligation to yourself and others is to determine ahead of time that person's ability and agenda. Are they competent? Are they rooted in care and consideration for others? And then to take time to periodically reassess that person's ability and agenda to make sure they remain "clean." Even the best have blind spots. I follow the directives of my Chinese medicine practitioner because I have neither the time nor inclination to do the work she has done. But the reason I chose her is because I've done enough work to recognize the benefits of Chinese medicine and her competency. If the medicine she prescribed me was either ineffectual or harmful, I would then start start to question whether I should be following her directives, taking care to evaluate the situation from all angles.

With the shadow side of authority, we get to control the activities of people we don't like, or their ideas. If we can't achieve authority in our own terms, we collectively place what authority we have in the hands of a particular person or party, with the expectation that they will do the controlling for us (something we call democracy).

A musician is not (or needs not be) of lower social value than a teacher but there is a difference between the two. It's a question of how each expends their energy. A simple thought experiment is to ask yourself, "Is it a good use of a teacher's energy to spend time performing as a rock star?" Or, "Is it a good use of the rock star's energy to teach high school?" Are they adding more value to their lives and to the world by doing the other's work? Are they demonstrating superior competence in fields they know little about? Since human beings aren't two-dimensional but multi-faceted creatures, the answer may sometimes be yes. For example Jack Black's character, Dewey Finn, in the movie *School of Rock.* There's always nuance. But, as a rule, we identify those people who are the most competent (soft skills as well as hard skills), then empower them to have hierarchical authority to exercise those skills in the best interests of others.

The more skillful gurus, masters, leaders, teachers, mentors, etc, by their merits, are external authorities. But not our internal authority. They are the person who can hold us true to ourselves through their compassionate challenging of our thoughts and actions. In the end, their influence over the contents of one's mind has to be subtracted so that the mind functions on its own terms.

The idea of death, the fear of it, haunts the human animal like nothing else; it is a mainspring of human activity—activity designed largely to avoid the fatality of death, to overcome it by denying in some way that it is the final destiny for men.[290]

—ERNEST BECKER

46 Why do Men Participate in their own Enslavement?

It's estimated that in the course of human history, approximately 75 percent of the humans that have existed have been slaves. Many in spiritual communities will have heard the sentiment that for centuries, and across all nations, there has been an imbalance favoring masculine energy and that now is the time for female energy to arise and lead us into a glorious new age. But the reason that men have been accorded the greater role in the creation of civilizations is that they were more useful "tools" than women. They were used by the ruling elite to access and control resources. Their minds, which focused more on "things," logic, and systematized thinking, were better suited to the extraction and modification of the Earth's resources—a pyramid scheme which benefited those at the top the most. Women were mostly seen as agents to manage the mood and morale of men and to provide future slaves, if they were given much thought at all. They were the cookie that men could look forward to—the sweetness to

290 Ernest Becker (1997). "*The Denial of Death.*" Free Press; 1st edition.

make life bearable. Without women's softness, care, and love, men would have had little reason to toil for their masters and continue with their existence. Why would they bother? Those women were pregnant more often through their lives than today's women, died in greater numbers in childbirth, had less upper body strength, and thus were less suited to ruthless exploitation.

Men have been controlled by "the carrot and the stick"[291] method. With women and family being the carrot, the stick involved the threat of death. Because of our capacity for abstract conceptual thought, and unlike other animals which live only in the here and now, humans can be threatened with death.[292] Death is the static on the radio dial—it's always there in the background as we twiddle between stations. Faced with the choice between his death and any other unfavorable course of action, a man will almost certainly choose the latter. If the choice is between "game over" and "leveling down," the choice is logically to preserve his existence with the hope to level up again in the future, however unlikely. Procreation and death are at the heart of what it is to be a human being. When you can hack into these programs, you can control humans.

Our masters are also prey to the same fear of mortality. They cannot conscience the fact that they might die without significance. They see their existential presence as vital to the project of humanity and seek immortality through ever-expanding power to tame their world and defy its reality. Billionaire banker, Lloyd Blankfein, once said he was just a banker "doing God's work."[293]

Increasingly, modern women are both the stick…and the stick. Which also means that conscious men have less reason than ever to participate in a paradigm that offers them so little.

291 The phrase "carrot and stick" is a metaphor for the use of a combination of reward and punishment to induce a desired behavior. In politics, "carrot or stick" sometimes refers to the realist concept of soft and hard power. Wikipedia.

292 This includes the threat to withdraw the means of survival from our lives—e.g. currency or access to currency via employment.

293 Citizen Truth Staff (July 15, 2019). *"Bernie Sanders Blasts Goldman Sachs' Claim It Does 'God's Work."* Citizen Truth. https://medium.com/citizen-truth/bernie-sanders-blasts-goldman-sachs-claim-it-does-god-s-work-936798278e6c

Profane space differs from sacred space in that it has no fixed point or center from which to gain orientation. Profane space has no axis mundi, no cosmic tree or pillar leading to the heavens. This is the experience of modernity: people unable to locate their center[294]

—ROBERT MOORE

47 Disconnection

The world we live in has been constructed and maintained by the suppression of our true natures. As outlined in the chapter, *Feminist Myths and Narratives,* this has not simply been feminine aspects but masculine also.

Especially for men, our society particularly places great value on only one type of consciousness—the heads-up, alert, problem-solving state of consciousness which is considered the most productive for extracting value to serve the needs of a fast-paced, technological, capitalistic world. More spiritual states are less easily monetized. Additionally, more heartfelt, open, compassionate, and humane individuals do not have the necessary acumen for ruthless exploitation of people and planet. The dominant model of consciousness favors "human doings" over human beings, and this is problematic. On the one hand, we've been able to craft a world of amazing complexity and abundance (for those who can afford it), and on the other we've used our intellect to escape the feeling of being part of a

294 Robert Moore (2001). *"The Archetype of Initiation."* Xlibris, Corp.; 1 edition.

world we cannot control. We've domesticated the planet so that we never have to worry about going hungry, being eaten by a predator, or staying cool in the summer. We've created industrial agriculture which destroys the soil upon which we depend. We've killed off the giant eagles.[295] We've created a national power grid fed by fossil fuels to run air conditioners in the height of summer in places where humans would not otherwise choose to live.

We discovered ways to be less dependent on the Earth and on each other. Our survival is no longer dependent on the survival of our friends and neighbors. We are no longer in primitive tribes where subsistence-level survival could only be achieved through unity. As long as we have enough money, we can buy our way out of trouble or pay for a lifestyle where we can avoid interacting with unwanted humans—our place in the sun. People either stand in opposition to our needs (they covet our stuff or mess with the way we want to live) or they are tools to get what we want (we transact with them for goods and services). "Just take care of Number One" is the mission.

Men and women have become disconnected from themselves and the natural world so that we create living environments which do not take into consideration the needs of our fellow species nor ourselves. For example, our urban environments are mostly ugly, noisy, dirty, overcrowded, and alienating and which evolved not from human need but from the requirements of the production-driven class system, squashing people together around offices and factories, rather than uniting them. The result is a "behavioral sink which means an increase in pathological activities due to the stress involved in high population."[296] These people feel a sense of accomplishment when they get their bills paid and their mortgage paid down. They feel they've arrived at a point of successful living.

---

295 Natasha Ishak (October 6, 2020). *"Meet The Haast's Eagle, New Zealand's 'Lost Giant' That Went Extinct 600 Years Ago."* All That's Interesting. https://allthatsinteresting.com/haast-eagle. These eagles predated on 6 foot tall bipedal moas (giant birds) and no doubt found 6 foot tall bipedal humans to be equally tasty.

296 Kim Mia (September 3, 2020). *"The Horrifying Study That Predicted Human Extinction."* Medium. https://medium.com/history-of-yesterday/the-horrifying-study-that-predicted-human-extinction-244fa185087b

Properly-speaking, there is no longer any world, there are only fragments of a shattered universe, an amorphous mass consisting of an infinite number of more or less neutral places in which man moves, governed and driven by the obligations of an existence incorporated into an industrial society[297]

– MIRCEA ELIADE

The contesting of resources over the course of human history has given a false picture of toxic masculinity that feminists would like us to buy in to. Such competition was not for the benefit of men so much as it was for the benefit of their nearest and dearest—women, offspring, tribe. Yet the contesting of resources (from skirmishes, to wars, to assaulting Mother Nature herself) inevitably produces disconnection and a scarcity mindset. It "otherizes." If others are less worthy of consideration then it's okay for us to have their resources.

As always, the story is nuanced. It should be noted that hunter-gather societies were not idyllic. In order for the social structure to hang together, conformity was the rule. Many who advance ideas of reconnecting with the values of such societies would need to realize that non-conformity would not be tolerated. As we lost "survival through compelled unity," we gained perspective. We stood far enough away from others to be able to get a sense of ourselves—away from the tribal/societal pressure to conform—to be able to sense the stirrings of our true natures. Solitude, explored by individuals, has always been a powerful tool as part of a spiritual path. As a species, though, rather than doing so consciously, we've largely entertained societal atomization with fear and frustration. Perhaps we could not have done otherwise given our level of cosmic conscious awareness and given that we are human organisms living in a world not fit for human consumption. Yet this multi-millennia long exploration of independence is leading us back to unity. Unity is now a conscious choice where once before it was the unobserved and conformist water in which we swam (see *Unity Consciousness,* chapter, *Conclusion*).

297 Mircea Eliade (1987). *"The Sacred and The Profane: The Nature of Religion."* Harcourt Brace Jovanovich.

Popular culture is a place where pity is called compassion, flattery is called love, propaganda is called knowledge, tension is called peace, gossip is called news, and auto-tune is called singing.[298]

— CRISS JAMI

48 Conclusion

As it stands, it is impossible to live freely within an oligarchic plutocracy. The plutocrats will simply continue buying up power by creating oppressive laws and "legal" extortion rackets that keep the people without wealth and power in a permanent state of poverty and powerlessness. Factoring in special interests and their lobbyists, and the illusion of a free democratic republic, what remains is a nation desperately believing that they can vote their way to a better life, or dreaming of the day when they don't have to choose between the lesser of two evils.

When taken together, a full account of scientific findings indicates that species extinction is happening at the highest rate ever, short of the massive meteor(s) that once slammed into the planet. When we consider the impact human activity is doing to the natural systems we depend on for our existence, the data strongly suggests that we are committing ecocide. The world's plants are disappearing five hundred times faster than they should. The global animal population has decreased by sixty percent since the seventies. And the United Nations predicts that a million more

298 Criss Jami (January 8, 2015). *"Killosophy."* CreateSpace Independent Publishing Platform

species will go extinct within a few decades. Oil, natural gas, and coal extraction is reaching its peak with little chance of renewables being able to adequately replace the concentrated energy form found in hydrocarbons. With the earth's temperature rising at a frightening speed, the political will needed to implement broad-scale, organized efforts to change our ways is woefully insufficient.

It should be noted that environmental destruction isn't driven by human nature but a mistaken idea. It is an inevitable consequence of a system built on the acquisition of profit above all other considerations. But if we were to get rid of the ruling class and all the mechanisms of control they utilize, we would sooner or later be faced with the same paradigm all over again if we fail to do our inner, conscious work.

Certain groups of conscious men and women are considering what might be a replacement to the status quo. Groups like the Zeitgeist Movement, The Venus Project, Ubuntu Contributionism, Charles Eisenstein's Gift Economy, the degrowth movement, Free World Charter, the permaculture/regenerative agriculture movement, One Community Global, New Earth, and many others. But, being largely powerless, what little implementation there is of their good ideas is just a drop in a bucket. They are mostly just effective in raising consciousness.

Everybody is sick of the system. Even the people who are running the system—those who are deeply embedded, deeply unconscious, not practicing spirituality, not on the path of awakening—even they are sick of the system. It's actually a problem. Because if everyone is desiring something completely different, what usually ensues is the complete destruction of what is. Pretty much all humans are actively desiring this society to end, quite literally. The human race will certainly have to purge itself of all the things that are maintaining the old system to usher in a new system. But, given our current trajectory, that purification process is not going to be particularly pleasant or coherent.

Part Seven

The Divine Feminine

If you want to change the world...[299]

If you want to change the world love a man; really love him.

Choose the one whose soul calls to yours clearly; who sees you; who is brave enough to be afraid.

Accept his hand and guide him gently to your hearts blood

Where he can feel your warmth upon him and rest there

And burn his heavy load in your fires.

Look into his eyes, look deep within and see what lies dormant or awake or shy or expectant there.

Look into his eyes and see there his fathers and grandfathers and all the wars and madness their spirits fought in some distant land, some distant time.

---

299 With permission

Look upon their pains and struggles and torments and guilt; without judgment
And let it all go.
Feel into his ancestral burden
And know that what he seeks is safe refuge in you.
Let him melt in your steady gaze
And know that you need not mirror that rage
Because you have a womb, a sweet, deep gateway to wash and renew old wounds.
If you want to change the world love a man, really love him.
Sit before him, in the full majesty of your woman in the breath of your vulnerability,
In the play of your child innocence in the depths of your death,
Flowering invitation, softly yielding, allowing his power as a man
To step forward towards you…and swim in the Earth's womb, in silent knowing, together.
And when he retreats…because he will…flees in fear to his cave…
Gather your grandmothers around you…envelop in their wisdoms,
Hear their gentle 'shusshhhed' whispers calm your frightened girls' heart,
Urging you to be still…and wait patiently for his return.
Sit and sing by his door, a song of remembrance, that he may be soothed once more.
If you want to change the world, love a man, really love him.
Do not coax out his little boy
With guiles and wiles and seduction and trickery
Only to lure him…to a web of destruction.
To a place of chaos and hatred
More terrible than any war fought by his brothers.
This is not feminine, this is revenge.
This is the poison of the twisted lines.
Of the abuse of the ages, the rape of our world.
And this gives no power to woman, it reduces her as she castrates him
And it kills us all.
And whether his mother held him or could not,
Show him the true mother now.

Hold him and guide him in your grace and your depth

Smoldering in the center of the Earth's core.

Do not punish him for his wounds that you think don't meet your needs or criteria.

Cry for him sweet rivers.

Bleed it all back home.

If you want to change the world love a man, really love him.

Love him enough to be naked and free.

Love him enough to open your body and soul to the cycle of birth and of death

And thank him for the opportunity,

As you dance together through the raging winds and silent woods.

Be brave enough to be fragile and let him drink in the soft, heady petals of your being.

Let him know he can hold you, stand up and protect you.

Fall back into his arms and trust him to catch you,

Even if you've been dropped a thousand times before.

Teach him how to surrender by surrendering yourself,

And merge into the sweet nothing of this worlds' heart.

If you want to change the world, love a man, really love him

Encourage him, feed him, allow him, hear him, hold him, heal him.

And you, in turn, will be nourished and supported and protected

By strong arms and clear thoughts and focused arrows.

Because he can, if you let him, be all that you dream.

If you want to love a man,

Love yourself, love your father, love your brother, your son, your ex-partner;

From the first boy you kissed, to the last one you wept over.

Give thanks for the gifts of your unraveling to this meeting,

Of the one who stands before you now.

And find in him the seed to all that's new and solar,

A seed that you can feed to help direct the planting

To grow a new world, together.

– LAUREN WILCE

Surrendering, receptivity, passivity, opening, allowing/accepting, letting go, healing, love, nurturing, understanding, compassion, diffuse awareness, flow, softness, dissolving, formlessness, the sphere, restoration, life, fertility, renewal, creation, connection in the form of relationships, harmony, insight, intuition, knowing-based wisdom, forgiveness, the Moon, and sensuality.

49 Traits and Qualities

In the next two chapters, we're going to be examining the nature of our respective genders according to both masculine and feminine energetic principles. In how they relate to their lives, men and women benefit in different respects when they are attuned to their respective personal energy systems.

Rather than seeing certain traits exclusively as the domain of one sex or the other, it's more accurate to say that they fall on a continuum with sometimes a big overlap of traits and abilities between men and women. Women can be exceptionally intelligent and rational and men can be exceptionally nurturing and verbally expressive. Sometimes, the way women are verbally expressive (or nurturing, etc) is very different from how men are verbally expressive, so there is nuance within traits themselves. At a population level, though, men demonstrate a higher propensity for masculine traits and women for feminine traits.[300]

---

300 Interestingly, studies show that men are both dumber and smarter than women. The most intelligent humans tend to be men, women are largely grouped in the middle of the spectrum, and more men with lesser intelligence than women comprise the other end of the spectrum.

Just as men and women differ in terms of their physiology, so too do they have different energetic systems. Or, I should say, we both have the same energy structure (the chakra system) but we have different strengths and weaknesses according to certain characteristics. Particular chakras resonate more with either a feminine or a masculine quality. Our needs are often based upon the imbalance we naturally have in ourselves. The masculine seeks the feminine, and vice versa. In order to bring himself into balance, men can cultivate more female energy within themselves, and so too is the opposite true for women.

When a woman is in her divine feminine, she is able to connect with and embody these attributes and allow them to flow with and through her without resistance. Each and every woman is a unique and beautiful fractal of Divine Feminine; the heart of the soul. What this means is that no woman should serve up a cookie cutter version of herself which matches every other woman. Just like men, women are looking to access their core essence, their true nature, which would allow their own uniquely expressed representation of divine essence to flow through them. Neither traditional nor modern gender roles and identities have allowed women to be who they really are—the civilized world has never had the goal of allowing the full flourishing of either sex.

Women who are in their divine feminine come from a place of flow. In other words, they are not in resistance to what they don't resonate with but with what they do. They are living in alignment with their life force energy. Most women have been conditioned to live their lives with their minds rather than their hearts. The divine female has learned to live from her body and the life force which animates her. This interior force has a greater intelligence for her than her logical, linear mind; something more suited to the divine masculine.

If women stop shaving their legs because they are in resistance to expectations of feminine beauty then they are out of alignment. If they continue shaving their legs, resenting the fact, but do so because of these expectations, they are still out of alignment. If they enjoy their hairy legs because it makes them feel like an earth goddess, say, then they are in alignment. And if they shave their legs because it brings forth in them a sensual aspect in their nature, and/or a delicious appreciative response they adore from their man, they are also in alignment. It depends on the individual.

Women like to decorate their existence. Whether it be choosing nick-nacks or wall coverings for the home, knitting garments for a boyfriend, selecting a baby beanie for her infant, or having "everything on the side" when eating out in a restaurant. Of course, she also decorates her body with hairstyles, clothing, and beauty products. She'll name her car and give it a personality. Her main course is her life which she decorates with side dishes.[301] Whereas a man decorates his life with internal values and opinions[302] (see *A Man's Code of Honor,* chapter, *The Divine Masculine*), a woman doesn't have a code of honor in the same way. She does have a set of values which she expresses externally and which are a signal to others about how to think about her and treat her. They are a mechanism by which other people can establish who she is as a person.

Women who have, or are in the process of embracing their singular divine feminine nature, will express some aspects which fit the traditional view of femininity, some aspects which are post-traditional, and some which are neither. The divine female will have taken the time and done the work of decoding her own organism and feeling into what works for her and what doesn't. Moreso, she will have embodied the divine feminine traits and qualities and allowed them to express themselves through her being, without resistance. She doesn't have to cultivate or claim her womanhood in the way a man might claim his manhood. It's not a process of clearing resistances in order to work towards becoming a woman. And it's not that resistances relative to her femininity, or aspects she identifies as female, never arise. But she is aware of them when they

---

301 Girls too like to decorate their lives. A doll's house is her fantasy plan to choose and decorate a lifestyle for herself, lived vicariously through playing with her dolls.

302 When a man decorates his life, it is usually an expression of an egoic nature or his wounding. He'll decorate his life with a Tessla or an apartment in the fashionable part of town, or by bulking up. And maybe a trophy wife. Or he'll grow his hair long, wear wooden beads, etc, to signal his rejection of typical male clothing in favor of the feminine. He's has rejected traditional masculinity but has yet to discover a new form of masculinity.

do and turns towards them with loving acceptance and enquiry, in order to set them free. These resistances often express themselves as "negative emotions." In the end, the divine female trusts herself to know how to be and how to do because she is fully aligned with her process, centered on her feminine essence.

Many of the recognized spiritual practices that are offered are very useful and beautiful—for men. They have been developed and practiced by men over millennia, and have, perhaps unwittingly, focused on that which serves the divine masculine. Whereas a man's spiritual practice may be to empty his mind (and his testicles!) to touch pure presence, a woman's is to experience fullness and radiance—to feel as fully as possible—hence the trope, "Live, Laugh, Love!" A woman will always be insatiable—she exists in an amorphous state of yearning. This is why she has a shopping list of needs from a man and also is attracted to "man, the provider" until her cup runneth over. Her spiritual path is to integrate her felt sense of being less than full—to resolve herself to the feeling of being existentially unsatisfied—both for her own equanimity and so as not to drain her man of his life force energy just to assuage her thirst.[303]

For women, the empty state can be hard to achieve because to have an empty womb and an empty heart is challenging enough. For a woman to achieve the calm, centered state of the infinite—to become the infinite—is to become divine. At her essence, and at the highest order, her deep spiritual connection to her feelings and emotional nature allows her to tune into and align with divine energy— to be a gifted healer, mother, lover, and consort—to experience herself as love, in the knowing of herself as love.

A woman's two places of power are her heart and her womb. The womb has a cyclical aspect. By menstruating once a month, expelling and purging old blood, a woman's energy is restored—not only at the physical level but spiritually as well. The "time of the month" is an energetic calling to the woman to purge herself of any accumulated resistances and blockages. When a woman gets a little "crazy," this is really an opportunity for her

303 Hence the appeal of feminism which promises women more. More than they previously had, and then more again. Equality is no longer sufficient because she still feels empty.

to do her inner work—and she needs to feel safe, validated, and held in order to feel supported to let go what arises. She may choose to sit for a day in a candle-lit room with a glass of water or with her "sisters."[304] A woman in her divine essence knows how to handle her increased spiritual energy during menstruation because she is in tune with her body and has consciously devoted time to do so.

All women are different and approach their inner work in different ways. What is common to them is that at their center is love. So no matter her practice, as long as she comes back to her love, the methods by which she does so can be numerous. Love has its own gravitational pull. Love is pulling love to love.

304 Anita Diamant (1997) "*The Red Tent.*" Wyatt Books for St. Martin's Press. The book's title refers to the tent in which women take refuge while menstruating or giving birth, and in which they find mutual support and encouragement from their mothers, sisters, and aunts.

I taste him, and I realize I have been starving.

— JODI PICOULT.

50 Sex and Relationships

There is a value and importance for a woman in her divine aspect to address her sexuality as a core feature of her spiritual path. Sex is a way a woman can maintain her equilibrium, if she approaches it consciously. In order for a woman to awaken to her own true nature, she requires life force energy. In order to move past inner resistances, trauma patternings, or blockages, sex is the most powerful energy available to her.[305] It will help her encounter those blockages with both her breath and a somatic intelligence which calls for her full awareness. She is able to liberate anything which is not based in love, anything which she is disowning in herself. Unleashing her sexual energy allows her to direct it towards her physical health, mental clarity, longevity, and spiritual work. When she allows herself to surrender and feel, her own energy body directs its self-expression naturally and normally, without concern for how it may be regarded or received. Without interfering with or manipulating her natural self-expression, she can also learn to raise up her "lower" vibrations and direct them upwards to open her energy centers; her heart, throat, third eye and crown chakras.

305 A man loses his sexual energy through ejaculation, a woman through menstruation and loss of the life force energy of the blood. She loses energy once a month, often feeling irritable, tired, crampy, and bloated.

The more she allows herself to remain present and relaxed, resting in the intelligence of her body, the more aligned she becomes.

One of the prevalent beliefs is that all men want is sex. Yet women like sex as much (or more) than men.[306] Indeed, their "female erectile network"[307] has solely evolved for her pleasure (unlike a man's penis which is also used to pee). Nature designed women to enjoy sex. They are aroused by more and various stimuli than men, and in some cases don't even realize they are feeling aroused.[308] Sex is more of a woman's thing than a man's thing! If she's with a man who can fully bring her to heightened arousal, she'll slowly rise to her peak and then ride a plateau for hours to come. Few men have yet discovered this because few men can keep up with her. A woman's multi-orgasmic nature points to an evolutionary history where she fucked whoever she wanted to, for as long as she wanted to, whenever she wanted to (and the men in that tribe were happy!). She evolved for "rapid serial consortship." "After an orgasm, a woman may be anticipating a dozen more. A female body in motion tends to stay in motion. But men come and go."[309] Generally speaking, it takes guys five minutes to come and women twenty minutes to come. This is frustrating in a paradigm of monogamous relationships but it makes complete sense if we evolved where women shared themselves with multiple partners (either that or our hunter-gather ancestors were tantric masters able to "hold their seed!").This was the natural order of things and consequently the planet was a lot more sane than it is now.[310]

---

306 Meredith L. Chivers, Katrina N. Bouchard, Amanda D. Timmers. *Straight but Not Narrow; Within-Gender Variation in the Gender-Specificity of Women's Sexual Response.* National Center for Biotechnology Information. https://www.ncbi.nlm.nih.gov/pmc/articles/PMC4667912/pdf/pone.0142575.pdf

307 Sheri Winston (August 13, 2020). *"Women's Anatomy of Arousal."* Chronogram. https://www.chronogram.com/hudsonvalley/womens-anatomy-of-arousal/Content?oid=2169839

308 Interestingly, many women wake up with a hard-on, just like men, but their "erect" clitoris is hidden from view (it extends beyond the visible head/glans of the clitoris, about 4 inches).

309 Christopher Ryan & Cacilda Jethá (2010). *"Sex at Dawn: The Prehistoric Origins of Modern Sexuality."* Harper.

310 This is in counterpoint to what some Red Pill commentators call the 1000-cock-stare, which refers to women who purportedly have become so inured to the cock that their eyes glaze over. Despite access to numerous males (through hook-up apps), these women's disconnection derives instead from a deficit of social and emotional connection with male partners, rather than having had one cock too many. https://www.mgtow.com/definition/thousand-cock-stare/

Women also have different desire styles. Whereas a man can go in a straight line (from desire to arousal to plateau to orgasm), a woman places value on the setting, the mood, the level of intimacy or love with their partner, etc, which then informs her level of arousal. The first stages of desire may even precede, rather than follow, foreplay.[311] But, just like men, women in their natural state need novelty and variety or else they become bored. Not necessarily wanting a different partner but, if she just gets sex-by-numbers, it may push her in that direction. If sex is listless, spiritless, or bloodless, she begins to wilt and fade. Heat and passion and connection is her currency of love. She needs to feel alive!

~

In an evolved partnership, a woman will have reached a degree of self-awareness whereby she is conscious and compassionate in her choice of words and actions towards herself and others, and hence her man. These words and actions reflect a certain gentleness and acceptance without negating her own subjective or emotional frame. "This kind of gentleness, like water, can seep into and penetrate the cracks in a man's armor, awakening the deep, powerful masculinity within him."[312] She can deal with times of sadness or upset without blaming, shaming, becoming vindictive or emasculating. She is comfortable in her own skin, recognizes where her boundaries are, and enforces those boundaries with compassion for her beloved.

She is the force multiplier who can take him further than he could go by himself.

The Divine Feminine uses her good judgment, leading from her heart. She allows herself—her body, mind, and spirit—to be led by a man. As in partner dancing, the man leads and the woman follows. It is a voluntary act where he attunes himself to her and she submits to his direction,

---

311 Many women, who are "not in the mood" for sex, will report having enjoyed intercourse if they initially push themselves to do so. But there are also those women who regard this as "service sex," and this doesn't feel good for them *nor* their partner. It's a state of mind.

312 John Welwood (1990). *"Journey of the Heart."* Harper Collins.

moving with grace, living in joy, being spinningly lovely. If she doesn't like it, he'll soon know and she won't put up with a tyrant or narcissist. But she understands that he has her best interests at heart and she will make this "submissive" gesture to be in partnership with him. This is *his* strength. A Divine Man's intention is to lead them both to a good life, a crafted life, one day at a time. She embraces his heart and guards it within the castle walls, and he maintains his castle.

She gets to be a woman and he gets to be a man—not rigidly but fluidly. Since men have a feminine aspect, and women a masculine aspect, there are times when a man needs to step into his feminine. There are times when the king needs to hang up his sword, release his tears, and lay his head upon the breast of his queen. The Divine woman feels no fear that he will dwell in his feminine in preference to his masculine. He will return after he has discharged and integrated whatever shadows are causing him to emote. She can stand in her masculine in service to his pressing needs.

The best smell in the world is that man that you love.

— JENNIFER ANISTON

51 Evolutionary Programming

For the sake of brevity, I'll focus on just one aspect of evolution's contribution to femalehood.

For a woman in her divine feminine, her senses are exquisitely sensitive. Her olfactory sense in particular! Women can perceive odors better than men, especially those associated with male pheromones.

MHC, Major Histocompatibility Complex, allows humans to differentiate between cells that are produced in their own bodies and cells that come from another organism. It's why our farts smell okay(ish) to us but other farts reek! MHC also allows women to pick up immune system information from a prospective mate and how genetically dissimilar he is to her. What ends up happening is that she is attracted to a man who can give her the best chance to produce a healthy baby.

In a particular experiment, a number of men wore t-shirts for three days, then removed them, and put them in plastic bags. Soon thereafter, women of childbearing age, selected at random, opened each bag, and sniffed the sweaty t-shirts! They were then asked to rate the men's desirability on a scale of one to ten. All they had was their sense of smell to perceive the male's attractiveness and no other information was presented. The results produced very definitive "nos" and "yesses." They were attracted by some smells and repulsed by others. After the researchers had determined the differences in the genetic make-up of both the men and women, they found that the women's sense of smell had invariably selected potential mates whose particular genotype would most likely produce offspring with a potentially strong and healthy immune system, conferring on them the best chance of resisting illnesses and disease. By simply using their noses, these women were able to accurately infer vital information about a potential mate's suitability and fitness. One even begged to take a t-shirt home with her![313]

In parts of Greece and the Balkan states, some men carry handkerchiefs in their armpits during dances and festivals. These are then offered to women as tokens prior to an invitation to dance. Once we see past this as a weird and somewhat gross social custom, the practicality and ingeniousness of it becomes clear.

313 Christopher Ryan & Cacilda Jethá (2010). *"Sex at Dawn: The Prehistoric Origins of Modern Sexuality."* Harper.

Part Eight

The Divine Masculine

I know men and recognize them by their behavior, by the totality of their deeds, by the consequences caused in life by their presence.[314]

– ALBERT CAMUS

Generally speaking, men have more masculine and women have more feminine divine aspects, as you might expect.[315] All beings have aspects of both the divine masculine and the divine feminine within them and, ultimately, what we're all reaching for is integrating both fully within ourselves.

---

314 Albert Camus (1955). *"The Myth of Sisyphus and Other Essays."* Vintage Books

315 Because of how women have become masculinized over the last few generations, they may well find themselves going through these stages, especially if they have a high level career.

Male energy is outwards in its focus; in manifestation, in materialization, and in form. By setting goals and focusing on the prize, whatever that might be, and in acting from one's true nature and unique frequency, the divine masculine can bring about it's heart-dreaming and heart-purpose. This goes through several stages of development, and there is a divine inherent in each stage. In other words, it's not something that can only happen to a man having lived a full life.

~

Dreamers. Males in their first stage (boys) are dreaming of being swashbucklers (the next stage). They are interested in learning about the world and how it works, testing themselves to the point of destruction, reaching mastery over their bodies, jostling for status with their peers (mostly playfully), and fantasizing about life as an adult. Many boys (and younger men) spend a good deal of their time fantasizing about being superheroes. But it's not simply about having amazing powers. It's about learning how to control their power and have the responsibility in wielding it fairly for the greater good. The best superheroes (Batman, Spiderman) undergo an internal struggle with their past which, through reconciling and surmounting, makes them even stronger and more noble.

Swashbucklers. Swashbucklers live for the moment. There may still be some strings attached to their parents but, for the most part, they have finally become free agents. They live for adventure, for challenge, for conquest, and for what fun there is to be had. They are passionate and reckless and immature and irresponsible. Swashbucklers don't pick up their dirty laundry—they are who they are. Those who remain stuck in this stage and fail to grow up are the Peter Pans; the Puer Aeternus. Many modern men are stuck here because society has yet to convince them that there is something more worthy of their attention and struggles.

Pioneers. At this stage, men are characterized by an energetic investment of their time to build, establish, or carve out a place in the world for themselves. A swashbuckler has little direction in life (except for short term goals) but a pioneer starts to feel a compulsion to figure out where and how he might devote his energies in a more focused way. This means picking something (usually income-generating) and sticking with it. The question is what to pick? If his circumstances in life allow him to, and he doesn't just have to settle with what's available, this is hopefully in alignment with his core. Only by testing out his choice will he get the feedback (from his organism) to understand whether or not he's on the right path. And once he's happy with his choice, he may pick a woman who wants to go down that path with him (or wait until later when he has found "fame and fortune"). This stage can last many years until the man feels "he's arrived."

Mid-life crisis. Up until this time, a man has had relatively stable certainty about who he is and the direction he is taking. Not any more. He starts to question which parts of himself he left behind by his dedication to his path. Is he really so two-dimensional? Are his choices only two-dimensional? These, and many other existential questions, bombard him. Only...there is no "him" any more. He doesn't have a sense of who he is. He must reinvent himself through trial by fire. A fire within him that burns away redundant parts of himself and reveals other more promising aspects, so as to emerge phoenix-like from the ashes. Not all men pass through this stage (or it may be less personal and more spiritual). The more conscious, especially, those who never lost track of themselves, may progress to the next stage fairly easily.

The Boss. This is a man in his power. He may not be particularly powerful in life, or notable, or renowned, or even a boss. He *is* boss. He is fully possessed and grounded. It makes him wholly unlikely to behave inauthentically, as this would be inconsistent with his core. He may have to suck it up for a while with, say, an asshole business partner but this would draw down his reserves and he would place a renegotiation of the relationship at the top of his list, even if it hurts him financially. He has done his work in terms of how he sees the world, and opinions from others don't move him to change his mind—only proof that he is off track (should he be open to hear it). His life perspective, the result of his own internal and external inquiries and deliberations, has been forged by his own mind and is now "formed." It is iron-strong because he himself brought himself under his own command; no one else. Because he is so clear about himself, he doesn't "waste his time" with extraneous activities because they don't relate to who he is or what he wants to accomplish. They don't feed his soul. The Boss derives enormous satisfaction from providing value to others. Not just any sort of value—something that resonates from within that he is conscious of and wishes to honor and share. He is sharing part of himself.

Sages. At this stage in a man's life, he is more interested in contributing his gifts to the next generations than in finding and meeting challenges and embarking on adventures for himself (not that they disappear). A Sage is still fully in possession of himself, as he was as a Boss, but is less "penetrating" with his masculine essence. He is softer, calmer, more humble and equanamous, less interested in making change happen. He is more of a resource to others and, instead of actively providing his wisdom and personal qualities to them, will wait for them to search him out for input, insights, and advice. Even then, instead of giving direct answers, he might ask questions which, rather, lead them to find the truth for themselves.

No matter how old they become, men always have a boy or a swashbuckler in them waiting to emerge if the moment seems right.

~

The Divine Masculine, at whatever stage of his development, spends his time cultivating himself. He is committed to being effective in how he employs his talents long after the mood he decided them in has left him. He is strong, patient, stoic, capable, and accepting. He acts when he is able to and accepts the situation when he can't. He sees the wrong in the world but does not let it puncture his world, or personal domain. He also sees the wrong in himself which leads him into self-defeating patterns, and eradicates them. Once his mind is firmly secured by its rightful owner, he sets it to good use, as and when he feels his masculine nature compelling him to take on additional tasks, roles, responsibilities, projects, etc. He is able to do this because he cultivates his will, his strengths, and his capacities so as to refrain from becoming ineffective. He doesn't bite off more than he can chew, whether emotional, relational, physical, financial, or spiritual, etc. But if he does, he will readily unburden himself. He builds his inner and outer life, conquers his fears and foes, fails willingly, succeeds graciously, and constantly learns.

He has also integrated his feminine aspect. For example, his meditation is a practice of surrendering to the divine feminine within. In other words, a state of beingness which is receptive, formless, accepting of all that arises. Meditation is not a penetrative act.

Being divine seems to imply a certain state of perfection. Maybe that's true but I'm going to suggest that you don't need to be perfect to be divine. You just need rest in your own sense of self and what's important to you—your rightness/honor, owning what shit is yours to own, and being present with where you are at each moment, meeting yourself with clear non-judgmental yet discriminating acceptance. You say, "This is where I am. This is the wounding I carry having lived this life on this Earth, with these people, with this body, under these circumstances, with these evolving values and beliefs. This is how all of that it affects me in moments as they unfold. And knowing all this, I love and accept myself as perfectly imperfect; committing myself to stepping towards my higher self, however I might stumble." This philosophy can then be applied to any stage of a man's life.

You are perfect as you are, in other words, and there's always room for improvement.

Strategic, self-disciplined, discerning, precise, grounded, structured, rigorousness, authority (in its pure sense), form, action, directed, directness, responsibility, strength, focus, fatherhood, the sun, generosity/giving, encouragement, material abundance, clarity, intellect, transformation and growth.

52 Traits and Qualities

Holding space. Witnessing without judgment. These two additional traits allow "life to occur" in that space. It's like providing a blank canvas to an artist and making sure the wind doesn't blow it away by holding it steady. It's about allowing others to reach, develop, and express the fullness of their being without allowing one's own ego-needs to flavor the interaction. It's how a father plays ball with his child. How a lover may hold back his own orgasm to wait for her to reach hers. How an elder steps aside to allow someone younger to make a mistake (even when he knows what to do to avoid it) so that they learn for themselves. This is the ability of a man to stay steady with his own sense of being. This doesn't denote an inflexibility but rather indicates that, at this point on his timeline, he is fully in possession of himself and cannot be swayed or manipulated by others away from what he knows. He is in alignment with his personal code.

A man's power is in his mind—his perception, discernment, logic, reason, rationality, and intellect. When a man works with his feminine side, such as spontaneous creative energy, and combines it with his mind, intelligence is guiding creative energy as a form of expression. A man makes meaning out of his raw emotional energy through the application of his mind.

Wisdom is related to intelligence but there is not a direct correlation. There are plenty of smart guys who are dumb! A wise person is someone who can determine a pathway forward while weighing different truths to account for their importance in the full context of the circumstances. They've edited the information available. It takes wisdom to ignore simplistic explanations for a particular effect and point to something perhaps more counter-intuitive. Cognitive biases and logical fallacies, for example, can mask a truth which lies hidden behind an appealing fiction—it took a wise man to sniff them out.

Self-discipline permits a man to become a master and is his friend in his direction and path. It means being able to do something, even if he doesn't feel like doing it, when it's in alignment with his core values.

The masculine trait of strength is internal, rather than a feature of his muscles (a man might choose to work out and bulk up as compensation for a deficit of internal strength). Character strength is the ability to be unshakable without being rigid—when he has the courage of his convictions as well as the courage to challenge his convictions.

The trait of directness reflects knowing one's own mind and clearly revealing that to others. Not by being arrogant, belligerent, or overbearing. Being direct simply means being economical with one's words, to get to the point and not waffle. There is a simplicity, an elegance, in directness even when complex ideas are being expressed. When Emperor Joseph II complained to Mozart that there were "too many notes," in *The Abduction from the Seraglio,* Mozart replied, "There are just as many notes as there should be."[316] In other words, despite the complexity of his work, Mozart felt he was being direct—that there were just as many notes as required, neither more nor less.

Each man needs to find out what it is for him to align with at his core—what traits, masculine and feminine, can he embody and to what

316 Bernard, Andre; Fadiman, Clifton (2000). *"Bartlett's Book of Anecdotes."* Boston: Little, Brown.

extent. Adopting the traits of an alpha male, say, will certainly attract women. But if it's out of alignment with his true nature then all the pussy in the world will ultimately leave him feeling as though he's missed the boat. Accepting that he is never going to be a chick magnet might be part of him coming to back to himself, but only after having done the work of exploring alpha traits from his own perspective. He may challenge himself to be a leader. But if his capacity for first leading himself and then leading others doesn't much resonate with his core being, he needn't beat himself up about it. He just needs to realize himself fully for what he is, not for what he is not.

Ultimately, a man needs to be profoundly satisfied and deeply content with his own experience on his death-bed. He may have been dealt shitty cards in life but he played those cards to the best of his ability while remaining in alignment with his core essence.

A Man's Code of Honor

A man does what he must – in spite of personal consequences, in spite of obstacles and dangers and pressures – and that is the basis of all human morality.

– JOHN F. KENNEDY

A man's code of honor relates to what is most sacred to him and to what he devotes himself in honoring. It's his personal moral philosophy.

Honor is not something men are born with. It cannot be given but has to be earned. It can also be lost. To men, honor means doing the right thing in spite of how they feel. This puts men at odds with women, where doing the right thing often means honoring how they feel. For example, when a man meets the right woman, sometimes he'll even say to himself, "I'm not ready for her yet." He recognizes that there is something he needs to accomplish in his life before he is ready to commit to this particular woman, and may even sadly let her go to honor his path (or she may let him go because she can't wait until he's ready).

If you want to predict a man's behavior, find out what his opinions and positions are. Unlike a woman whose behavior can be predicted from her feelings, a man will not let his feelings get in the way of doing the right thing, as he sees it.

If I say that a woman is less honorable than a man, generally speaking, this may well be something a woman takes offense at. It's not that women are not honorable, it's just that men are more attuned to ethical (as opposed to moral) conduct than women. Men are less concerned with being socially correct. When women align themselves with strong men, bad boys, or even gangsters and mafiosi, they are less concerned with ethical behavior than with their personal safety and the ability of the man to access resources, through his domination of others. These particular men, though unethical, are better able to give these women what they want. More conscious and socially aware men recognize that this paradigm does not foster a healthy world in which both men and women as a whole can live in harmony. It's not that a man of honor is immune to his shadow aspects. But when he realizes he has committed a transgression, he will apologize for it and make amends. He is accountable. He rises above himself when he chooses to confront those shadow aspects that momentarily took the best of him. A conscious man will have a code of honor even if it disadvantages him, as the standards which govern his life will trump his more base desires. He can embrace the pain of personal failure through radical acceptance and vulnerability, denying nothing. It is the spiritual victory that matters more than the material one. To fight a good fight and die a good death. A good death follows a life lived honorably, which may mean living a truth outside of civilized norms.

How does a man of honor act virtuously when injustice is done to him? To quote Marcus Aurelius, "The best way of avenging thyself is not to become like the wrongdoer." Those with more power may determine the circumstances in which we find ourselves but our mind remains our own. We are always free to make choices even if some choices suck. A man's code is to "show those qualities then which are altogether in thy power—sincerity, gravity, endurance of labor, aversion to pleasure, contentment with thy portion, and with few things, benevolence, frankness, no love of superfluity, freedom from trifling, magnanimity...Free yourself from imaginary constraints and see how every trial becomes an opportunity for virtue and purposeful action."[317]

These are qualities, or energies that can be embodied by any particular man and may be prioritized or colored differently from one man to the next. Sometimes a man might die or suffer greatly in standing in his truth. But, to a man of honor, it's better to die at someone else's hands than by his own, should he abandon his code simply in order to make his life easier.

A Man's Purpose

There is nothing noble in being superior to your fellow man.
True nobility lies in being superior to your former self.

— ERNEST HEMINGWAY

A man's purpose in life is to put into practice the potential he has developed/is developing, based firmly on the truth of his nature and his core principles. He needs to feel like a person of worth in a world of meaning. A man who chooses to "go with the flow" is living in his feminine essence. This is not a bad thing when it is in alignment with his own deep impulses of Being, and at certain times in his life when it is profitable to his wellbeing. Most men who go with the flow, however, are signaling their spirituality for the approval of others when, in fact, they are aimlessly drifting and allowing things into their life which don't serve them. They profess their desire to accept the moment and what it has to offer without employing any discriminating awareness.

Conscious men with a purpose have a vision for what they want from life. They are self-determined. They are, in the best sense, a law unto themselves. They choose their own path, direction, mission, and destiny. A man "is concerned with something out there in the world; is concerned with someone out there in the world—a work to do, a job to complete, a

317 Marcus Aurelius (1997). *"Meditations."* Dover Publications. 1997.

task, a meaning, a mission in life waiting for him."[318] He knows he needs to develop and apply a degree of focus, competency, and effort to make his ambitions more than just a dream. On his journey from Dreamer to Sage, his vision and direction will change according to the fulfillment, sense of achievement, and satisfaction it brings him.

Innate in masculinity seems to be the desire to have an impact in life. Is there a way to be heroic? To make a difference? To help others? To provide a service or deliver a solution? To be the cavalry and save the day? What is the victory of life? Some believe that you can't claim to have lived a life of purpose until you have improved the world in some way. The service you give to life has to raise a portion of the earth. The calling for men is to give the gift that resides in their hearts, in a practical way, with practical solutions. A conscious man's path is not a retreat from action into passive acceptance—it commences in the heart and moves to a fire in his belly. So that he can look skyward and cry, "I am here! And I am here to win victory!"

318 Viktor Frankl, in interview.

If what you are wanting is overall wellbeing and happiness within the relationship, the choice of who to partner with must be a multi faceted choice and a conscious choice, not a compulsive one…it will be an exhale, a relief and relaxation… It will feel like coming home…[319]

— TEAL SWAN

53 Getting Ready for Divine Union

The well-rounded, conscious man who embraces all aspects of himself—his shadow and light, his masculine and feminine—is a man who can have positive essential qualities and also make space for other men and women to have those same qualities. His level of self-authorship has enabled him to provide to a woman those aspects of himself which permit her to relax, unfold, and blossom.

The first point to bear in mind is what value do men find in being with a woman? This is a question a conscious man must ask himself and is obviously specific to the individual. Clearly the presence of sex, intimacy and possible offspring are key motivators but, in their absence, what value would she add to his life? Unless he has answered, to the satisfaction of his own mind and heart, what he is looking for in a relationship, he must continue to act from unconscious desires. How will he know that she is capable of the kind of loving work that he wants to do? How will he assess

319 Teal Swan. "*Attraction (Why You Are Attracted To The People You're Attracted To).*" https://tealswan.com/resources/articles/attraction-why-you-are-attracted-to-the-people-youre-attracted-to-r375/

how skillful she is at compassionate relating or how willing to learn?[320] Does she still exist for herself when he is talking or does she constantly interrupt to assert her own talking points? Is she someone who is looking to discover him, ask questions about him, probe, and resonate herself with him? When he shows her his vulnerabilities, is she comfortable and interested and lets him know that he's safe in her hands? If she lies about little things, is she also going to lie about bigger things? Do they agree to create an environment in which they are both willing to explore and mine the cave of shadows together, carefully and compassionately? How will he set the stage for this to happen? It can turn into a mudslide if either clings to their dysfunctions or relates unskillfully. Does he have boundaries? Is he willing to let her go if she ignores them?

What does he do internally to get himself ready to be in a relationship with this highly evolved female? What aspects of his character does he have shame around? What elements of his personality are not serving him? Has he tamed his inner critic? Is he honorable? Is he radically honest with himself? Does he have clarity or confusion? Has he largely integrated his shadow side? Has he mostly decommissioned his conditioned ego? Is he able to express his essential being without fear of judgment or inner resistance? Has he gained insights from the past, can plan for the future, and can live in the present (which I would call wisdom)? Has he fessed up yet and forgiven himself his failings? Can he ask for forgiveness from others when he realizes that he has transgressed upon them? Does he want to constantly be the light that helps reveal his lover to herself? Her rock?

The list could go on. All told, there is ever an opportunity to become the best version of himself, even if this woman never materializes. If she does though, can he reveal to her that he has done his work and has the character to be trusted? That his actions outwardly and truly reflect the

320 Recommend authors are:
Stan Tatkin, thepactinstitute.com
John Gottman, gottman.com
Keith Witt, drkeithwitt.com
Alison Armstrong, alisonarmstrong.com
Dr. Sue Johnson, drsuejohnson.com
David Deida, deida.info
among many others.

authentic man he's become? His opinion of himself is more important than the credence he gives to a woman's opinion about himself.

If this sounds like you, may you be inspired to recognize her when you see her! Remain aware of what you need so that, when she does come along, you recognize her and feel the freedom to take action on what is before you. In other words, have good game.[321] Only push where something is going to move. If it doesn't then let it go. If it will, push at the point where it moves the most. Then sit inside of the question, "What can we become?"

The conscious man needs to be ready to be loved by a divine woman because she sees more in him than any woman ever has. She can love him with a depth approaching the infinite that his whole being has longed for.

Claim yourself so that you can claim her, as complete in your own true nature as you can muster.

---

321 Recommended are:
James Marshal, thenaturallifestyles.com
Dan Bacon, themodernman.com

Sex is an emotion in motion.

—MAE WEST

54 Sex and Relationships

Part of living with integrity and from the heart is to come into alignment with his core essence, which fully embraces both the masculine and feminine within him. A man in his divine essence is unconcerned with "becoming more masculine" or manly for the purpose of attracting a woman. He wants to be the best version of himself, present *that* best version to the world, and draw into his life women who are attracted to his own unique expression of himself. He is certain about himself. Resolved. Comfortable in his own skin.

Whilst women are the gatekeepers of sex (she gets the final say on whether it happens), men are the gatekeepers of relationships. For many men, the central meaning in their lives is their woman. For the divine masculine, this is unlikely to be the case—she is *a* central aspect but not *the* central aspect. Yet men derive renewal and energy merely from the presence of a contented woman for whom he cares. She need only be vibrant and happy for him to receive what might be considered nurture. She need not even be focused towards him but happily be doing her own thing. What she values most in a man is his sense of certainty and safety which gives her the opportunity to live most fully in her feminine aspect. The trick is to care about her while not caring what she thinks.

How much work has he done? How equanamous can he be in the face of irrationality, criticism, reproach, willful delusion, drama, shit tests, condescension, contempt, or any other form of relational aggression? If you're like me, no one ever warned you about wounded women (see *Wounded Women,* chapter, *Modern Women*). If a man is wanting to experience a sense of wellbeing and happiness within a relationship, he must consciously (as opposed to compulsively) screen out some women and choose others with that purpose in mind.

At the center of his relationship must be his masculine core values. At the edge of these are his boundaries—things he won't tolerate in a relationship and, at which point, he walks. No matter how many fine qualities she may possess, no matter how much he likes, loves, and lusts after her, a conscious man's first duty of care is to his own value system (based unalterably on his true nature). Another name for this is self-respect. Needless to say, he will have spent much time and effort deconstructing and reconstructing himself to rest in this place of certainty—a certainty which is paradoxically open to change when new insights are revealed. She is free to leave—or choose a different type of relationship with him. That's not to say that there isn't any give and take in the relationship. In fact, neither gets their way every time but each is sensitive and attuned to the level of need in the other and it's degree of strength or urgency. Each person's needs are mostly balanced with their partner's for most of the time (although they may ebb and flow). And neither party is covertly angling to get more than the other.

Our intimate relationships are most often the ones which cause us the most conflict. Despite the joy they may bring, they also bring us face to face with our deepest emotional pain and woundings. And because society provides to men little guidance or support as to how to journey through these dark tunnels, it is at this point that many relationships crumble (see *The Practice of Love*, chapter, *The Divine Union*).

Being aware of the consequences for a man in today's world, in the post-#MeToo era, means recognizing that he could be ruined through the choice of woman he associates with. It's never been quite so dangerous to have the wrong woman in his life. He could have everything he's worked for stripped away; his children placed in the hands of an ex-wife who might poison their impressionable minds against him, and half his shit filling up her new condo. This is not hyperbole, this is a daily occurrence for many good men. The Divine Masculine has a firm understanding of such a reality and adjusts accordingly.

Most relationships have a shelf life. In the end, trying to preserve a long-term relationship at all costs is not the answer, especially when the man finds himself trying to wring out any last drops of positive connection—when the relationship is no longer capable of regenerating the loving energy it needs. When that is the case, it's probably time to move on. It's more productive to have the attitude of improving his relationship skills with another (and with himself in relation to another), opening his heart, and taking each day as an opportunity to expand himself and his beloved. Quality rather than quantity is the theme.

~

If a man in his divine essence has done his spiritual work—integrating past traumas around any mother and father wounds, any shame or guilt he carries about his masculinity, has fully reclaimed his sexual energy, and has connected to his purpose—the way he interacts with his woman is transformed. If he has connected with his essence, with why he is on the planet, with what he is here to do and bring, with his passion for life, his sex with her is *only* in the context of the fullness of his being. In a sense, he is a law unto himself because his integrity is priceless—it cannot be bought or bent.

The secret to great sex is in the way a man treats his lover—as if she were his lover for life, even if the meeting is casual. He meets her without fear and with an internal commitment to meet her with all of his heart, presence, and body. Resonance is the unspoken discourse of intercourse. Pure, passionate, deep, healing, love-making. His orgasm is a prayer which singles her out, in a moment of clear ecstasy, as the divine recipient of every ounce of his being. Just for her. She surrenders to his focused attention. Such an experience is hard to convey in words.

Part Nine

The Divine Union

Oh, the comfort, the inexpressible comfort of feeling safe with a person; having neither to weigh thoughts nor measure words, but to pour them all out, just as they are, chaff and grain together, knowing that a faithful hand will take and sift them, keep what is worth keeping, and then, with a breath of kindness, blow the rest away.[322]

– DINAH MARIA MULOCK CRAIK

Because we live in a universe based on duality and polarities, we experience a certain melancholia of feeling separate. Knowing ourselves as separate, we reach for connection. When we think we've met The One, we

322 Dinah Maria Mulock Craik (2010). "*A Life For A Life.*" Nabu Press

experience a form of liberation from our own singularity—no longer are we condemned to walk through life alone. Yet connection seems insanely problematic. Why is it so hard for human beings to make relationships work? Why do they often end up as a "battle for your soul?" When we start a relationship of any kind with another human being, it generally starts out well enough. Good will towards the other greases the wheels. Yet inevitably there are bumps in the road when either the relationship ends, continues poorly, or differences are resolved and the air is cleared. With long-term relationships, this can and does happen again and again. And at any time there may be an obstacle too large to overcome, and the relationship ends. A lot of people simply don't know how to make them work and yet they are the fabric of human existence. In this chapter, I hope to offer some insights as to how to develop high-level relationship skills and mindsets. Beyond that, I hope to shed light on the way to reinvigorate intimate partnerships by approaching them as sacred paths.

This disconnect between individual and group interests helps explain why the shift to agriculture is normally spun as a great leap forward, despite the fact that it was actually a disaster for most of the individuals who endured it.[323]

— CHRISTOPHER RYAN AND CACILDA JETHA

55 Growing up Together

Evolutionary psychology attempts to explain how men and women have co-evolved. Here's the story so far:

Through natural selection/mating strategies, men selected certain kinds and types of women they desired. And vice versa. Those lucky winners then passed down those traits generation by generation. Men and women would meet, be attracted to one another at a sexual, emotional, and chemical level, which mother nature facilitated by washing the brain with hormones and chemicals (adrenaline, testosterone, estrogen, dopamine, serotonin, oxytocin, and vasopressin) to get the two procreating.

Men are the way they are because women found certain traits appealing. For example, it's thought that women selected men for their hunting prowess to provide for themselves and their offspring which favored traits such as height, aggression, and spacial awareness (accurately perceiving their prey's movements and their own kinesthetic awareness in their pursuit).

323 Christopher Ryan and Cacilda Jethá (2014). "Sex at Dawn." Harper.

Female gametes are eggs which are large but few in number. Male gametes are sperm which are smaller but numerous. This puts a higher premium on those "fitter" male gametes selected for the available female gametes—essentially a buyer's market. The thought is that females are, consciously or unconsciously, selecting those gametes which would offer her offspring a greater chance of future survival. She selects the best mate she can find which would include his ongoing contribution to her and her child's wellbeing. The naked ape with the biggest ju-ju got the most bananas. The suggestion is that these choices are made at an individual level between males and females considering copulation.

But since we are a hypercooperative species, and since we know that in hunter-gatherer societies men and women freely engaged with each other in relative sexual promiscuity, my hypothesis is that natural selection (by Mother Nature, not by humans) was made at the group level. Evolutionary fitness would then be determined by how effective each tribe was in meeting the demands of its environment. Selection took place at the level of the group rather than individual. If the individuals in one tribe, born of the ubiquitous sexual choices made therein, were collectively "unfit" to survive, then the whole tribe would be effectively removed from the gene pool. So we have competition (in the evolutionary sense) between groups/tribes of humans rather than between individual men and women in those tribes, hoping to maximize their potential to produce future offspring.

Since our co-evolution has also been shaped culturally, as well as our biological drives shaping culture itself, it all becomes very messy.

Since the dawn of civilization, getting in-laws has been one of marriage's most important functions.[324]

— STEPHANIE COONTZ

56 The History of Unions

One of the problems that men and women are encountering at this stage in their co-evolution is that we've achieved our biological objectives. In terms of procreation, there are plenty of humans on the planet. More won't make things better. In terms of men creating a world in which women are protected and provided for, technically speaking (even if there is no political will to do so) we can now provide a good standard of living for every family living. We don't because it would undermine the global market economy. Yet never has there been a time when women were so cared for materially. In very limited terms, we have achieved our objectives. Women can no longer fully celebrate their role as being 'God's creator on Earth.' It's not really as big a deal as it used to be historically—7.7 billion people now compared to 1.9 billion, only a hundred years ago.

In the past-however-long, coupledom in the form of marriage was primarily an economic arrangement without any particular commitment to intimacy. Because we have more choice about what we bring into our lives—where we live, which community, which employer, which partner(s)—we are no longer confined by norms of the past. We can choose

324 Stephanie Coontz (May 19, 2005). *"Marriage, a History: From Obedience to Intimacy or How Love Conquered Marriage."* Viking Adult.

who to be with. But this brings with it concerns and anxieties. We are now struggling to transform coupledom into a higher-order arrangement with greater degrees of emotional, sexual, mental, and spiritual connectedness. Sex is no longer mainly about procreation. It has become the property of the self, a skill to be developed, and a way we define ourselves. We've brought love into unions, and sex into love.

Judging from the higher rate of break-ups, this is no easy task. Whether its possible or not, we are engaging with all aspects of our beingness in and through an intense union with another—a mechanism for expanding our consciousness through love. Perhaps we are struggling to reintroduce those aspects of our humanity which had been lost to the sands of time? A more innocent age? Or a more conscious one?

The concept of marriage itself is struggling because of the expectation that one person can fulfill all the roles that were previously part of tribal social dynamics more broadly. We expect sexual satisfaction to be provided by just one person. We want commitment, and family life, and social status, and economic support provided by just one person. We want that person to be our best friend and trusted confidante. We want them to meet our needs for security and stability, yet also meet our needs for stimulation and adventure. We want reliability and predictability, but also novelty and spontaneity. These needs arise naturally from within and pull us in different directions at different times yet we try to harmonize them within one relationship.

In a practical sense, men and women come from "constructs" which involve relational patterns, developmental orientation (straight, gay, etc), unconscious influences and trauma patternings. Yet neither men nor women enter a relationship expecting anything other than happy relating.

When people are ready to, they change. They never do it before then, and sometimes they die before they get around to it. You can't make them change if they don't want to, just like when they do want to, you can't stop them.

— ANDY WARHOL

57 Types of non-Divine Relationships

The sensory relationship. In this relationship, a man is more focused on adventure, challenge, conquest, and fun. This is also where the participants are more focused on the physical side of the relationship, of doing fun things together, perhaps a little romance, but heavily weighted towards having sex. They're interested in the heat of a passionate relationship—the fire and sparks, the vitality of it. There is a chase for erotic polarity and dopamine hits. Although superficial, these relationships are a hell of a lot of fun while there's fun to be had—there is an intense feeling of aliveness and living in the present. The polarity of self and other is at its most pronounced.

There is some codependence but the bonds of codependency are not particularly strong. They're also are usually short-lived, lasting for a few months once that "new car smell" goes away, often ending explosively, and often with the participants diving right into the next sensory relationship.

The growth relationship. Here the participants have reached a level where they've become interested in their responses, patterns, and perceived deficits in relationships and (mostly unawarely) see the other as a potential teacher in transcending those issues. The couple often has unrealistic expectations of their partner and expect them to be a certain way or meet certain needs. They may be constantly angling to get their way, sometimes by battling, sometimes by tripping over themselves to be a nice guy or a good girl to get their prize. The principle purpose is to find a new inner equilibrium, calibrating their inner masculine and feminine essences as well as attuning to the inner masculine and feminine essences of their partner. New ways of being and relating are adopted or rejected, not just with the other but also with themselves. The polarity of self and other is still intact, though a little softer.

There are strong bonds of codependence but, rather than dopamine, the drug of choice for this style of relationship is oxytocin (which promotes safety and bonding). These relationships can last many years but may become stale and mundane. As mirrors for each other, lessons are learned and, at some stage, one or the other reaches a point where no more learning takes place and the relationship dissolves or dies on its feet.

The partnership relationship. Participants here are more fully integrated and have reached a level of appreciation and respect for themselves and their beloved. They are highly attuned to themselves, their partner, and the forces and factors which surround them. They are able to recognize their reactivities and surf the waves of their emotions when triggered by their beloved, and more primitive drives have been reconciled, either internally or through communication with the other. They are able to quickly reconnect with themselves, become present, and self-soothe. Self-control rather than repression is the order of the day.

There is a patience and acceptance that flows around them and a confidence in allowing the process of partnership to unfold at its own pace. Reciprocity flows freely. Each person's needs and desires are energetically balanced with the other's.

This is an inter-dependent relationship based on peaceful, mutual benefit and trust. Their reliance on external forces (children, family, home, etc) are of lesser importance to the personal connection which bonds them. There is generally less polarity in this relationship because the couple's inner worlds have taken precedence over the physical, and they have moved more towards each other psychologically, creating safety rather than excitement. The couple is both comfortable apart and together—they're neither threatened by intimacy nor by fears of being abandoned. There is little clinging nor discomfort about being close. Forgiveness comes easily as they give their partner the benefit of the doubt in their intentions for the other's well-being. Sex is holistic—a synchrony of the physical, emotional, and spiritual. Compassionate communication is the norm.

Creating the sacred balance. Growing the bonds of intimacy.[325]

58 The Divine Union

The vertex of the Divine Union is a place of deep knowing where both recognize they are with their "rightful" partner. There is a connection to "that in each other" which is—and was already and always complete. It is a part of their true nature which is neither evolving nor improving but reflects the beloved's deepest essence. It's a shared-heart relationship of true intimacy where the interests of the other are of equal importance to the interests of the self. It's almost literally their other half, or opposite half—themselves reflected as the opposite sex.

This is a relationship between more than just two personalities—it is between two souls. Harmful or challenging aspects of the personality which intrude into the relationship are regarded as separate from the soul connection itself—they don't get in the way. The relationship rests at this deeper level.

This couple is completely unbreakable. This is a dependent relationship. A consort relationship.[326] They are dependent on each other in the sense that they are so much better together than they would be alone,

325 Intimacy can be defined as a familiarity in union, founded on seeing the other for who they are and accepting them as they are. Both partners trust in the other in regards to physical, psychological and emotional safety and concern.

326 A consort is one who catalyzes in us, by her loving presence, key aspects of our humanity which we would have a hard time doing so by our own efforts.

even though they would be fine alone. There is a symbiosis created that serves them both better than they could otherwise serve themselves. Their individual qualities based in masculine wisdom and feminine wisdom combine into a whole, larger than the sum of its parts. This then lends itself to a creative force which can be used in the service of others. Just as there is a celebration of true intimacy, it doesn't remain as a divine couple-bubble but is turned outwards in service of people or planet or existence itself, in big ways or small.

There is an inherent sense of ease and graciousness in the relationship because both are committed to watching out for the other's best interests. Both can relax knowing they are safe in the other's hands. "If what you are wanting is overall wellbeing and happiness within the relationship, the choice of who to partner with must be a multi faceted choice and a conscious choice, not a compulsive one. The way you will experience the relationship with that other person within in your own body is that it will be an exhale, a relief and relaxation in your body. It will feel like coming home as opposed to an inhale, a tension and an excited craving."[327]

In the divine union, neither gives up aspects of themselves in order to mold themselves into the perfect mate. Each brings out the fullness and totality of their organisms—the animal and the divine, and their authentic natures. Neither needs to subtract from their true nature in order to hide, mask, disown, or appease. The question of one partner reducing themselves for the comfort of the other never even emerges. They are celebrated rather than tolerated.

327 Teal Swan. *"Attraction (Why You Are Attracted To The People You're Attracted To)."* https://tealswan.com/resources/articles/attraction-why-you-are-attracted-to-the-people-youre-attracted-to-r375/

We come to love not by finding the perfect person, but by learning to see an imperfect person perfectly.

— SAM KEEN

59 What is Love?

Why does True Love appeal to us so much? Why does it have such a strong appeal? When we love we want to merge our self with another self. When we desire love, we want a relationship-bridge leading to somebody we can rendezvous with on the other side. The entertainment industry has long-realized it had a sure winner in putting this scenario in front of us—from romantic novels (a $1.5 billion/year industry), to chick flicks, Romeo and Juliet, and you-are-the-one love songs. At one level, we know we are being presented with a fantasy. At another, the reality is that this feeling of love is woven into the fabric of our existence. It feels real.

But those who rely on their feelings to generate action are at the mercy of an inner substance that ebbs and flows.

Love is primarily an action. It's a combination of two purposes—"I want to understand [this person]" and "I want to care for [this person]." When these are fused together, love means taking the other person's best interests as your own—their best interests, in practice, as having no less nor more importance than your own. The feeling of love, the warm fuzzies of the heart, are not to be disparaged but are concomitant to the action of love.

Romantic love is all about the feeling of love. Here, the action of love follows the feeling. We start by being carried away by a sea of love-chemicals, by our hearts, and by our hopes. The world suddenly seems brighter, cleaner, and more optimistic as the other person's singular presence awakens us from the mundane. Love reveals itself when something is profoundly evoked in our core, a powerful and mesmerizing force, simply though being in the presence of another. Sometimes we meet someone who checks all the boxes but does not move us to love. At other times, we meet someone wholly unsuitable but who sends our hearts a-reelin.' Love doesn't care about being sensible or wise but, like a child, may step into the road with no mind for oncoming traffic.

The feeling of love draws in the beloved. She is infused into our body, into our own Beingness, just like tea in hot water—gently permeating and gracing plain water with flavor and color. To stretch the analogy, there is a recognition by both water and tea that they can experience a transformation by mixing themselves with each other, to merge, to know a sweetness of existence never before known, an aliveness that transcends the mundane. When fully steeped, they know each other as One. This is why we have fear in love relationships, as well as joy. What if we are imbibing something toxic rather than nourishing? It's the ego's job to keep us safe—to separate ourselves from that which may harm us. It's Love's job to expand us—to unify and integrate within ourselves all aspects of reality, regardless of the harm it may do. Life is the dance between the two.

A supreme challenge of human life is reconciling the longing to fulfill ourselves in union, in partnership, in love, with the urgency of fulfilling ourselves according to our own solitary and sovereign laws.

— D.H.LAWRENCE

60 The Practice of Love

A relationship with an intimate partner can throw into relief what it means to be masculine or feminine, what it's like to be alive to another's nature, and compels us to investigate and connect with our own aliveness more profoundly. It's like an enthoegenic trip—one which can shoot us into hyperspace or which can bring demons racing towards us. It can knock down walls which prevent us from coming into our powers and potentials. Or leave us bleeding as we knock our heads against them. As relationships become more evolved and conscious, so too do each other's shadow aspects become more evident—and more welcomed. In order for them to see the light of day, these shadows need to be met with unconditional but critical acceptance. The fears, annoyances, and difficulties that are catalyzed in the presence of another are embraced as essential components to love's path.

After the expansive honeymoon phase of a relationship, difficult emotions get stirred up as the couple's competing needs begin to manifest with some urgency. It feels like something is going wrong with the relationship, and maybe they shouldn't even be in that relationship. Suddenly all the expectations of a life filled with light and love are thrown into question by the very person with whom they envisioned such a life. "Now, if only they could change into who and what we want them to be! Be the sort of person we want them to be! Get with the program!" Suddenly all that forward progress comes to a stop and the deep-seated needs that had been lying dormant and desperate start to assert themselves. What has happened is that an attachment to the divine aspects of love has captured the ego.

We bring to a relationship all the conditioned aspects of our nature that have not yet been integrated—our worries and concerns, likes and dislikes, and a slew of personal needs. Love is a spiritual path precisely because it reveals both the angels and the demons of our nature. Our hearts seem to expand and burst upon the world, only to fall earthward in a death spiral.

But we don't have to crash and burn.

An essential attribute of this new relating style is to allow both lovers to be the aegis[328] of each other's shadow aspects. Their role is neither to sit in judgment nor ignore, enable, condone, or mollify. They are an empathizer who holds in sacred trust the wounds of their lover and tends them with gentle medicine, without allowing their beloved to bypass their own inner work. As emotionally charged as some moments might be, each person is at peace with what arises.

This work is not for the faint-of-heart. It requires willingness, commitment, and effort simply as starting points. Having the mindset that strong emotions will inevitably be aroused by the beloved, and will be for the rest of their lives, means that the relationship will not automatically be derailed when they do. And they will arise. So a conversation needs to be had before the first one appears, even in its mildest form—the mildest disappointment. So that the work of conscious relating can begin, when all ample good will is still present, to prepare the ground and set the standard.

Imagine taking divorce (or break up) off the table. Imagine using the time you would have spent doing something of personal interest,

328 The modern concept of doing something "under someone's aegis" means doing something under the protection of a powerful, knowledgeable, or benevolent source.

instead on someone you find interesting. It's not that you are bound to those choices, in reality, but mentally etching them in stone gives you a different mindset. It also requires developing certain inner resources to meet love's journey, such as clarity, forgiveness, charity, and bravery. The ability to self-reflect without illusion, denial, suppression, or repression, and the ability to hold space for the other is essential for a couple's evolution. The ability of walking towards our pain, rather than running from it, and experiencing it as it is. It's about embracing the totality of our unwanted experiences. Of course, only masochists enjoy feeling pain. But to be informed by pain that emerges from a relationship is to offer oneself to the process of continuous improvement in the service of oneself and the beloved.

Being a conscious man following this path is to be a warrior of love. When he can sit in his pain and allow his awareness to rest with it gently and with tender benevolence, the body knows what to do. By surrendering his pain to forces he cannot conceptualize, he begins to experience relief, then strength, then stability. If his woman allows him to process his pain with gentle acceptance, cradled in her love, he can then fully integrate it all. By managing her fear as he crumbles before her, she gets to have the man of her dreams as he arises from his own ashes.

The process is both somatic and cognitive. By courageously questioning himself with gentleness (i.e, not beating himself up), he gives voice and energy to his organism for an answer to emerge. One process is by using RAIN—Recognize, Allow, Investigate, Nurture.[329] He then lets go an expectation of a reply. Maybe he'll get an answer there and then. Maybe in the shower. Maybe when he goes to pee. Insights usually emerge when invited, not demanded.

While it may seem I'm advocating complete honesty in expressing painful feelings as soon as they occur, there is nuance here. What's not often emphasized in a relationship is "timing." Sometimes it's healthier to sit with one's own experience, bringing attention to it, and fully flushing

329 Tara Brach (2019). *"Radical Compassion: Learning to Love Yourself and your World with the Practice of RAIN."* Penguin Life. Also: https://tarabrach.ac-page.com/rain-pdf-download

it out before authentically expressing it, having achieved a greater understanding. If every moment is an opportunity for venting or self-revelation, it's also an opportunity to overwhelm and exhaust our partner. Because, before all the other desirable elements of a relationship, surely the most important is to be expanded by the simple joy of just being with each other? What is the point of being in a relationship if you're neither adored nor adoring?

The dance between the Infinite and the Finite (see *Unity Consciousness,* chapter, *Conclusion*) occurs with the practice of love. We neither want to be so in love with love that we have our heads in the clouds, nor do we want our relationship to be so entirely earthbound and arduous that we never again touch blissful union. We neither want to be proud, solitary, and wild nor meekly domesticated. Mature love is to stand in paradox.

It is honoring each other's incompleteness whilst at the same time celebrating the struggles each lover engages with to remove the obstacles to the full expression of their true natures. "You are perfect as you are, and there's always room for improvement," as the Zen saying goes. What is represented is a profound alliance for mutual wellbeing. If I'm being cute, it's like being your football team's biggest fan, as they continue to struggle with divisional aspirations.

The red-hot minute.

61 Triggers and Reactions in Relationships

The red-hot minute refers to that moment when something gets said or done that quickly escalates one or both people into a state of hyperarousal. When a couple is simply reactive in a relationship, nothing positive happens for the most part.

When we become upset and it's out of proportion to what is happening in the here and now, this is an almost certain indicator that there is a negative procedural memory that was formed by trauma. It enters into our state of being without it being consciously tagged as "this is coming from the past." It often doesn't bring up pictures like a flashback. All that is brought up is a heightened emotional state without determinable past reference points.

Your partner may catalyze certain angry feelings in you and the temptation may be to punish her with cruel words. If you can do so calmly, share that temptation with her! But reassure her that you're owning this temptation and that you're mature enough to safeguard the integrity of the relationship. Ask yourself if you can be kind. If the answer is no, then don't say anything. Or say it in a different way. Loving kindness doesn't mean that you don't express your anger but that kindness informs how you choose to express it. You can throw daggers at her. Or you can explain why you're hurt and angry, taking ownership for what's yours. If you're too fired up, wait until you aren't and start to integrate your experience through taking a walk, working out, or journaling, or whatever works for you, in order to parent yourself from the inside out and be in a place of receptivity when you reconnect with your beloved. Of course, it's easy for me to say...

Equally, if you are expressing that pain, behaving respectfully, and owning your shit, the worst thing she can do is preemptively lash out at you, offense being the best defense. Or else break the connection and distance herself through fear. This is a big one for women whose operating system is fear-based. Can she sit with your anger while you express it *without* the intention of wounding her? Intentional wounding is how we arrived in this fucked up place over the course of history. This doesn't mean squishing pain but it does mean avoiding turning pain into a weapon.

It's important that we learn to regulate states of arousal, like fear, emotional shut down, and anger, so that we aren't totally dependent on our partners. But at the same time a healthy relationship also involves what's called co-regulation. This is the "warm and responsive interactions that provide support and that help someone understand, express, and modulate his or her feelings, thoughts, and behaviors."[330] The most important role a partner can play in a relationship is signaling safety. When the nervous system is triggered, it needs to resolve itself back to a baseline of ease and well-being. By holding space for when our partner has been captured by a threat response, they will feel more capable of negotiating that reaction for themselves in the future.

Or how about if you are feeling anxious, unsettled, or fearful? Can you ride the waves of your emotions to let her know what you're going through and ask her to please hold you? If she is in a relatively composed state herself, then she would most likely want to offer that to you. Her ability to be there to offer you external regulation then translates into an increased ability for you to regulate yourself when a similar state emerges in the future. So what's going on is that certain procedural memories are

330 Beth Newton (February 12, 2019). *"Moving From Misattunement to Coregulation."* The PACT Institute. https://www.thepactinstitute.com/blog/moving-from-misattunement-to-coregulation

being transformed by the benign and loving influence of the beloved, something many men and women may have failed to receive in their formative years from their primary caregivers. This co-regulation enhances and secures the relationship. Many women have been asking for this kind of vulnerability from men. But when push comes to shove, can she suffer the temporary loss of her confidant manly-man? An emotional rock of a man is profoundly reassuring to the female psyche around whom her emotional waves can crash and roil without knocking him off balance. She doesn't want an emotional brick wall as traditional males had exhibited. But is she evolved enough to stand in her own strength when he is not able to?

Beware of those women who weaponize trauma. It's a sneaky tactic used during heated exchanges to claim that a man is abusing her verbally. By playing the victim and essentially throwing an adult tantrum, she can seize the moral high ground and place you in the role of perpetrator. By eliciting a sympathetic response, the hope is that you'll then apologize so that you know you're the bad guy here. It's another way of avoiding being accountable to herself for her own set of issues.

I agree that it's important to have healthy boundaries and to recognize the fear that might arise in the form of "punishment-by-disconnection" subsequent to verbalizing those boundaries. The trouble is, this punishment aspect is often the default response by others. Our world is so fragmented and the separation paradigm so entrenched that speaking up for oneself and sharing one's needs is perceived as an obstacle to the other person's contentment aspirations. Clear and compassionate communication often doesn't work in a world of walking wounded.

I love you not only for what you are, but for what I am when I am with you.

– ROY CROFT

62 Dependency

In traditional relationships, the woman dedicated herself to her man. She supported him emotionally, and did the cooking, cleaning, and homemaking. He was dependent on her for these things and she was dependent on him to protect and provide for her. Both were in survival mentality, though, and neither could get their needs met fully. Both felt constricted by their roles. They took care of each other at the end of the barrel of a gun, so to speak. In this post-feminist world, both men and women are going their own way, claiming independence from each other, or else warring with each other within a relationship. Neither is dependent on the other. Neither dedicates themselves to each other. Both are alone together.

Yet dependency in a relationship can be a good thing. In nature, many creatures are dependent on each other for their wellbeing, which we call symbiosis. For example, a bee pollinates a plant by transferring pollen (benefiting the plant) and the plant provides nectar which the bee uses as a food source, honey (benefiting the bee colony/keeper). We don't characterize them as being "excessively dependent" on one another, even though they are. They caretake each other. Even within our own bodies, we have a mutual relationship with our microorganisms (such as gut bacteria). We are dependent on them for our health. It's my contention that men and women also do much better in life by being mutually dependent, even "excessively dependent." When we hear the term "dependency" in the context of a relationship, we automatically think of "codependency." This, in itself, is instructive because it underlines how distanced and antagonistic men and women have become from each other. A codependent relationship is where there are one or more wounded people hoping unconsciously the other will fix them in some way—where they are unconsciously trying to heal from the abuses of childhood.

But here's the nuance.

It's okay to be dependent on someone to help you heal, as long as she is comfortable doing so, it enhances her life, and it's not a cop-out for you doing your own work. Doing it consciously, rather than unconsciously, is the key difference. The corrective experience is the adult coming into his agency in lieu of the child who had little.

The phrase, "you complete me," is usually taken to indicate an unhealthy dependence on another where one is lacking or deficient. A lot of human beings have a felt sense that there is this one person "out there" who would complete them. The feeling itself is entirely natural (just as the feeling of love is common to all humans), although today it mostly springs from a wounded heart. In the context of a codependent relationship, "you complete me" patches over the cracks and underscores the personal work that was never done.

But when two fully integrated and self-possessed people meet each other in intimacy, it doesn't mean that they have little need for the other. They need completion with "that which they are not"—that which does make them whole. That which completes the circuit. North and South complete each other—they are dependent on each other. Neither are deficient. They are excessively dependent on each other to reveal to themselves their positive and negative aspects (in the magnetic sense). Looking for someone to complete you is contextually healthy where the masculine and feminine energies meet to create a dynamic whole.

A man's heart is like a campfire before which a woman rests. He enfolds her, envelops her, and protects her in the warmth that emanates from the flames of his love. He glows upon her and takes pleasure in seeing her sense of relaxation and comfort as his loving attention warms the air around her and caresses her skin. But this doesn't keep the fire going… What keeps any fire going is being fed fuel. A man's campfire is dependent on the woman placing a few sticks in the middle.

Your heart's desire, even if you haven't realized it, is to live every moment in the wonder of worship.

— DAVID JEREMIAH

63 Putting Each Other on a Pedestal

Being in partnership with a significant other is perhaps the most difficult spiritual path you can undertake. For better or worse, the union between men and women has become less about duty, sacrifice, and procreation, and more of an intensely focused wrestling match with our angels and demons.

Yet with this challenge there lies an opportunity to see the path of intimacy as a sacred path. As a path of ascension involving a whole new level of intimacy. In modern times, intimate relationships have become the new temple that brings us face to face with each others' shadows and light, and offer us a chance to relate consciously. They allow us the opportunity to explore and cultivate the unformed and unintegrated aspects of the beloved (and ourselves), as well as the stuff that makes our hearts sing, and consciously work with what's there to create more unified human beings who adore each other. They allow us to evolve our consciousness.

The answer is really simple as to how to relate. It's called worship. Putting the pussy on a pedestal, idolizing her, without recognizing his own power is a common problem of modern men. Sometimes there is a battle for control over who gets to be on the pedestal. But both can put each other on a pedestal by celebrating the divine in each other—the name for that is worship. It has to be as unconditional as possible and it has to be a heartfelt commitment from each person. It means not only accepting her "Buddha nature" but also those aspects of her conditioned ego and dysregulated nervous system she might carry. If our own journey is to integrate our own shadow aspects, then so too must we take the integrated/unintegrated other as part of ourselves.

When we think of worship, we think of getting on our knees and acknowledging something more powerful than ourselves. This is not bending the knee as a supplicant because of being less worthy. It's kneeling from your power as a man in front of a woman's power. You have a feminine aspect within you but her feminine aspect is more powerful than yours. It is worthy of being honored and worshiped. She will worship you in the same regard, if you've made the right choice in selecting her to be in your life. Both are admitting to the other that there are aspects in the other that are more powerful which deserve to be honored, respected, and adored. There is a sense of humility which serves to check our more self-aggrandizing instincts. It is a recognition of the heart that we worship that which we are not—that which is more than us.

The question they ask themselves is, "How many moments can we make sacred?" There is always the possibility of slipping into irreverent forms of relating where we "veg out" and where we're careless with our words. We may mindlessly "hang out" with each other. Everyone needs to relax and recharge and it's impossible to be fully present all the time. But given that caveat, the divine relationship is intentional. It is a practice of "divine relating." Each person recognizes that each moment is an opportunity to be fully present with what is and to savor each moment as "god-given."

Men need to pray on women and women need to pray on men (not prey on each other). And this is the key; we need to make it a daily practice to worship each other. Both. At the same time. It doesn't work if one person gives all the time and the other takes a back seat—it would be a labor of love but it wouldn't be a divine union.

The divine union is where both see each other for who they are; at the soul level, at the animal level, at every level. It's seeing god in each other. It's the relationship where you can be accepted for who you are. Not in the naive sense where any behavior is acceptable. But in the embrace of the process of being who we are now, with how we are evolving and improving.

Giving does not only precede receiving; it is the reason for it. It is in giving that we receive.

— ISRAELMORE AYIVOR

64 The Gift

What hurts in a relationship are expectations. You have needs and you have expectations that you believe your beloved will want, desire, and take action to fulfill, because she loves you. It sounds beautiful. And it is. It is your heart embracing the poetry of love, but in an immature way. Rather than having expectations, instead offer whatever you have to offer as a gift, choosing to be devoted to each other without feeling enslaved to each other. How much can I give rather than how much I can get? If both people share this perspective there is no giver-taker relationship—only giver-receiver. Both give and receive according to their ability and in accordance with the needs of the beloved, never having to sacrifice themselves in the process. Neither feels an entitlement to something which was never offered nor which fell under some unspoken, supposed agreement. "It is better to be honest about an expectation, or to not give something to someone at all, than to give something that is laced with unexpressed and subconscious expectations."[331] And in the spirit of a gift, it is given not as a transaction (I give you this if you give me that) but as

331 YouTube channel, Teal Swan (December 26, 2020). *"Giving and How to Give in Relationships."* https://www.youtube.com/watch?v=Nst89AYlgZU

a love offering, and an invitation to reciprocate in kind at some future point with a love offering of their own. There are no demands, only offers.

But, as in all of life, this is nuanced too. Men need women and women need men, as sustenance for each other. And as catalysts for growth in each other.[332] They are designed for each other, despite our contemporary levels of dysfunction—they are not optional extras for each other. In this physical, human form, its impossible to not have needs. Just try not to breathe, to move, to eat, to sleep. Seems obvious at that level—but we're not just flesh and blood creatures, we have needs at the energetic, mental, and spiritual level too.[333] In a relationship, there do exist certain requirements which have to be present for the healthy functioning of that relationship. It's actually harmful to one's health to not be loved, to not be attuned to, to be used. This is not a limiting belief that we can disprove by just thinking otherwise—by just having a positive mindset. In fact, the power of positive thinking can adversely impact our lives because it alienates ourselves from our pain and wounding, and from our normal and natural human needs. It produces a state of dissociated happiness. A layer of shame under a veneer of spiritual work that sends the message that the only way we can resolve unmet needs is by pretending that they don't belong inside you.

If you decided to acquire a dog and wanted to be a responsible pet owner, at minimum you would be obligated to feed it, pet it, and walk it. You wouldn't just gift it those things when moved to do so. If you want a relationship with healthy teeth, you need to brush and floss daily. Yet with human relationships, we never consider what the baseline is for meeting its minimal requirements.

This is especially true in intimate-partner relationships. There are certain things which a man or woman needs which are either related to their sex or to who they are as a unique individual, in order to function well

332 Without the presence of our sex opposite, change might not occur (just like without a catalyst, a particular chemical reaction cannot occur). A man with a growth mindset would do well to choose a woman who can catalyze him to be the best version of himself.

333 The trick is to dispense with those needs that do not serve our true nature.

within a loving dyad.[334] If one person or the other is either unwilling or unable to supply those things from their heart (rather than as a duty), then now is not the time to be in a relationship (or at least an intimate-partner relationship). Or if one has a surfeit of needs which the other can never hope to meet, then any reliance on him to meet those needs is doomed to failure. Privileging the relationship without first privileging your own needs means that you end up having less in the tank to offer your partner. There's no shame in not being ready for a relationship—it's simply the time to do the necessary individuation or self-work beforehand (see *Getting Ready for your Divine Union,* chapter, *The Divine Masculine*).

"Ask for what you want."… You'll hear this a lot from relationship therapists and counselors. It sounds obvious, and it's a good idea, since your partner is not a mind-reader. And usually, if she can meet a need, she will—because she hopefully has ample good will towards her beloved and the health of the relationship. But it can be tricky. You want your partner to know what your needs are so that she can of her own free will choose whether or not to offer to you something in the moment. The danger comes when she gives you what you want without it emerging from the core of her being. She may be stepping more into a performative role where she's giving you something in order to please you and almost, from a once-removed perspective, is asking herself, "What would make my partner enthralled with me in this moment...what does he want to hear?" She is not "moved" by his experience but is managing the relationship. In the moment, his needs may be being met, but by an inauthentic partner. It's a picture of love, rather than the real thing.

In a Gift relationship, there is a middle path between asking for what you want and expecting the other to be a mind reader. Attunement. Attuning to another is like learning to skateboard. You have to place your awareness in the way you need to balance on a board with wheels. You need to feel through to the ground, lean into the curves, understand the limitations, scan for clear paths forward, etc. If you disregard any

334 I'm limiting myself to monogamous arrangements but the same is true of polyamorous, since the individuals within such an arrangement for the most part relate one-on-one.

essentials and become lost in your own experience, reality can bring you crashing to the ground. In a similar way, you can tune in to your beloved by observing her, feeling how she moves when she's in your arms, listening to what she says, what she doesn't say, trying to actually feel what she feels, understanding the limits of her abilities, understanding what she means/what's important to her, all the while keeping yourself centered and balanced. Imagine her joy at you being so perceptive of her lived experience! Imagine what it would be like for her to truly be seen and how positive it would be for the relationship. When conflicting needs arose, imagine how secure and safe she would feel knowing that hers wouldn't be disregarded or downplayed and how open she would be to hearing yours? Imagine if she attuned to you too—how "at one" with her you would feel. A relationship of this sort simply requires the decision to live this way, a practice to develop attunement skills, and forgiveness when mistakes are made or when one participant needs personal time.[335]

How many times have you heard it said that the only person responsible for your happiness is you? Or similar sorts of New-Agey ideas? And it's not that it isn't true; you have to be attuned to yourself and be actively integrating all aspects of yourself to understand what it is you need to lead a rich and fulfilling life. In terms of the Divine Union, I'm going to suggest quite the opposite. I'm going to suggest you need to take responsibility for her happiness. And, crucially, she needs to do the same for you too. It's not a one-way thing and it cannot work if it's just a one-way thing. By taking full responsibility for the happiness of your beloved, you are disinclined to fall back into the position of separation or selfish self-interest (as opposed to enlightened self interest). It's so easy to protect yourself by simply focusing on your own needs, expressing your own needs, requesting a change in behavior of the other, and hoping the other will accede to your request. But if both parties in the Divine Union take responsibility for the other's happiness, then there is a reaching out,

335 One caveat. During the man's "Pioneer" stage (see *The Divine Masculine*), it's natural for a man to focus considerably more energy on what he is building which leaves him relatively depleted when it comes to attunement.

a reaching across, a meeting, and a connection which is not achieved when we focus predominantly on our own happiness. If both take full responsibility for understanding and actualizing the unconditioned needs (the needs which derive from true nature rather than conditioned egoic needs) of the beloved, then we take her best interests as if they were our own best interests. A different 'felt' sense is then created in the relationship. It means it won't be okay to see her suffer any more than it would be okay for her to see you suffer. It's not about two individuals striving and competing to get their needs met who may have differing degrees of desire for connection. But rather starting out at that place of devoted connection—making *that* the starting point—of hard-wiring loving engagement into the relationship. The realization is that we are dependent on each other, rather than co-dependent, or two side-by-side individuals, and that we're not going anywhere without the other person. It's a healthy symbiosis.

I should re-emphasize that this requires an equal commitment, or else you get a giver and a taker—a doormat and a primadonna.

Of course, meeting her needs doesn't always mean meeting her wants. It sometimes means giving her the gift of saying no to her—giving her what the moment needs in order for her to rise to the next level and expand her beingness. Saying no means that, when a divine man does say yes, it won't simply be coming from a place of accommodation. He will mean it with all his heart. Being solid in his convictions and having healthy boundaries can also be a gift because it gives his women a sense of his steadfastness, allowing her to rest in her feminine (even if initially she doesn't like it much).

We need to celebrate men and women for what they have to offer—what they can offer themselves as well as those around them. We need to celebrate their gifts no matter how small and without judging by comparison.

Your hand opens and closes, opens and closes. If it were always a fist or always stretched open, you would be paralyzed. Your deepest presence is in every small contracting and expanding, the two as beautifully balanced and coordinated as birds' wings.

— RUMI

65 The Dance of Merging and Separating

From the age of two, a human being begins to keenly feel his inner self, the I Am, and the outside world. As he matures, he recognizes that his interiority is unalterably his own, cannot plainly be revealed to others, and that he is achingly separated from them. Language seems a poor mechanism by which to articulate and reveal the fullness of his nature—to be fully seen, understood, and accepted by others. There is only one person he is guaranteed to have a relationship with for his whole life—himself. And so he struggles to express what he values most—his desires, thoughts, and feelings—searching for a fundamental connection with others who might love whom they see.

Men and women find themselves presenting their exteriors, their personas, to each other—their souls perhaps briefly meeting in ecstasy—only to fall back to earth, away from each other. And so the dance of merging and separation continues and evolves... "Do you love me?"..."What are you thinking about?"..."Are you here for me?"

In this mortal realm, the Divine Union is never in a conclusive state of oneness. The best we can hope to achieve is smoothly moving back and forth between separateness and togetherness. A living relationship is like walking—it is continually out of balance and, only by tipping first one way and then the other, can we put one foot in front of the other. There is an ever-present tension, a dynamic equilibrium, as we are neither gods nor animals but divinely human.

Come closer, until I no longer know where I end and you begin.

— UNATTRIBUTED

66 Sex

Of course, when we start to address the topic of sex, we can take any number of approaches and go off in countless directions. For many, evolved sex is spiritual (and I don't mean mind-blowing, out-of-this-world orgasms!).[336] Expressing our sexuality is fundamental to our spiritual work. Sex is our life-force energy. It is the energy that created us. And any sexual dysfunction, anywhere we have an issue with sex, is an indication of the degree of our inability to align with our true nature. More simply, sex is about connection—that's all it really is. Yes, there are moving parts but it's not an action—it's not a "sex act."

Full-bodied, skin to skin contact is transformative. Skin acts as the meeting point between two lovers. It is the point where we connect to each other physically, yet at the same time it acts as the barrier that separates us—a somatic paradox. It is the edge where two beings, "trapped" within their own bodies, meet and communicate through sensual touch.

Learning how to be sexual creatures, the practical application of sex, is largely left to trial and error, with a little help from porn sites, magazines,

336 Tantric sex is a method of heightened consciousness practiced either alone or with a partner. There are 108 practices of tantra which help to connect with the Divine. Most of them don't have anything to do with sex. Some of these tantras were yogic or breath or meditation or consciousness practices. It is important to come with an innocent mind, a beginner's mind, to spiritual sex.

friends who claim to have some experience, and a minuscule amount from school. At the beginning of the last century, sex ed started out merely as education about venereal disease and prostitution before scratching the surface of sexual relations. And because of large-scale social opposition, it has never really come close to equipping young people with the information and techniques they need for a happy and healthy sex life.

We're now at a crisis point where, after thousands of years of confusion and adverse societal conditioning around sexual expression, it seems that we're as far away from understanding and awakening to its divine expression as we could possibly be. In the current climate of fear, even the most enlightened sexual arts teachers and practitioners (of tantric sex) have to be aware that they are one step away from a claim of abusive behavior to being out of business, or worse.

Yet restoring our alignment with our sexual life-force energy is crucial for our spiritual work, not to mention the shared joy it can bring. In some indigenous cultures, the women of the tribe would select a male adult whom they trusted, who embodied qualities they valued as a sexual partner, the most empathic and talented, to instruct post-pubescent girls in love-making. This would be his sacred duty, not an indulgence for him to experience. He was a guiding force for her to discover what was right for her own organism. Yet, were one to propose such an arrangement in our culture, I've no doubt it would automatically be called "grooming."

When pubescent boys start to experience a testosterone surge, they need to be able to experience a safe outlet for this energy—it has to go somewhere, dammit! The role and value of the temple priestess has been lost to antiquity in purifying, energizing, and balancing men and boys through sexual arts. These were women who had a natural inclination and access to sexual wisdom who would train these boys in the art of love-making. The term "whore" used to mean "the holy one." As a tantric priestess (whore), Mary Magdalen, in her relationship with Jesus, demonstrated a tantric relationship which supported him on his personal journey to access his power as a spiritual leader. Coming from her divine feminine essence, and through her heart, she supported the raising of his kundalini through ecstatic enlightenment. Today she is regarded as a whore, in its modern derogatory sense, who fortuitously received redemption. Yesterday's *Pretty Woman.*

With young men and women being trained by caring sexual practitioners, both would then be able to experience a sexual encounter with the opposite sex in a way which was knowledgeable, attuned, and mutually beneficial.

No matter whether or not these two examples accurately reflect a more attuned way of relating sexually, there are certainly missing pieces in how modern men and women meet each other between the sheets. Poetry, rather than prose, would come closer to describing what is required for the divine union of two lovers. But since I'm not a poet, I'll attempt to do so by metaphor.

As described earlier, sex is more of a woman's thing and intimacy is more of a man's thing. Both aspects are expressed and received but are either dominant or non-dominant. A woman receives the man's lingam, and the man receives her love (non-dominant function). Or conversely, a man penetrates the woman by his lingam, and she penetrates his heart with love (dominant function). It's not that the woman is sexless nor the man heartless—clearly both are capable of giving and receiving either. They are built by nature to offer their gifts in different ways and at different levels. In love-making, the divine union is realized when a flow of energy circulates through the lingam, up through her heart, into his heart, and down to his lingam. A sacred electrical circuit! A pranic circuit, more clearly. The less resistance in this circuit, the more open, receptive, trusting, and relaxed both are, the greater the flow of energy. Both the woman and the man meet each other with receptivity. They are receptive to their own inner experience and to each others.' There is no "wrong" outcome unless one or the other is in denial of their experience.

Women and men have anatomical differences that serve a purpose. A woman flows where a man does not. Both can flow from the tear ducts, their mouths, their noses, urinary tracts. But women also cry more easily, flow from their vaginas (vaginal discharges, amrita) and their womb (menstruation). Their bodies regularly purge themselves of unwanted waste products and toxins. Men's do not do so. Men have only women to flow through (from their semen) which is women's sacred gift to men. Men find healing from a woman accepting his flow as part of her own. Some believe that women are absolutely essential for a man's full being and healing. She takes care of herself so that his poetic heart finds poetry in her appearance and essence. She can "fuck the war out of him" and recalibrate him to peaceful ways. In Sanskrit, "yoni" (vagina) means "sacred space." It is a privilege to enter that space.

Passion derives from polarization. "Sexual attraction is based on sexual polarity which is the force of passion that acts between masculine and feminine poles."[337] In long-term relationships you naturally become depolarized as she becomes more like you and you become more like her. The chemistry comes from polarization. Presence is the antidote—when you're totally feeling her, thinking her, empathizing fully, and your mind's not wandering.

The dance between sexual partners is occurring all the time. Indeed, foreplay begins the moment after orgasm. It's in their daily conversations, the way they exchange small touches of care and reassurance, the small acknowledgment of each other's experiences, etc. There is a vibrational ebb and flow between their respective polarities.

---

337 David Deida (2004). "*The Way of the Superior Man.*" Louisville, CO. Sounds True Inc

CHARLIE: *"A man takes a drop [of whiskey] too much once in a while, it's only human nature."*
ROSE: *"Nature, Mr. Allnut, is what we are put in this world to rise above."*[338]

67 Meeting our Instinctual Drives

We live with all kinds of archaic messages and conditionings that we embody, that live side by side with more modern scripts about masculinity and gender roles. In the movie, *The African Queen*, prim and proper Rose Sayer, played by Katherine Hepburn, seems to regard the human animal as something to reject in order to achieve a more spiritual perfection. On the other hand, Charlie Allnut, played by Humphrey Bogart, seems to accept that a man's essential needs and desires are a part of his nature and cannot be overcome. I think a more nuanced position would serve to bridge this divide.

Rising above our nature is not to be confused with suppressing, rejecting, or denigrating it. At times, overcoming our primitive drives, instincts, hormonal imperatives, desires, etc, is not to deny nature but to exercise free will in making optimal personal decisions in the full knowledge, recognition, and acceptance of those drives and instincts.

A simple example; we evolved to crave sugar. In prehistory, our ancestors' primary concern was to obtain calories to survive and reproduce.

338 *The African Queen* movie (1951). Starring Humphrey Bogart and Katherine Hepburn.

Foods which tasted sweet were a good indication of high calorie content. With easy access to modern sugary foods, it's now all too easy to consume more than is necessary or healthy, and "suppressing" the urge would be wise. Another example is "neoteny." Prehistoric men favored women who retained juvenile features into adulthood which they may have interpreted as being better-suited for reproduction.

The physical and social environmental conditions in which modern humans find themselves are entirely different from yesteryear. There is less likelihood of an early death through predation, injury, or disease, less of a social imperative to reproduce, and relationships with women have trended more towards long-term, intimate, and monogamous (which is "unnatural"). Yet, given our biology and given the opportunity, we still would want plenty of sex with young, hot, cute, neotenous women.

The vikings were savage warriors and in times of war would rape, pillage, and plunder. They often remained in the villages they'd conquered but they would then become nurturing, caring parents, and the next generation of men would be far more civilized. Humans have an incredible adaptability. Today the Scandinavian countries are amongst the most peaceful and happy. Men curtail much of their nature and biological drives all the time. A prime example being the suppression of our drive to "spread seeds" (we use condoms or abstain from sex). This suppression of male nature is, in fact, a cornerstone of marriage. Men do so willingly and lovingly.

Some men find contentment in aligning themselves with their biology, who we might call players or pick-up artists. And some find contentment by, say, caring for a long-term partner in chronic pain for whom they no longer feel any sexual attraction. In the first example, the difference between an unconscious man and one who is conscious is that one is either ruled by his dick (or mother wounding), and the other has made a lifestyle choice which celebrates sex. In the second, an unconscious man may resent being "tied down" through societal expectations and the loss of his freedom, or he may place more value in his code of honor, freely chosen for himself.

Finally a unique creature, in nature, standing with some dignity and nobility and transcending the human condition; and then he is good only for dying.

— ERNEST BECKER

68 The Single Man

Many men are experiencing a crisis of masculinity. Men, as a whole, are considered contemptible. Fathers are subject to "divorce rape" and to having their sons and daughters removed from their lives. Sons who grow up without those fathers may become antisocial and rudderless. The presence of men in colleges is declining and those that make it in are one step away from a false allegation of sexual abuse, a tribunal to determine guilt, and subsequent expulsion. Levels of testosterone are decreasing. And male suicide is increasing.

Advice is in short supply as to how they can face their challenges. One such source many turn to is Dr. Jordan Peterson.[339] He comes from a perspective which has a traditional focus—becoming self-disciplined and accountable (which I don't have a problem with) in order to compete for work and wife (which I do). I have a great deal of respect for him but, surveying the social and political landscape, I would have to say that he is doing men a disservice by recommending they do what has been done before. He considers marriage to be a "positive good and a path to inner

339 Jordan B. Peterson (2018). *"12 Rules for Life: An Antidote to Chaos."* Random House Canada; Later Printing edition.

freedom" which, in an ideal world, it might be—but, unfortunately, getting married to the wrong woman can lead to a man's ruination in this day and age. I consider it profoundly unwise for men to choose to become legally vulnerable to the court system through marriage. And, going further, in this post-#MeToo and #BelieveHer era, a man needs to be exceptionally vigilant about opening up his life to a woman, whether it leads to a committed relationship or not.

Appreciating fully all the obstacles and insults to realizing his own humanity and masculinity can send even the most highly conscious man into a funk, if not a rage. A good man can feel cheated by life when his best efforts are denied, exploited, or received with tepid approval.

It could be assumed that this book privileges the idea of being in relationship with a good woman. For many men, the idea of a stable, long-term relationship is neither part of their immediate path, nor ever will be. And this is to be respected. Some have decided to forget about understanding what women want and require from a man, and how they might acquire those things, and simply focus on their own personal aims and desires. They have decided for themselves what is valuable in their lives, and if that might detract from their value in the eyes of a woman, then so be it. Perhaps they choose to share their time with other men who appreciate their ideas and experiences—a form of platonic love. But their principle concern, if they are a man of character, is to maximize how they might go about being a good human being and reaching towards their fullest potential, which may or may not mean developing qualities that are appealing to women (or other men).

In fact, when the single man works on himself to approach life equanamously yet with detached engagement, he becomes sufficiently self-possessed to shape and direct this world with wise intent, to stand his ground, and act upon his convictions based not on his feelings but on his devotion to form and function rooted in truth. He occupies his space without apology or reservations, yet without arrogance.

It's okay to be who we are naturally, despite what anyone else may think. The more loving, conscious, and awake we are as men, then the people and situations in life that present themselves to us become more likely to resolve towards their own greater integration and true nature. By his very presence, there exists an implicit invitation for them to express their own completeness that the conscious man had also realized (mimetic theory).[340] That is the power and potential that we all have, the gift we have to give, should we choose to embrace the opportunity. Each one of us can become a redemptive force in the world, in ways large and small.

There is a growing social movement of Men Going Their Own Way, or MGTOW. In its broadest definition, it is basically men saying that their aim is to focus their life around their own pursuits and exclude from that equation a woman, or women. They believe, with a lot of evidence, that engaging with a female "significant other" is a recipe for disaster which cannot otherwise be successfully mitigated. I believe that they are correct—that it is unwise to do so for the majority of modern women. A lot of men are disgusted with the paucity of options that are available to them. But they are excluding, by implication, women who would be suitable candidates for pair-bonding, thereby making both themselves and those women losers in the game of life. They may also be cutting off their hearts to spite all women (to adjust the idiom).[341] To repress part of his masculinity is to risk not be fully in his masculine essence (even though it might seem eminently wise to do so) and rest in a state of spiritual contraction. Modern men need to develop advanced selection criteria and skills to successfully avoid and screen out women who don't pass the sniff test. To always be screening yet never give up hope.

To make your external relationships even better, it is necessary to listen to and understand yourself. Having a great relationship with yourself is not so you don't have to have a relationship with a woman. Or any relationship. The quality of the relationships you have is a mirror of the improved quality of the relationship you have with yourself.

To live a good life, you need to constantly survey and learn from the

---

340 YouTube channel, ImitatioVideo (December 17, 2018). *"René Girard Explains Mimetic Desire."* https://www.youtube.com/watch?v=OgB9p2BA4fw

341 Cutting off one's nose to spite one's face.

ever-changing social landscape, and then be prepared to change your understanding when new information presents itself. It's also important to reflect upon and discover your true nature so that you can engage with life with personal integrity and authenticity. Honor your personal path of mastery—of thought, word, action, and intent. Focus on what works best for you—you as the unique individual that you are. Your unique aptitudes. This is the path of purpose. Having the self-awareness to figure yourself out and the courage to live that expression. To take what life has to offer you, good or bad, and use it to temper[342] your whole being.

Just imagine living in a world where society's highest priority was the maximization of potential. What sort of person would you be if you could access the resources you needed to undertake a chosen endeavor? What sort of person would you be if (should you decide to include one) your intimate partner in life was optimally skillful in terms of being in a relationship with you, and you with her? What sort of person would you be if you had time, and you didn't have to sell your body and soul in order to generate an income, just to pay bills? What sort of person would you be if you could penetrate this world with sacred masculine intent, in a way that was both safe and dangerous—that allowed you to fail without incurring a mortal wound (physical or psycho-spiritual)? What sort of person would you be if you were allowed to fail and where failure was not punished and instead recognized as an opportunity to learn and grow? What sort of person would you be if you had had an ideal education? What would that look like? Why didn't you get it? What sort of person would you be if you had had parents who honored you for who you were, without imposing an agenda of their own on your existence? What sort of person would you be if you were surrounded by friends, coaches, teachers, lovers, community members who were themselves optimized? What sort of person would you be if you had the loving, wise, and intelligent advise of those people around you who could help you on your journey?

In life we're dealt the cards, and we have to play the hand that we're

342 Dictionary definition: the state of a substance with respect to certain desired qualities (such as hardness, elasticity, or workability)

dealt to the best of our ability. What sort of person would you be if you were dealt a really good hand? And you didn't have to play out a crappy hand? In the end, the point is to do your best with what you have and expand yourself and others in the process. But it's important to recognize that potential can go to waste. And there's no good reason for it to go to waste—either through personal choice or through accepting an inferior world not optimized for our wellbeing.

In the world as it's been created, a man is judged by what he does—for society, for women, for family, for country, etc. Little empathy or consideration is given to him for simply being a virtuous man. That doesn't pay the bills, and it doesn't compete with "getting shit done." Conscious men would do well to work towards creating the fundamental conditions where society places more value on the intangibles (wisdom, authenticity, integrity, compassion, courage, etc) than it does on resource acquisition, status, and power—all wedded to ego needs. Imagine a world where we selected our leaders by such criteria! If, indeed, we needed leaders in the traditional sense. It's easy to incentivize people through the market system by rewarding them with money for the goods and services they produce. I wonder by what mechanisms a new society could instead incentivize the production of fully realized people—an optimized humanity?

Part Ten

Conclusion

Nothing exists by itself alone. We all belong to each other; we cannot cut reality into pieces. My happiness is your happiness; my suffering is your suffering. We heal and transform together.

– THICH NHAT HAHN

A problem fully understood is a problem half solved. I hope that I have gone some way to presenting the fullness of the problems which face a conscious man as he walks through life and will now go on to suggest some half-solutions in this conclusion.

69 Challenging our Programming

Without understanding all the ways our humanity has been violated in this world would be to be blind to the ways human consciousness is cabined, cribbed, and confined by its control systems. “It’s much easier to fool people than to convince them that they have been fooled… Breaking free of the ancient, historical ‘constant’ of mind control is an ongoing process of waking up out of a state of denial. Spiritual emergence and awakening involves a physiological break from the consensus social agreements of our planetary cultures.”[343]

All beings are doing the best they can, in proportion to their level of conscious awareness. That given, humans now need to move towards preventing separation between themselves and aspects of themselves, and separation between themselves and others. Life is about relationships—relationships with oneself, with one’s beloved, with family, friends, community, etc. And since we are all of divinely equal merit, ultimately we need to move towards treating those most distant from us as lovingly as we treat those closest to us. A healthy human is one deeply enmeshed in intimate relationships. But quality is the key, not simply the presence

343 Karlos Kukuburra. thetemplate.uk.com

of greater enmeshment. The quality of our relationships determines to a large extent the quality of our lives.

Challenging emotions are markers by which we can examine our shadow side. Just this morning, I put leashes on my two dogs to take them for a walk. One refused to leave its dog bed. I dropped its leash and took the other for a walk but found I was annoyed at the first. I discovered I had an expectation for appreciation and that the dog was being ungrateful! Here I was, offering my time when I would rather have had a coffee—I was doing something nice and the dog snubbed my efforts to take it for a joyful walk, to give it healthy exercise, and to pick up its poop. How ungrateful! So I had an agenda. It was less important to be attuned to the dog than with my own agenda. I simultaneously see myself as flawed and at the same time hold myself in high regard.

I saw the dog as "irrational." Living mostly from my masculine essence can color my perceptions. I can think to myself, "*I'm* rational. It's a good way to be. Why aren't you rational too?" And it means I don't always bring "beginner's mind" to a situation. I can perceive lack of rationality in others (or dogs) as an actual obstinate refusal to be rational. How do you regard women when they are "irrational?" Wouldn't it be better if women were more rational? Of course, I hear you say! It would make life so much easier. But does that make me worth more than her because I'm more rationally minded? Not at all. Men and women have equal worth, in my mind. But saying that men in general are more rational than women is to invite howls of disapproval. Yet saying that women are more nurturing than men would not be met by an equivalent disapproval. Recognizing our sex differences is a political act! How men and women react to the objective reality about our sex differences is telling. Women can fly off the handle and call men misogynistic for daring to suggest that women are less rational overall than men, or men can become frustrated when women act irrational, or "crazy." Neither reaction is warranted.

In a sense, there are many male attributes which women find baffling. Why can't men be more socially outgoing? Why can't they create the same sort of social networks? Be more expressive, more verbal, more emotional? Recognizing and accepting each other for who we are and *how* we are means that a man could reply, "Yes, I'm less adept in these key respects than you are. Can you accept me for that?" and not suffer any disapprobation. It means we can play to our strengths instead of writing each other off.

Society is collapsing, and people are starting to recognize that the reason they feel like they're mentally ill is that they're living in a system that's not designed to suit the human spirit.

— JIM CARREY

70 The Age of Healing

Traumatic events in a person's life don't automatically create a traumatized person. Trauma is what happens when an organism is not conditioned to meet these events in a way that dissipates a painful experience. When the world in which they live is fast and furious, stressful and antagonistic, even the most well-put together person can be overwhelmed and overtaken by trauma. And when this has been the norm for generation after generation for thousands of years, we're basically left with all of us being basket cases. When we're all walking-wounded, our bodies, our nervous systems, know the score. But we think that we're all mostly normal.

If men and women were automobiles, they would be trying to run around with empty tanks and flat tires. Because they have been run low by the demands of a stressful life and the generations of trauma and suffering. They want more than they can give. Men are generally more stoic—they would rather not ask for what they need, if they see that it would deplete the resources of those they love. So they suffer in silence, even to the point of taking their own lives. Women get "screamy and crazy" and imagine that men are deliberately being antagonistic by not giving them what they need. So they cling to the notion that they must be victims of Patriarchal privilege.

So many are clamoring to get their needs met because they are in so much pain and personal deficit (just like a narcissist). Those who actually experience chronic pain understand how their world contracts around them, making them self-centered. You can see this with other animals which, when sick, get quiet, still, and seem to turn inward. It means they are conserving their energy for their own well-being. They can't spare any of their precious energy to engage fully with others.

Traumatized people hurt people in many ways—emotionally, physically, sexually, verbally, etc. Sometimes this extends into criminal behavior. Yet when they are prosecuted, justice requires that they are summarily punished, rather than acknowledging that these people are victims of their traumatic past. It's not about justice so much as it's about compensatory revenge. In a sense, their crimes are perfectly understandable because they never got what was needed to ensure their contentment by a society optimized for their wellbeing. But locking them up is a police activity, not a therapeutic one, and rehabilitation is mostly given lip service. As a society, we're just happy to keep them out of sight and out of mind with the responsibility for their behavior being entirely their own—"if you can't do the time, don't do the crime." It is not a technical fault of their own making—it is a social and spiritual crisis in society—and it cannot be solved at the level of the individual making reparations to the State.

The next age has to be an Age of Healing—like we had the Information Age, the Steam Age, the Space Age, the Atomic Age, etc. We need a Healing Age as a species if we're not going to tear ourselves apart. Certain key components need to be identified for this stage of healing. We need to be cognizant of and apply the laws of life, the laws of nature, to the extent where we submit things to the organism which are healthy, rather than toxic. Certain things are toxic to the human organism and we need to design-out of society those things. This is absolutely no easy task but the first step is to become aware of what those things are and then trust the process.

So what are those things which are toxic? They are essentially "abuse." Such things as physical and sexual abuse are easily identified, but also those things a human being needs in order to be healthy and whole but which are intentionally absent. Take, for instance, solitary confinement where the lack of human contact leads to mental health problems. Or emotional abuse... Or structural violence...[344] If you grow a plant from seed, then step on it, what you'll get is a stunted plant. If you're looking to maximize its genetic potential, you need to understand that there are certain factors which are needed in order for it to grow tall, strong and healthy—matching the environment to the stages of development. In the case of the seedling it would be water, light, air, soil, soil microbia, soil nutrients, and not being stomped on. In addition to other forms of nourishment, love and belonging are crucial elements for humans which need to be underpinned by knowledge and wisdom.

We need to treat our bodies well. We have this crazy modern idea that we can deal with any kind of inhumane behavior without it affecting our organisms as long as we change our thinking about our experience and by discarding the persecutor/victim perspective. Yet the body knows the score. The body understands when it is out of integrity with the mind—when it is overridden by the mind. It withdraws itself from the mind. It carries the tensions, stresses, aches and pains, the origins of which remain ignored and unresolved. And as long as the body doesn't give us a hard time of it, we can thankfully ignore it. Until cumulative stresses develop into conditions where we start finding it harder and harder to function. An athlete understands how to disconnect/dissociate from the body, to push through and past pain and muscle towards the finish line. But whereas an athlete may also nourish and repair the body, most of us pay it little attention other than as a tool for attracting the opposite sex. We're not in

344 Gernot Köhler and Norman Alcock (1976). *"An Empirical Table of Structural Violence."* JSTOR. https://www.jstor.org/stable/422498?seq=1
Structural violence refers to the adverse impacts of social inequality that is the inevitable outcome of our competitive stratified society. Poverty is a form of material violence. Psycho-social stress is a form of relative violence. Both are unnatural and arise from the way society is structured. The fatalities due to structural violence are the leading cause of death globally, far in excess of fatalities resulting from civil and international conflicts.

relationship with it. Even with practices like working out or yoga, there is a danger of going through the motions irrespective of the "opinions" of the body. As we get more into relationship with our body, we become conscious of it and become conscious of the subtle resistances it carries. At the same time, the body "reaches out" to the mind and begins to talk in its own language.[345] Just like we clean our teeth daily, we can "clean" our body daily—a process known as somatic hygiene.

~

We need to treat each other well. The number one factor which predicts longevity is not exercise and diet, nor is it refraining from smoking. It's not even access to good medical care. It is whether or not you believe you are embraced by a community of people who have an interest in *your* best interests. The best thing we can do for ourselves is to be there for each other. When we raise children according to their best interests, they're going to do well. If we don't, they won't. It's so simple it almost seems childishly simplistic. The fact that we don't take seriously the work necessary to bring about healthy humans and, by extension, a healthy society shows that we don't even have a handle on this most basic concept. If we do, we don't understand how we can resolutely overcome the obstacles in so doing.

One such obstacle is that children are seen as private property, with parents having almost complete freedom to determine the direction and quality of their lives.[346] This also includes the freedom to be ignorant, and remain ignorant, which trumps the rights of the child to receive loving, attuned, intelligent parenting. The State would be even more useless in this role. It's said that it "takes a village to raise a child." This widespread proverb has its origins in African tribal cultures where extended families

345 The kriyas which may be experienced in a Kundalini awakening may also be connected with the neurogenic tremors associated with trauma release. It's the body and mind being released from their cage and realizing that once-lost relationship of humans in their true nature.

346 Since one in four children now live in a single-parent household, and that person is substatially more likely to be the mother, these children are considered the mother's chattel property.

have long been the norm. The fact that the phrase has hung around in western cultures without implementation is a testament to the power of its message. Children are sovereign individuals in their own right for whom the community has a duty of care and stewardship. That means that the community needs to be accessible to them, skillful, and resourced. Their interactions need to be underpinned by knowledge and wisdom.

Love, connection, and belonging are crucial elements for humans to thrive. We have to approach each other with love, rather than hostility or indifference. This means that the asocial and antisocial are not made to feel excluded but are regarded with understanding and compassion. They need to know it's truly safe to come out from behind their protective coating. It also means developing a community-wide "immune system" to effectively deal with people and processes which would be harmful to collective wellbeing.

I believe that our true nature is to live in harmony with ourselves and our fellow man. To do so, we have to learn how to "put the human being back together."

I do not want the peace that passeth understanding. I want the understanding which bringeth peace.

— HELEN KELLER

71 Living Together Harmoniously

The War of the Sexes

There cannot be peace between men and women as long as there is war in love. Love is what will heal us but we need certain higher virtues that support loving energy—such as wisdom, intelligence, clarity, intuition, compassion, care, honesty, awareness, etc.

Male/female relations are tragically broken. There is a war against men. And I do not mean this as a metaphorical flourish. The sooner we name the poison, the better. And that is Feminism. The feminist narrative is that if you weaken men, you will make women stronger. This, while simultaneously trying to assert that women are as strong, powerful, and independent as men. Feminists pit women against men as if they were warring nations which have no interest in suing for peace. Or it's like we are in a three-legged race together, with women trying to outrun men.

If feminists were smart, and wanted a stable, female-dominant world, they would emulate bonobo society[347] where females guide and steer the social order by building and maintaining loving, long-term relationships.

347 Elle Beau (February 29). *"How Much Like Bonobos Are We?"* Medium. https://medium.com/sexography/how-much-like-bonobos-are-we-6b175b918aa7

Incidentally, a society where every male is sexually satisfied (which male bonobos are) is one which is peaceful and happy (in comparison to chimpanzee social orders which are thuggish and stressful). The benefits of intimacy and loving relationships (including sex) are indispensable for the health and well being of men and women. And while neither sex can declare themselves entitled to such relationships, the ambition to pursue them recognizes a fundamental human need which we need to make easier, not harder. If women make use of their unique strengths and advantages, they then become fully empowered. Shifting the perspective that men and women are not in competition with each other, but live in symbiosis, is crucial for our well-being.

Yet a hidden war is waged on ordinary men and women by the ruling class, using and funding feminist groups as a proxy to divide and conquer them. It's a phony war. Men and women have historically cooperated with each other, however dysfunctionally, our interests being aligned. Men cannot be egged on to fight women but women can have their fears inflamed enough to regard men as their enemy.

Men and women are predisposed to different types of fears and traumas. Women fear being overwhelmed by male power and dominance in the form of physical and sexual violence. They also latch on to the notion of patriarchy, as they fear social and economic powerlessness. Men's Achilles heel is their tender hearts. Their fear is of being emotionally cut by a woman where, unlike physical wounds which heal themselves, they bleed out on the inside. Women fear for their external safety, generally speaking; men, their internal safety.[348]

Unlike our grandfather's generation, most men have stepped up to the present and acknowledged the mistakes of the past—of women who suffered sexual abuse and disrespect in all its forms. The flip side does not yet exist. There is no expectation of women to own their role in men's pain (mostly emotional/relational abuse). You could even say we live in an

348 Even though almost as many men as women are victims of physical domestic abuse, they do not tend to fear this going into a relationship.

emasculation culture (the male equivalent of rape culture) where "male tears" are mocked.[349]

Yet in the darkness, there is one candle. A video project created by conflict resolution expert, Dr Hanna Milling, *From Women To Men*,[350] in which several courageous women express remorse for how they have treated men in the past and lovingly accept their own lack of accountability. These women were able to come to terms with their past and forgive themselves.

Saying "I'm sorry" is to demonstrate accountability. "Accountability is the only real way a person can demonstrate proof that they actually care about someone else. And a lack of accountability is proof that whatever level of caring or love a person professes is questionable."[351]

Only with forgiveness from and for both sexes can we truly start to move forward. Only then can we begin to heal and apply ourselves to the serious task of developing relationship skills which neither devalue nor overvalue the other sex.

Until that time, it's wholly necessary to take the job of screening out women very seriously when choosing an intimate (or even when asked to mentor a female associate).[352] Otherwise, men are just playing Russian roulette with their lives and reputations.[353] It's also imperative to be highly aware that the world is more gynocentric than it is misogynistic and that, in order to preserve their wellbeing and to step fully into their masculine essence, conscious men will need to confront it (or at least cope with it). Men have never feared oppression by women, financially or politically, though that is changing. Women are taking advantage of a misandric world in an attempt to enrich their lives at the expense of men.

---

349 Christine Rosen (September 2018). *"Man-Hating Goes Mainstream."* Commentary Magazine. https://www.commentarymagazine.com/articles/christine-rosen/man-hating-goes-mainstream/

350 Dr Hanna Milling (Aug 3, 2018). *"From Women To Men."* Authentic Love. https://www.authentic-love.de/

351 Paul Elam (December 8, 2019). *"Teach a Woman to be Accountable in 5 Steps."* https://www.paulelam.com/teach-a-woman-to-be-accountable-in-5-steps/

352 Kim Elsesser (January 1, 2015). *"Sex and the Office."* Taylor Trade Publishing.

353 A return to the Victorian practice of chaperoning can even be imagined where a dispassionate third party directly supervises conduct between a man and a woman to restrain "immoral conduct."

In most walks of life, kindness in the face of unkindness is a social good. But in these times, in this culture, with these wounded/indoctrinated women, the kindness good men naturally want to extend to them will most likely be seen as something to be exploited and to which they believe they are entitled (rather than something to be appreciated, emulated, and reciprocated). As mentioned in *Domestic Violence* (chapter, *Feminist Myths and Narratives*), without the tool of physical coercion, compelling a woman by force to behave herself, men no longer have any tools with which to hold women to account for bad behavior (social institutions show little interest). Meeting bad behavior with bad behavior is, and never was, the answer. This is a predicament perhaps best addressed only by loving firmness and the power of "no" from men. And sisters taking sisters to task for ruining it with men. Certainly, appealing to wounded women's better nature seldom produces a result.

Men use power overtly and women covertly. It's easier to confront male power because it's more blatant. But how do you shut down whispers and passive aggression? "We really ought to be looking to shut down all of the illegitimate uses of traditionally gendered power of any sort when we come together to try to work together."[354]

Although the state of affairs these days is very discouraging—it's almost an impossibility to find a woman who is capable of living in harmony with a man—my hope is that men and women can take a path forward where we collectively own our shadow aspects, celebrate what the opposite sex brings to our lives, and co-create a new way of being that brings out the best in each other. A world in which both sexes feel respected, safe, and excited to be in the presence of the other. Where women can fully inhabit their feminine aspect as much as they choose. Where men can look to each other as brothers rather than adversaries. Where we can love freely and vulnerably.

The world that awaits us does not belong to women. And it does not

354 Evolutionary biologist, Heather Heying. YouTube channel, Tom Bilyeu (December 10, 2020). *"Evolutionary Biologist Reveals How Society Is Losing It's Grip on What Makes Us Men and Women."* https://www.youtube.com/watch?v=t79O-4U8X3k

belong to men. It will be revealed by men and women coming into their divine essences. It arises from the dance of merging and separating, and of co-creation from the best version of themselves.

Complimentary Arrangements

> *The healthiest relationships have room for both male and female strengths.*[355]
>
> – SHAWN T. SMITH

I'm in favor of discrimination between men and women!

It's okay, you can breathe easy…It's important not to read the term "discrimination" as implying a judgment which negatively impacts one sex or the other. To discriminate simply means to observe differences and to act in ways which recognize those differences. Like discriminating between taking a bus or a plane. It's a separate issue whether an act of discrimination is right or wrong. Once it was fine to discriminate between men's and women's access to a credit card, and later it wasn't.

What is the most optimal form that men (or women) could achieve in their life, given optimal conditions—one where we are able to maximize our potential? And how would we go about redesigning our material existence so this might become a reality?

We don't yet have any idea of what a new paradigm of harmony between the sexes might look like. I'm quite certain it would bear little resemblance to the current reality of animus-possessed women and demonized men. Nor would it be the old, traditional model of proscribed roles and responsibilities, although that was probably in greater alignment with men's and women's expressions of sex-based choices. Many modern women claim that hearth, home, husband, and child leaves them unfulfilled. No doubt, that's true for many. But of those women, how many are in acting accordance with their true nature? Probably not even they know.

---

355 Shawn T. Smith PsyD (February 2, 2014). *"The Woman's Guide to How Men Think: Love, Commitment, and the Male Mind."* New Harbinger Publications; 1st edition

This is something that will just have to be left to the organic process of unfolding as we liberate ourselves from our shackles, mental and societal.

Should we have a more gynocentric society or a more patriarchal society? If we have something more egalitarian with a symmetry of influence, and if we recognize that men and women are both similar and dissimilar, how do we arrange ourselves socially? What would that look like? Perhaps we should meet situations with whatever is most appropriate for that situation. If it's most appropriate to be rational, then that person (usually the man but not exclusively) should take the lead in this respect. If it's more appropriate to be nurturing, then perhaps it should be the woman. It really depends on the conditions in the moment. Men and women rather than being able to meet any eventuality with equal effect, can be seen to be better adapted to play to their respective strengths in a complimentary sense. Neither is belittled or demeaned for being less adept in whatever respect.

"A man is usually more successful if his firmness is in the foreground, supported by an underlying quality of gentleness, while a woman is often more effective if her gentleness is in the foreground, rooted in an underlying quality of strength."[356]

Should men lead and women follow? If that sounds like it favors men then why should it, if men are also acting for the benefit of women? Consider partner dancing. The man leads the woman around the dance floor, mindful of the space available to them. They are attuned to each other and to a center point of balance. They lean towards each other, away from each other, sway, release and hold each other, and place their feet so as to coordinate with the requirements of form while avoiding stepping on each other's toes. The man indicates through body signals an invitation for the woman to execute certain movements, like spinning under his arm or transferring her weight for her to change direction. He decides what happens and she submits and responds—not as an automaton but in her own creativity, interpreting her inner desires through bodily

356 John Welwood (1990). *"Journey of the Heart."* Harper Collins.

expression. Does she feel oppressed? Not if he is skillful, sensitive, and attuned to her. Not if he is willing to learn from his mistakes and later receive her requests for different moves they've not yet explored. It's true that a woman could lead and a man follow. But it doesn't "feel" right, or look right, visually. They might have fun switching and experimenting, usually with a ton of laughter, but as a game and no more. In the end, what's created is a flow of energy which transports both dancers towards union and away from separateness.

Another analogy. Which is more important—the violinist or the violin? The violin has no agency. It is at the mercy of the violinist! Yet without a violin, his talents remain unexpressed. Without the violinist, the sweet sounds of the violin remain silent. They are not equal. One plays and the other is played. Is the violin oppressed? Or is it "natural" for it to receive instructions from expert hands? Would the violinist be worthy of the name if he was unskillful and unaware of how to bring out the tones and resonance inherent in the violin? If he's sensible he'll take care of the violin by keeping it away from moisture, adding rosin and cleaning the bow, keeping his nails trimmed, etc.

All analogies break down at a certain point and I simply present them for further thought.

The world that we decide to create for ourselves is not the property of men nor women. It's the product of men and women in their divine aspects arising to their full potential.

Living Socially

Only he who does not seek to be ahead of others is capable of living in harmony with everyone.[357]

– LAOZI

We certainly need to make great changes if we are to step into a New Earth paradigm—to create innovative technological, ecological, spiritual,

357 Laozi, 6th-century BC Chinese sage

and social mechanisms. Treating men as if they were women and women as if they were men, as gender-neutral, is a recent social construct that defies our true nature. Our current society is overly equalized because of political correctness. What's good for one is not always good for the other. Yet, more than anything, we need a loving and harmonious coexistence between men and women. We need to build trust in each other which also means calling out those who seek to break the bonds of loving kindness, of loving connection.

So we go through life, all of us, with unmet needs—needs which were not met by our caregivers when we were young. Childhood experiences need not have been adverse, even (see chapter, *Wounding and Trauma*)—it's just a fact of growing up with adults who did not particularly attune themselves to those needs. We carry these unmet needs into adulthood and look to our significant others, our relatives and friends, but more likely our beloved, to play a part in meeting those needs. And we do so consciously or unconsciously.

I favor doing so—consciously!

We need each other, no matter what. Our biology is wired for connection. I believe we are a social species and we are here to love and support each other. And, if that's not the case, that we are simply independent units walking around working on ourselves, that means that others are basically free to fuck off and die. A popular spiritual myth that is peddled but which is largely damaging is that "everything you need is within you." Such spiritual practitioners themselves emerged from a childhood where their needs weren't met. In order to address their pain, they turned to spirituality for an answer to that pain and derived a "spiritual" rationalization for not needing people—people cause pain, therefore omit people's influence because, hey, "I choose to be happy." Such folks are in denial that we are a social species and that how we treat others impacts their happiness. Such spiritual gurus exhort us to transcend our animal nature and often throw the baby out with the bath water. The funny thing about spiritual teachers is that they are right about a lot of things, but never always right about everything (since they also disagree with each other). Yet many devotees hold their words as sacrosanct.

So this doesn't make sense. It makes sense to embrace solitude and quiet reflection in order to check in and be with what is alive within us. The capacity to be at peace with oneself when alone is to be emotionally mature. Indeed, those who are happy to live alone make the best intimate partners because they can allow their lover to be themselves. They know if the relationship ends, their inherent contentment will carry them along as they are less likely to be "insecurely attached." Yet joining with others who are simultaneously improving themselves creates a force-multiplier effect potentially larger than whatever it might be we could accomplish alone. This creates connection, intimacy, and social cohesion. True intimacy can be fostered not just with a beloved but with others too. It allows us to profoundly understand and empathize with another.

It's also necessary to recognize and integrate the shadow aspects of living socially. There is rightly a fear of being engulfed by the body politic. There is a greater responsibility for others' wellbeing which is largely absent in a society ruled by separation mentality. This can produce a degree of anxiety or tension between individual actualization and community responsibility. A life of service to others can be draining for a person where giving, self-sacrifice, and self-effacement may receive little in the form of support or reciprocation. This can lead to burn-out.

Under what set of social and material arrangements do we need to live so that children grow up happy and whole? Those on the regressive left see the state as a substitute for the absent father—something that has deep pockets and will stay out of the child's life except to pay for needs identified by the single mother. Those on the right see the nuclear family as indispensable—a little-house-on-the-prairie picture of conformity, obedience, and respectful behavior with a breadwinner at the helm and stay-at-home mom at his side. For 95% of human history, neither of these social arrangements was the norm…

Gender Roles

We must live together as brothers or perish together as fools.

– DR. MARTIN LUTHER KING JR.

We live with all kinds of archaic messages and conditionings that we embody that live side by side with more modern scripts about masculinity and gender roles.

Ultimately, men and women should be free to choose their own path in life—the freedom, energy, and joy derived from their core that they need to express in the world. However, it's necessary to depoliticize the concept of gender roles. The problem arises when some sort of special value or status is ascribed to a gendered role. A change of perspective allows back the complimentary natures of men and women and acknowledges sex differences without being proscriptive about what men and women can and can't do. There's nothing wrong with a woman being a homemaker and a man being a breadwinner if that's how they want to choose to arrange themselves. Or a woman being a nurse and a man an engineer, etc, as long as the man has every opportunity to be a nurse and the woman has every opportunity to be an engineer.

Above all, men need to build the bonds of brotherhood and fatherhood. Men do best when they are called to purpose—what the Japanese call "Ikigai." Rather than succumbing to service of the ruling class by calls of patriotic duty, men can choose to express their warriorhood by standing up to the threats of feminism, especially in regard to reclaiming a significant presence in their children's lives after divorce. They can mentor young men (who can simultaneously mentor younger men/boys so they too find value in responsibility). They can share their secrets, hopes, struggles, vulnerabilities, and joys with other men (in men's groups) who will hold such things in sacred trust. They can drop their masks, at least for a while, which their culture would rather them wear.

Consent

♫ *I ought to say, "No, no, no, sir" (Mind if I move in closer?)* ♫

– BABY IT'S COLD OUTSIDE[358]

On the question of consent, I recall my first act of love-making with Naomi (name changed) which, in this day and age, would no doubt be considered date rape.

To cut a long story short, she and I had become very close and ended up in bed together. Going with the flow, we both removed our clothes. There was no prior talk of sex—we were exploring sensuality and doing what felt right. Pretty soon, we were both enflamed by passion. She whispered, "No." Naomi's eyes gazed at mine with desire, her body was naked and open, her vagina wet, her "no's" soft. She said no. And, as she held me to her, I penetrated her.

Back then, there was a different mentality around sex. The closest thing I can think of to describe it, is the tongue-in-cheek Christmas song, *Baby It's Cold Outside.* Back then, if the woman said no and meant it, then she'd simply end the interaction. Naomi was enjoying the experience and, when I rolled over on top of her and slipped inside her, she recognized that we were simply on a different footing. There were no tears, no remonstrations, just sweet union. We went on to have a fully-loving relationship for many months thereafter.

If Naomi wanted to, she could jump on Facebook, like so many women do, and accuse me of date rape. Regardless that 30 years ago there was a completely different social ethos, I would still be judged by today's standards. Consent therefore, surprise surprise, needs to be more nuanced. It can't just be a verbalization of the word, no. I know you've probably had this drummed into you, "No means no!" but I suggest this "control device" should be challenged. Again, I'm advocating for nuance here (in times where nuance is despised). I'm not advocating at all for men to simply have their way regardless of the woman's wishes. Consent

358 Rod Skelton and Bett Garrett, 1949. Won Best Song Academy Award 1949. Popularized by Dinah Shore and Buddy Clark. Recorded by Johnny Mercer and Margaret Whiting.

has to come from the heart and the man has to pick up on that. If the heart is saying "yes" but the mouth is saying "no," should you ignore the heart's voice when no doesn't necessarily mean no? A latent fantasy of many women is "being taken against their will." This is what sells the majority of romance novels written by and bought by women. A woman wants to safely experience being taken and fucked open to God (to use David Deida's phrase)[359]—sexual agency resting with the man as she surrenders her will to his, in trust. So if this is a fundamental part of female psychology—the desire to be taken—then saying no can be an invitation to being taken "not-really-against-her-will." The woman desires to feel his power and, if she releases the tension by saying yes, then she has no opportunity to meet her needs because consent is openly and summarily articulated. So consent has to be a conversation between two hearts, not between two heads, or else passion and desire is lost.

Certainly in the eyes of society, and our western legal system which wants to ensure two people be clearly accountable for their sexual activities, this certainly muddies the water. I fully recognize this and I don't have a solution for it. All I know is that life is complicated and legislating behavior between sexual partners, trying to simplify it so that it can be regulated and managed, is not how this human spirit-animal works.

To feminists, sex is something that men do to women which is why men are being increasingly required to take all the responsibility to determine consent. The woman's subjective feeling is the determining factor in whether or not consent has been reached. A woman can be held responsible for drunk driving but not drunk sex. In fact, if both parties are drunk, the man can be charged with rape since she is considered too drunk to consent (yet he cannot consent to sex either and is not considered to have been raped). Why is it that only women cannot give consent while drunk?[360]

---

359 David Deida (2004). *"The Way of the Superior Man."* Louisville, CO. Sounds True Inc

360 Ashe Schow (July 22, 2015). *"Ever had drunk sex? That's rape, according to this university."* Washington Examiner. https://www.washingtonexaminer.com/ever-had-drunk-sex-thats-rape-according-to-this-university

Because of the stereotype they perpetuate, that all men are oppressive, dangerous, and violent, and that women as a result feel too fearful to say "no" to any sexual advance, the claim is that women go into a state of "tonic immobility" where they are unable to advocate for their own needs. For the most part, this is bogus, but life is messy. Sometimes women do indeed go into a state of fear but it usually has more to do with past trauma than the present moment. Unfortunately, her existing sex partner may well pay the price for the woman's lack of integration of her trauma patternings. If those men fail to pick up on her distress, they could then be accused of rape.

During sex, in long-term sexual relationships, if the woman becomes tense or frozen, the guy will most likely sense the change in her disposition and stop what he's doing. In a caring relationship, where vulnerabilities are shared, the woman might then relate her inner life, perhaps revealing to the guy a past sexual trauma brought on in the moment by something he was doing (he being a catalyst, not a culprit). It's a given that consent was withdrawn without her having to ask him to stop because he could immediately sense that she was not wholeheartedly present for love-making. They might then have a discussion where he listens to her experience because he cares for her and wants to help her heal. This happens frequently in growth-based relationships where both parties are accountable to themselves and their partners and are effective in dealing with their shit. In less mature relationships (either because the relationship itself is in its early stages or the parties are less mature themselves), the same triggers and experiences happen but are dealt with less effectively. If the woman's disposition changes and the guy doesn't pick up on it (or does, but thinks the best plan is to carry on giving her his love), the woman might then later tell him that she felt displeased with how he ignored her pain in the moment. A mature guy would then apologize and ask her to please let him know if it ever happens again. A less mature guy would become defensive and non-empathetic. This situation also happens frequently and is part of the whole growth journey. It's not rape, even though the woman might claim it to be. It's a scenario where the woman felt a degree of trauma but did not express it to the guy. He, being unfamiliar with her psychological make-up, was simply unaware of her signals (or lack thereof).

So relying on two hearts talking and consenting with each other is problematic if one heart is not listening nor the other speaking. Consent is sometimes not realized. And withdrawal of consent is sometimes not realized. If a woman gives a clear, heart-centered "no" but the man is not listening, he gives his own needs priority over hers. And if a woman's heart is offline and her mouth says "yes," she may well be disconnected from her own core and perhaps perceive the man as having taken her against her will. She may feel aggressed upon even though she consented verbally or physically. Consent needs to be wholehearted, quite literally.

Withdrawal of consent needs to be communicated effectively by the woman (or the man)—by whatever means: words, actions, and a heartfelt implicit or explicit "no." If a woman stops consenting, there should be an obligation for any withdrawal of consent to be clearly and unequivocally communicated. Men are not mind readers, especially when no sometimes means yes.

Women's experience of sex is supposedly all that matters in the post #MeToo era. But men also have negative sexual experiences, especially when they are learning about it for the first time. They often feel shame or embarrassment for not knowing what to do and how to be and this affects their experience in all sorts of weird and interesting ways. Sometimes sex just doesn't go right. Women are not the only ones who wake up the next morning with regret. But no man would blame the woman for fumbled mistakes. And not all bad experiences are the result of bad intent. So why is it only men who have to walk the knife edge? The correct thing to do is properly identify our experiences for what they are and refrain from jumping to pathologizing or criminalizing a man for unsatisfactory sex and using either the court system or social media as a form of therapy, oblivious to the real-life consequences for the man.

What if our religion was each other?
If our practice was our life?
If prayer was our words?
What if the Temple was the Earth?
If forests were our church?
If holy water—the rivers, lakes and oceans?
What if meditation was our relationships?
If the Teacher was life?
If wisdom was self-knowledge?
If love was the center of our being?[361]

– GANGA WHITE

72 Unity Consciousness

Many conscious men are used to teachings that are directed towards dismantling their attachment and identification with the constructed ego, or psychological self. This is a self which has been constructed through the mind and personal belief system and observes how emotions and the body interact. You are awareness. You are consciousness. Rather than being an organism which uses awareness as an information-gathering tool. Being in pure presence is one level of awakening but you won't really experience unity because pure presence is not experienced through the heart. It embraces a view of life which is akin to a dream, a secondary reality. Heart-based awakening occurs when one opens and surrenders to the Divine itself and a profound experience of intimacy occurs with

361 (c) 2007 Ganga White, Yoga Beyond Belief. All Rights Reserved, Used with permission. Whitelotus.org.

all that is. Being fully present in the moment is freeing but provides no orienting principle to engage with life at a heartfelt level; the level of intimacy, connectivity, and love. From a heartfelt connection with form (and formlessness) emerges an appreciation of the worthiness and value of all of life. And if life has value then an ethic appears which views the fullest expression of each organism as Good.

Even in pre-pandemic times, our lives were already socially distanced from each other—like we were just roommates in this house called Earth. Living in a world built by us, for us...and without us. The streets of empty cities during lockdown merely serving as a reminder of the social distancing and masking of our inner lives from others that had already occurred—had already separated us from our fellow men well before any coordinated response to a virus. We had became demoralized, fragmented, and dehumanized well before 2020.

When men meet in public, they unconsciously regard each other with a level of coldness and suspicion akin to hunter-gatherers from differing tribes[362]—having the energetics for possible physical confrontation. We need connection as men and we don't get it because the brothers we would expect to see on a daily basis, as part of our tribe, no longer exist. When women meet in public, they may smile or wave casually but are more presenting the illusion of connection as a way to cope with possible conflict. We live in a state of continuous tension, of fear and suspicion.

Our fears and anxieties have long since prevented us from thinking logically and responding lovingly. Yet even now, we continue to perceive unity through the heart. We are homesick for a world which doesn't even exist. And despite all efforts to seemingly break this connection, our heartfelt desire for unity—to live in peace, love, and understanding—endures.

~

362 Jared Diamond relates in his book *"Guns, Germs, and Steel,"* how, when two men meet on the trail who don't know each other, they either have to sit down and figure out some kin connection or else fight and possibly kill each other.

Are we made to take care of each other? As hominins, we once lived in a state of emotional connection with each other. Then we had an upgrade in our mental software and lost that connection. We became able conceive of ourselves as separate from others. The ego is essentially this concept—when we perceive ourselves as an "I." This "original sin" was not self-inflicted, as Christianity suggests.[363] It was the evolutionary result of how we interacted with our environment (by way of the glacially slow traditional model or perhaps at warp speed from having discovered magic mushrooms; the Stoned Ape theory).[364] Or, if you want to go that far, through the imposed hybridization of our species.[365] At the species-wide level, intelligence was an unwieldy, new tool in the hands of naked apes not used to feeling it's heft. We've had a little practice in its use since then—now we need to master it in the service of unity.

Our concept of ourselves as separate from the group is thus a relatively new concept in the course of human history. Coming to a crescendo in the 20th and 21st centuries, individual autonomy had become the cornerstone of our lived experience, certainly in the western world. People's greatest hope was to live their own life, on their own terms. Money was the mechanism by which to achieve such a dream. The hero was the self-made man, self-sufficient and capable of forging his own destiny, epitomized in the work of author, Ayn Rand.[366] The comfortable illusion was that the individual could break free from the external circumstances which otherwise might limit him. In periods of economic expansion (like the 1950s), his reality seemed to reflect his efforts. However, in periods of contraction, every failure was inevitably a personal failure. He was to blame for his own perceived shortcomings.

For the conscious man, the path is to be the author of his own life at the same time as acting compassionately for the sake of community, family,

363 The eating of forbidden fruit was the original cultural narrative imposed on us by "our creator." It was our fault, not His. This was the first instance of "victim-blaming."

364 Reilly Capps (August 18, 2017). *"Growing theory says magic mushrooms are responsible for human evolution."* The Rooster. https://therooster.com/blog/growing-theory-says-magic-mushrooms-are-responsible-human-evolution

365 Michael Tellinger (2012). *"Slave Species of the Gods: The Secret History of the Anunnaki and Their Mission on Earth."* Bear & Company.

366 Ayn Rand (1996). *"The Fountainhead."* Signet; Anniversary edition

and lovers—extending his concern and protection in an ever-widening circle. To recognize that he brings the best version of himself to the game of life while acknowledging that his failings, not to trivialize them, are a reflection of the world he inhabits. He recognizes that his life is deeply entwined with each and every other person's life. Personal fulfillment is deeply entwined with collective fulfillment and the advanced new culture he wishes to build and embody.

~

The spiritual community places a greater value in the heart than the head. I can't say I disagree, especially as my purpose in life is to align myself with divine truth, which is embodied love. However, much of this community also pathologizes thinking. After all, thinking about the past and the future detracts from being fully present in the moment, which is all we have. There is a reluctance to rely on our cognitive abilities for fear that they will be out of alignment with our heart—a form of anti-intellectualism. Yet this is not a zero sum game. Quite frankly, this world needs both more heart *and* clearer thinking. More heart-centered relating *and* greater rational and logical thought. Intelligence is a tool for wellbeing when properly applied. The mind explicates, the heart implicates. The world has not suffered through a surfeit of logical ideas; it has suffered because of a deficit of care and consideration for people and planet, born out of the agenda of the ruling class. The application of intelligent thought that has resulted in a poorer world has not happened because complex thought or the scientific method are inherently bad, but from a cruel world etched with wounding and domination structures.

~

Happiness used to be just for the afterlife. Now we aim to manifest our own happiness in this lifetime, following our joy and integrating our shadow aspects.

Everyone has experienced a lack of meaning to some degree in their lives. There is a struggle to figure out one's place in life; to understand why certain things happen, to us and to those around us. There seems to be a fundamental dissatisfaction at our core—an emptiness that begs to be filled. A sugar-rich diet becomes a substitute for the missing sweetness of care and connection. As society continues to atomize, the question arises "What is my place here? Why am I here?" There is a feeling of despair that arises from being immersed in the pain and suffering of daily existence. Of being disconnected and separate, with nobody to watch over us, silently remonstrating with ourselves for not being strong enough to escape what is causing us pain. For being inadequate and even undeserving of happiness.

Søren Kierkegaard was a Danish theologian, poet, social critic and religious author who is widely considered to be the first existentialist philosopher. According to Kierkegaard human beings are a synthesis of opposites, split between the Finite and the Infinite. The Finite corresponds to that which is earthly; to the concrete here and now, to one's own reality as a sentient being in this physical plane. The Infinite corresponds to the Divine; to the limitless possibilities and potentialities that can be brought into existence. He argued that our existential struggles were the result of not holding both these principles in correct relation to each other. He specifically warned of our tendency to be preoccupied with the Finite; for the search of ultimate happiness within limited means that could not be realized. Rather, he suggested, we should relate ourselves to earthly matters while simultaneously relating ourselves to Source, or to use his term, the Infinite.[367]

Our connection to the Infinite is determined by the recognition, realization, and acceptance that we all suffer in this life—which gives us a perspective of that which is "not-suffering." Just as gold is purified in

367 What he is describing is a nuanced existence. What we have is polarization. Advocates for a Finite existence would have us respond to life in states of limbic reactivity or through secular logic. Advocates of an Infinite existence reject the body, mind, and states of natural desire as illusory; as something to transcend as quickly as possible. Our mortal existence is a hindrance to realizing our divinity. I believe we are here to integrate both.

the fire, so the soul is purified in sufferings. The fire takes away all the impure elements in the gold ore; it loses all that is base. We are essentially born pure and whole, and from that moment forward, life breaks us down. Yet that which is broken and remade is then more evolved. Think of Kintsugi, the Japanese art of repairing broken pottery so that it becomes even more refined thanks to its "scars." As a philosophy, it treats breakage and repair as part of the history of an object resulting in a far more beautifully complex or nuanced creation. To be a conscious man is to join heaven and earth into the fabric of his daily existence.

But the level of suffering is not invariable. Even though we are living in an age of permanent illness and meaningless separation, we can shape our environment to shape who we are and optimize the human condition. Take, for instance, the war on drugs. Much of the impetus for social policy came from studies conducted in the sixties and seventies where lab rats were given the choice between water and water laced with cocaine. The rats chose the cocaine, became addicted, and died. It was surmised that, once cocaine (and other opiate drugs) got a hold of you, you would be at its mercy. One had only to look around and see the growing number of junkies on the street to see the effects of these substances. Then, in 1981, a psychologist named Bruce Alexander postulated that rats who were happy and "free" and which were not held captive and solitary in small, low-stimulus cages would fare better. He devised a study which would replicate those previous experiments. But instead of just offering water and cocaine-laden water, he would build them a big ratty-wonderland where they could live with their buddies, have plenty of sex, and have all sort of things rats like to explore and play with. He called it Rat Park.[368] He found that even when presented with unrestricted access to opiates, the rat village overwhelmingly chose plain water. Even rats taken from previous experiments, when placed in Rat Park, recovered from their addiction.

Addiction arises from *lack* of unity consciousness—where we are kept in isolation, alienated from each other, and subject to the whims of

368 Bruce K. Alexander. Department of Psychology, Simon Fraser University (1981) *"The Myth of Drug-Induced Addiction."* Testimony delivered to the Senate of Canada.

those who have power and control over our lives—where we exist in less than optimal conditions. Our natural state of being is one of abundance, freedom, and relative safety.

~

When we think of separation mentality, there is a temptation to ascribe human nature as its cause—that we are inherently self-gratifying, warrish,[369] selfish, greedy individuals in competition with one another. Human beings are incredibly "plastic" in their ability to adapt to changing environments. It's their human nature to do so. But just like war is unhealthy (people are killed and the people doing the killing often suffer from PTSD), so too are certain environments. It's more productive to think in terms, rather, of human behavior shaped by cultural influences (see *The Cultural Paradigm,* chapter, *Why You are a Slave*). Depending on which society we were brought up in, there are different factors which produce our behaviors, perceptions and value systems. What we consider human nature is what we observe when humans behave within a set of circumstances over a long period of time. For example, hypergamy can only exist within stratified social systems where women have access to a potential mate with greater access to resources than she, and is therefore of higher status. Since this has been the case for a few thousand years, we believe it to be human nature. But if we think in much longer terms, when humans existed in a form of primitive communism (hunter-gatherer societies), we find this cannot have been the case. Warlike "human nature" can only exist where there is competition for scarce resources (not to be confused with healthy aggression).

We need to unify as a species and begin to collectively care for each other's wellbeing, both at an individual and societal level. We can no longer afford to be rivals. Our present society almost commands that we

369 "...whenever men are not obliged to fight from necessity, they fight from ambition; which is so powerful in human breasts, that it never leaves them no matter to what rank they rise." Niccolò Machiavelli. Discourses on Livy: I, 37.

bring out the worst aspects of our biological nature. What kind of society would bring out the best? How can we stop warring with our family, friends, and lovers? How can we be good neighbors, globally?

Anybody can become angry - that is easy, but to be angry with the right person and to the right degree and at the right time and for the right purpose, and in the right way - that is not within everybody's power and is not easy.

— ARISTOTLE

73 The Current Level of Global Consciousness

We're at an important moment in our history, as an evolving species, with our current level of consciousness. The level of dysfunction is at an all-time high at the same time as is our appreciation of it. We are now living during an era of self-destructive mass delusion. When the majority is pursuing—even cheering on—behaviors that undermine its well-being. We have excruciatingly problematic economic, environmental, and political issues. Many are finally looking at how we can improve our condition in this world, and at the same time are contemplating defeat. For millennia we've got on with the routine business of the survival of living; and now more and more people are asking questions about our human trajectory. How do we regard ourselves and how do we regard others? Can we create a good society? Can we live together and how do we manifest that? What is the nature and purpose of this shared existence? Given that we all have our personal subjective realities, how can we cohere to create a unified whole? These are not necessarily metaphysical or philosophical questions—there are practical implications which we can coalesce around. We all have a mind and a heart. We are inevitably, consciously or unconsciously, part of the evolution of our own collective experience that we call society. As conscious men, can we contribute, according to our abilities, to the direction of enlightened coexistence?

In order to survive as a species, we need to take power back into our own hands. We need to create a new paradigm of collective and personal sovereignty. And we need to reclaim our own consciousness as freethinking, free-feeling men and women. This means no longer seeing ourselves as subject to the authority of our rulers and revoking our consent to be governed. It means delegitimizing the ruling class, and legitimizing ourselves.

~

All I know is that first you've got to get mad! You've got to say, "I'm a human being, god damn it! My life has value!"[370]

– HOWARD BEALE

The first step of this process involves righteous anger. This type of anger comes from a place of love and self-respect. At the root of such anger is optimism that's been frustrated.

There is a difference between vapid anger, which is self-concerned anger, and righteous anger. Someone cuts in front of you on the freeway, or someone beats you to the punch on a great idea, or you hear an unpleasant truth about yourself you'd rather remain hidden from view. It's different from the kind of chest-beating, antagonistic anger you find on Facebook or Twitter. These are examples of egoic anger—anger concerned with preservation of the ego—and are unworthy of the conscious man. Worthy anger has a different quality than "self satisfied" or petty anger. It is an emotional response that resonates with collective injustice. You can be outraged at police brutality, or political corruption, or by attacks on civil liberties, or by intentional acts of cruelty or indifference towards others, etc. This anger recognizes brutalities which reduce the quality of our lives, singularly or collectively.

370 Peter Finch as character, Howard Beale. *"Network"* movie (1976). Full quote...https://www.imdb.com/title/tt0074958/characters/nm0002075

The message from society these days is that anger is a negative emotion. This is harmful because anger can be used to shame men, since "toxic men" are just angry ratbags. And in more spiritual circles, it represents a vibrationally lower state of being—so anger, however it is formulated, is something to transcend as rapidly as possible. I'd like to suggest that it is okay to get angry, but without succumbing to or becoming trapped in that anger. Outrage can swamp and overwhelm us to the extent that it becomes harmful to one's mental health. Yet it can be an invaluable marker to our fundamental humanity.

Righteous anger lets the world know how we feel. It's personally useful because its expression is cathartic. And it's collectively useful because it gives others permission to stand up and voice their frustrations, and lets them know they are not alone with their own personal hell.

We are then free to move towards higher concerns.

~

Truth in itself is no power at all… Truth must either attract power to its side, or else side with power, for otherwise it will perish again and again.[371]

— NIETZSCHE

371 Friedrich Wilhelm Nietzsche "*535. The Dawn of Day.*" https://www.gutenberg.org/files/39955/39955-pdf.pdf

We can spend our lives letting the world tell us who we are. Sane or insane. Saints or sex addicts. Heroes or victims. Letting history tell us how good or bad we are. Letting our past decide our future. Or we can decide for ourselves. And maybe it's our job to invent something better.[372]

— CHUCK PALAHNIK

74 The World our Hearts Know is Possible

When people say that the system has failed, they are mistaken. The system has done exactly what it has been designed to do—to impoverish most of humanity while thinking the system is their own collective creation. By now, it should be clear that governments around the world have little interest in putting the needs of the citizens they claim to represent first and foremost. There is fraud and corruption at all levels, and in all major social institutions. Instead, their fealty is to corporations and big money—and behind them, the ruling elite. Yet we constantly expect that voting will one day work to make our lives better. We give them legitimacy by constantly listening to their voices and following their orders. We steadfastly believe the "truth" of one party versus the "lies" of the other and hurl projectiles at the other camp. Many are starting to challenge their own acceptance of the status quo and asking if they'd be better off determining for themselves what a more just world looks like,

372 Chuck Palahnik (2002). *"Choke."* Anchor.

especially in these controversial times where so much is being exposed and so much is clearly being hidden for fear of exposure.

The fundamental principles that move societies are shifting. For people and planet, we are at the edge of the abyss. Indeed, we may already have stepped beyond the precipice and, like Wile E. Coyote, have simply failed to recognize it. No matter how dire the situation continues to become, corrective action by those in power is either negligible or non-existent. It wouldn't be too hyperbolic to suggest that we are on the brink of civilizational collapse. It has happened in the past and it could happen again, sooner than most might think. The Aztecs, the Mayas, the Sumerians, The Egyptians, the Holy Roman Empire, the Greek Empire—they all collapsed. What makes our times different is that civilization now operates at a global scale. Thus the collapse will also be global. Our systems, trade, and economies are so interwoven that any significant dislocation (financial collapse, environmental collapse, resource depletion, nuclear war, etc) will impact us all. As dominant as the Roman Empire was, its collapse was still a regional event. The reason that collapse is likely is that we are behaving in exactly the same way previous civilizations behaved. The raping of the environment, resource acquisition which breaks natural systems, stratified social systems where the rich keep getting richer, warfare which destroys lives, families, and healthy nervous systems—all are debasing the systems on which we depend to a logical end-point. The principle difference between yesterday's civilizational collapses and today's is in magnitude and speed of decline. We are now the observers of our own misguided civilization of which we are also a part. If truly we have degraded beyond repair the living systems of the planet upon which we rely, then our most coherent course of action would be to grieve the loss of our Mother Earth and say our goodbyes.[373]

Whether or not our days are numbered as a species or there's an amazing turnaround just around the corner—a eucatastrophe[374]—it

373 Guy McPherson (2019). *"Only Love Remains: Dancing at the Edge of Extinction."* Woodthrush Productions.

374 A sudden, happy turn of events which pierces you with a joy that brings tears.

cannot be denied that this predicament permeates both our material and psycho-spiritual worlds. Those of us who live with peace in our hearts can barely face the shock of this existence, as the pain of our collective experience exceeds the scope of our comprehension. We watch news reports and conclude that the world is tragically insane.

> *The world's a hungry place. A dark place. Maybe there's more of them, or things like them. Or worse. But there are more people like you too.*[375]
>
> – DAN TORRANCE

The world is blessed with beauty and abundance. Existence is a gift. But the two are combined to produce some sort of paradise built in hell. This is not a kind world. Nature is not always kind. People are not always kind. Systems are not always fair. It's difficult to see how, if the universe is love, it spawned such unsatisfactoriness (duhkha). We dream of a more perfect world because, at a deep and knowing level, we recognize that, on one hand, such a world *is* possible and achievable, given certain circumstances and conditions. And on the other hand, we recognize that our existence here is insufficient, at some level, and that we can do better. Miraculously, there is sometimes kindness in this world. Kindness is an act of rebellion in the face of an existence which doesn't seem to care.

Everyday life has become merely an accidental byproduct of a global economic paradigm run by corporate and political pirates.[376] If we consider civilization to have been a net benefit, how is it that one in three young children are either undernourished or unhealthily overweight in the world?[377] This is not a sign of success. This is not a world that is thriving.

People feel powerless, so at best they focus on the local and the personal rather than the global, no longer believing they have any significant agency. They apply themselves to their own particular projects, private activities, and personal relationships where at least they can claim some

375 Dan Torrance, *Doctor Sleep* movie (2019). Warner Bros.

376 The secret society, *Skull and Bones*, where the elite collude was not named as such by accident.

377 UNICEF (2019). "*The Changing Face of Malnutrition.*" https://features.unicef.org/state-of-the-worlds-children-2019-nutrition/

degree of control over outcome. There are times when all that suffering in their lives and in the wider world seems too much to bare.

But within suffering, there is a message. Suffering tends to take us to a convergence of what is bearable and what is not—a do or die situation. We are now at that juncture where we are either going to do things very differently or face our demise. We've are reaching the final act of a species-wide experiment based on the deep premise of how to go about being humans together in relationship to the world. We are seeing this come to fruition everywhere. We are at a place and time where becoming conscious of our inner and outer realities is no longer an individual choice—it is an absolute necessity, collectively. This world cannot afford the luxury of unconscious men and women directed by inner programming and outer control systems. Tolerant people can no longer afford to tolerate the intolerable. So one by one we're waking up.

We have a choice. Either we can make ourselves fit into this degraded world we have created—a world which has little to no regard for the true nature of human beings—or we reshape it to reflect the true natures of men and women.

~

Now that I have given some idea in the preceding chapters of the obstacles facing a conscious man and the world in which he operates, the solution to the world's problems is, I would suggest, two-fold. A collective evolution through personal self-actualization and a systemic restructuring of the world we inhabit. Simple, but not easy. It means being clear-headed about the nature of reality whilst dismissing cultural and political narratives meant only to distract and confuse.

If our next step forward must begin with an Age of Healing, we need to manifest a dominant paradigm for the liberation of people and planet based on mutual care and consideration. And love. We need to reboot our world with a unified vision to achieve this end. In this new zeitgeist, we can come together around creating a world for fully functional, fully integrated, fully realized individuals as the premise for coexistence. A guaranteed wellbeing. For the full, free, rich, 360-degree actualization of human potential to be realized, you have to have developed the material conditions in which to do so. As, under conditions of oppression, exploitation, or scarcity, the exercise of people's own interests and inclinations will be stunted and forestalled.

It's therefore necessary to replace the current global economic system, which places profit before people, with something more evolved. Competitive trade has dominated human activities since neolithic times—we transact for goods and services and we transact with intimate partners, family, and friends for favors. I don't wish to get into demonizing its current container, capitalism, but to rather think of it as a late-stage iteration which has served its purpose and become outdated.[378] For many, it's easier to imagine the end of the world than an end to market capitalism. But capitalism is not the only form of economy. Alternative economies—people's economies—place human needs and relationships above competition and profit, and are based on the principles and values of cooperation, equality, self-determination and collective governance.[379] This is a hard pill for many to swallow.

Abolishing, or phasing out, the money system, I believe, should be a top priority because, as described in *The Money System (*chapter, *Why You are a Slave),* it is the presence of money (not the love of it) that is corrosive.[380] The ability to meet one's material needs is determined by how thick a person's wallet is. And since most of the world has rather thin wallets, most of the world goes without. Needlessly. We interacted with Mother Earth for thousands of years to provide ourselves with goods and

---

378 Returning to a form of "pure capitalism" fails to address the inherently unjust premise of exploitation of labor. Nor even that externalities have no worth, bringing the whole model into question. It's a linear system where, once all the resources provided freely by Mother Earth have been extracted, it dies on its feet. This is in contrast to the closed-loop dynamics of a self-sustaining ecosystem.

379 For example, groups like the Zeitgeist Movement, The Venus Project, Ubuntu Contributionism, Charles Eisenstein's Gift Economy, the Degrowth movement, OpenDemocracy, Free World Charter, the permaculture/regenerative agriculture movement, One Community Global, New Earth, and many others.

380 Even when having wisely opted out of the fiat currency system (by, say, investing in precious metals or cryptos), having more money than others reinforces separation mentality by giving you the comfort of knowing you're ahead of the pack. It's a smart way to cope with the existing world but does not create a better one.

services before civilizations emerged. Private property was unknown. Yet people today, who are in dire need, will defend to their last breath this "right" while having little of it themselves. Private property is comforting because it implies that your stuff cannot be taken from you by force (it is protected by law)—it's derived from scarcity mentality. Yet with open access to resources (a commons-based or resource-based economy),[381] all goods and services can be available to all people to pursue their interests, while contributing their efforts to the rest of humanity and Earth's natural systems.[382]

An open access world is good for masculinity. If access to resources is restricted by the ability to pay for them, then the entrepreneurial man can better make his mark when restrictions to capital are limited only by Earth's natural systems and adverse impacts to other human beings (see next section, below). A capital-deficient man is less able to express his masculinity.

Without private property, there would be no need to go to war over the Earth's resources, to place them in private hands. Without a money system, the fundamental issues of economy (what people make and do for each other) would have to be resolved. The title of this sub-chapter pays homage to the work of Charles Eisenstein who proposes a Gift Economy.[383] How would we connect the provider of a gift with the person who needs that gift? How would we recognize and honor those who give generously? How would we efficiently and effectively coordinate social gifts, as opposed to individual gifts? These sorts of questions can be resolved with intelligent deliberation.

~

381 The ocean is an open access economy. One which has decimated ocean fish and whales and is a place for the world's garbage. So not all open access economies are necessarily superior.

382 This is in stark contrast to the proposition put forward by the World Economic Forum to remove any rights to ownership whilst maintaining a stratified society. *"8 predictions for the world in 2030"* https://www.youtube.com/watch?v=Hx3DhoLFO4s

383 Charles Eisenstein (2013). *"The More Beautiful World Our Hearts Know Is Possible."* North Atlantic Books.

Because the human race operates within parameters designed to limit its awareness, our evolution has been stunted materially and spiritually. So we also need a special kind of investigation which actually tries to figure out, first, what the concept of healthy, happy humans consists of for a whole society and, secondly, how it is materially to be achieved.[384] Under what sort of material conditions could people achieve personal and societal fulfillment? At best, in this day and age, fulfillment is largely restricted to each individual marching forward as best he can in a separate space from others (those with whom he has no close relations and/or is indifferent). Taking care of Number One. For a world in which we take each other's best interests as our own, we have to see individuals as ultimately realizing their potential only through and in terms of the freely realized potential of other fellow human beings. Such a world would be structured to facilitate that.

In other words, individuals might only be permitted to realize those aspects of their potential which allowed others to realize *their* own potential as fully and as freely as humanly possible. Personal freedom is constrained only where one's actions would limit other people working to achieve their own potential. It's a two-way thing. It's relational. It's also non-egoic. It's limited only to the extent of adopting the concept of "doing no harm"—we are not free to harm each other (not just interpersonal harm,[385] but by structural violence). That would mark the difference between a traditionally liberal framework and a unity consciousness framework.

People balk at restrictions on freedom and there is justifiable concern about present-day insults to our civil liberties. Such restrictions only benefit the power elite. Yet remove our masters from the equation and the picture changes. Then we just work to benefit each other. It's not Me-focused or We-focused. It's a blend of the two. As it stands, if the freedom to say and do what we want—to lie, to peddle false narratives, to inflict pain with words,

384 Using the scientific method for social concern may offer some value. It is a feature of the work of the Zeitgeist Movement and also Sam Harris' book, *"The Moral Landscape."* Or would such a "tyranny of logic" exclude other forms of knowing? Is there a nuanced synthesis?

385 Higher Perspective (April 22, 2019). *"The Connection Between Verbal Abuse and Anxiety Everyone Ignores."* Higher Perspective. https://www.higherperspectives.com/verbal-anxiety-connection-2635238625.html

to defame,[386] to monopolize access to resources, etc— includes the freedom to self-destruct as a species, then we're obviously not making the right choice.

As long as we don't have a world structured in such a way as to facilitate a social dialog/inquiry as to what it is we really desire and how we can achieve it, then we won't find out what we really want. Nothing can be more mistaken than the spiritual notion that we simply have to release our resistances and integrate our shadow aspects to realize our true natures, despite the dysfunctional world in which we live. If our true natures are being effectively repressed or oppressed by our conditioning (and are therefore not self-obvious), it's a mistake to imagine we already know exactly what they are. If they have been repressed effectively, this will create genuine ambiguity among us about recognizing them. We won't find out how to walk through life just by looking into our hearts/heads, as much as I'd like to believe otherwise.

I'm not suggesting that we have to wait until conditions are perfect for self-realization. Think of it as a double helix with one strand being societal advancement and the other being personal empowerment. Each strand needs to match the other as energy moves from bottom to top, each entwined strand serving this upward momentum. New levels of consciousness supported by new levels of social improvement, which then supports new levels of consciousness in an ever-virtuous cycle. The last piece of this grand puzzle is put in place not by some thought leader, priest, or politician—it is put in place by us all. Indeed, that is the only way it can be accomplished.

For example, there is an insufficient number of trauma-release practitioners—body workers, energy workers, breath workers, somatic experiencing practitioners, etc—and not everyone who has access to one can afford one, nor knows about the best approach for their particular condition.

386 The casual, everyday defamation of men by women to their women friends is a ubiquitous assault to men's lives that has no legal sanction yet can be highly destructive to his reputation and opportunities. This also extends to female on female violence, where women seek to harm women in their circles with malicious gossip who do not conform to certain standards of behavior. Such "free speech" costs us more than we gain with the freedom to exercise it.

Because trauma-release is essentially in its infancy,[387] those practitioners that do operate are largely winging it because of a general limited understanding, not of their making (although they've already made wonderful progress). The external mechanisms are not in place which means that internal mechanisms are not supported and individuals are left clutching at straws. Flip it round and you can see that the more optimized the environment, the more people are empowered. And the more they are empowered, the better able they are to optimize the environment.

~

If we lived within a horizontal democracy, we would have a better chance at being free. No masters, no rulers, and hence, no chance for power to become concentrated in the hands of a few. Yet even here, there are limitations. A voter who is ignorant has as equal a say as someone who has devoted themselves to understanding a policy issue. The two, unfairly, cancel each other out.[388] And inevitably there are more of the former than the latter on any issue.[389] Democracy is very energy intensive—for it to work effectively, the majority of the populace must be capable of dispassionately synthesizing complex issues.[390] "The best argument against

387 PTSD and cPTSD have had very little research owing to big-pharma placing all the emphasis on drugs and talk therapy, neither of which are particularly effective.

388 The most optimal path forward cannot be achieved under such an arrangement—only a mediocre middle way born of compromise.

389 Not everybody is cut out for democracy. The assumption with democracy is that if we don't participate in it, we should have no complaint when decisions are made which are not in our best interests. There are so many different ways an individual can contribute to the collective good. Some of those people are bored to tears by big-picture thinking. Yet we insist they vote. All the lawmakers have to do is appeal to their ignorance with vague claims about a better world (Hope and Change, Make America Great Again) sprinkled with false promises, and those who are truly interested in grappling with real solutions are swamped by those who fall prey to platitudes.

390 Historically, democracies were few in example and were fairly short-lived. Monarchies, and the like, required less collective energy as decisions were left to a small group of people (the rulers and their courts). Less energy was needed to reach a plan of action or run a nation. Democracies require a large energy investment to create a high-functioning, educated populace in order to make sensible decisions. With other things in life to focus on, is it feasible for everyone to have a well-thought out opinion on every single policy issue under the sun? Perhaps this is something we can aspire to but we certainly do not yet have the maturity.
If democracies are fragile and dynasties unfair, how can we achieve a higher-order synthesis? Something both energy-conserving and fair? A constitutional republic might fit the bill but has been shown to be deficient (it's an oligarchic plutocracy disguised as a democratic republic).

democracy is a five-minute conversation with the average voter," said Winston Churchill. Likewise, if the people democratically decide to do harm (to an individual, a group, or the planet), does the democratic will of the majority trump all other considerations? Developing poor policy propositions and then getting people to vote on them, however cogent the public's thinking is, is also inadequate. Manufacturing consent for a change in the law may still occur between groups who have certain ideological agendas. What we can observe is that getting a populace to agree on the best way forward has been largely impractical. We like democracy because it *feels* like we can move forward together. Even if a populace was unbiased, rational, and well-informed, the complexity of modern life means specialists are essential to understand, generate, and guide everyday complex decisions.

The only way things improve materially is if the way people are governed changes structurally. The problems we face do not arise from particular laws or court rulings, per se, but from the way human beings manage their affairs collectively—the system itself.

Imagine you and several billion other people had just been dropped onto a beautiful, virgin planet, called Earth, as equals. There are no rulers and there are lots of resources. There are no systems in place to facilitate peaceful, productive cohabitation yet all of you were committed to finding the best option. If you could design this world from scratch for the full, free, rich, all-round development of human powers and capacities, how would you do it and what might it look like?[391] How could it be designed so that laws were irrelevant?[392] Laws are essentially "patches" to compensate for design-flaws in the system—they exist to compensate for or regulate exploitation. For example, laws which exist to punish crimes like fraud,

391 As an example:
Frank Rotering (August, 2018). *"The Economics of Needs and Limits: A theory for sustainable well-being."* Self-published.
See also, *"Face to Face with Frank Rotering and the Contractionary Revolution."* https://www.youtube.com/watch?v=JNSnCGBsSAw&fbclid=IwAR1Nd7_LH4xftE-4HQJWV3zN8sQ_wpm45sr-r1Cxp8-I77NaoWL3UaSW8uc4

392 As an example:
Peter Joseph (April, 2018). *"The New Human Rights Movement: Reinventing the Economy to End Oppression."* BenBella Books.

theft, burglary, tax evasion, etc—such laws exist to circumvent actors gaming the money system. What if there were no money system? How could a form of governance be created where, individually and collectively, people could see things as they really were (free from control-narratives) and synergistically satisfy the needs of humans and planet? How could people have more fealty to the truth than to their tribe? How could people with different value systems coexist peacefully, harmoniously, and accountably other than by looking down the end of the barrel of a gun? How could they build a system without design flaws?[393]

What are the virtues which, when fostered, produce the healthiest, happiest society? If, say, wisdom and competence were considered worthy virtues of a leader, how would we decide who amongst us most ideally represented those virtues—and s/he granted conditional authority?

The fact that we have to grope our way forwards, and hope that things get better incrementally inch by inch, is a monumentally sad way to live when we know a better future could be available to us tomorrow. If we could only find a way to collaborate with those who have a different version of the tomorrow we want. No two people are alike and our different perspectives and viewpoints cause us to squabble over different political and social agendas. Sometimes many of us agree about the problem but differ radically on the solution.

~

Perhaps you are shocked by my "socialistic rantings," dear reader, and would like to squabble with me? Do you feel like double-downing on your own hard won beliefs? What is alive in you right now, having read these words? How can I embrace you? How can I take your best interests as my own? And you mine? How can we develop sophisticated ways of resolving conflicting needs? How can we go beyond agreeing to disagree?[394]

393 The work of W. Edwards Deming may be useful. https://deming.org/

394 When agreeing to disagree, conflict does not go away. It simply gets shelved. Each party is then waiting for that moment in the future when the balance of power shifts and they will get their way. It maintains separation. It doesn't bring people together. In fact, it gives up on bringing people together.

Can we be open to having our minds changed when faulty beliefs are demonstrated? Or at least seeing something worthy of consideration in the ideas of another which appears to meet the metric of truth? How can we come into alignment and coalesce around a shared vision for the world our hearts know is possible?

There is an urge to defend ego needs where our positions are considered part of our identity. When evolved human beings can separate themselves from their thinking, from the ideas with which they have fallen in love, personal and social advancement becomes possible through cooperation. At such time, upon ego-death, it will not be the end of the world to lose an argument. In fact, it's to be celebrated because it means that we've kept our eye on the prize (our liberation).

We do what we can with what we have. With every small step, every thought, every action, every intention and decision, we can consciously align ourselves with compassionate fellowship. Even if you don't agree with my version of tomorrow, how might we be brothers? How might we actually *start* to change the world?

~

Do not comply!

The great Howard Zinn wrote, "Historically, the most terrible things—war, genocide, and slavery—have resulted not from disobedience, but from obedience."[395] In other words, you get what you accept. At what point do we ask ourselves, "When will enough be enough?" At what point will we decide to disobey?

I'd like to suggest that the only way to change the system is by not accepting it—by not participating in it (rather than fighting it) and withdrawing consent to be governed (which is our right).[396] How do we collectively refuse to engage with the system? Refusing to pay taxes and

395 Howard Zinn (1997-2009). *"The Zinn Reader: Writings on Disobedience and Democracy."* Seven Stories Press.

396 "Governments are instituted among Men, deriving their just powers from the consent of the governed." Thomas Jefferson. The founding fathers, however, never articulated just how consent could be withdrawn, short of revolution.

fines, refusing mandatory vaccinations, refusing to obey orders which are not in our best interests, refusing to pay rents/mortgages, refusing to accept the legitimacy of those in authority? Refusing to work for the control system—the military, national guard, and police, the intelligence agencies, the prison industrial complex, etc? Refusing to honor the religion of private property—occupying the land, the streets, and the workplace? How about nothing more than taking a walk in nature, on this god-given planet of ours, on land owned by a multimillionaire? Radical stuff. But the baby steps forward have produced too little, I would suggest, and time has run out.

The history of non-compliance, both nationally and internationally, has been shown to be highly effective. Non-violent, collective action against egregious policies or regimes, such as the boycott of South Africa under the system of apartheid, the Boycott, Divestment, Sanctions (BDS) movement against Israel's treatment of Palestinians, the Montgomery bus boycott of 1955, are examples of people uniting for justice. The challenge is to extend the scope of this type of single-issue action to challenge the power structure itself.

The way out is through the door. Why is it that no one will use this method?

– CONFUCIUS

The reason is that the door has armed guards (see *The Police and National Guard,* chapter *Why You are a Slave*). Heroes, like Julian Assange, Ed Snowden, and Chelsea (Bradley) Manning have shown us the way. They have also shown what can happen if you try to walk through the door alone. They did what they had to do because they were men of conscience and to have done otherwise would have been psycho-spiritual suicide. If wildebeests were to cross the river one by one, the crocodiles would target and converge on them. Only by swimming across en masse can they hope to confuse the crocs by presenting an indistinguishable and unstoppable sea of bodies. How would such a feat be achieved for human salvation? How can we do better than mass protests which appear to be nothing more than citizens going cup in hand to ask for more?[397] How could we get that kind of balls-out level of commitment needed to save us all? How can we end the business of flapping our wings (and our lips), and actually take off to go somewhere better? How can we resolve the fear that tethers us to the ground and the ignorance that prevents us flying off in the right direction?

397 I was part of the largest peace-time demonstration in UK history to protest entry into the war against Iraq. Prime Minister, Tony Blair, was unmoved. If the people simply shake their fists without using them when they are ignored (metaphorically-speaking), then protests are delusional.

I can think of no right more fundamental than the right to peacefully steward the contents of one's own consciousness.[398]

— SAM HARRIS

75 Final Words

Hard times are upon us, whether we want them or not. To be a conscious man, to remain a conscious man, will increasingly bump you up against those forces which seek to limit that consciousness and punish you for insisting on being its arbiter. Win or lose, our task as conscious men is to remain balanced and heart-centered through the shit storm we call life. When adversity strikes and you feel yourself reeling, forgive yourself (and others) and gently come back to your center. You are what this world needs, whether the world knows it or not. You are the way forward.

Everybody wants to go to heaven but nobody wants to die. So it's no good simply to feel righteous. "The espousal of humane goals and loyalty to ideals are admirable, but are grossly inadequate…to achieve freedom."[399] We have to use our masculine essence to penetrate the world. To use our systematizing brains to be strategic rather than reactive—to be not passive spectators but active participants in the way we organize our world—to actually take action to do good, not alone but collectively. By choosing to safeguard our status as free-thinking and free-feeling men,

398 Sam Harris (2015). *"Waking Up: A Guide to Spirituality Without Religion."* Simon & Schuster; Reprint edition.

399 Gene Sharp (2012). *"From Dictatorship to Democracy."* Serpent's Tail.

and in matching our actions to the contents of our minds, we become the unstoppable force that pushes the immovable object towards our liberation.

The desire to determine how the world is shaped has governed the lives of men and women for millennia. And behind us lies an ocean of misery bringing us to what now appear to be "end times." Through all the wars of conquest, through enslavements, through plunder and pillage, through injustices, degradations, and dehumanizations, there remains in each and every one of us an inextinguishable flame of goodness—something which is imperishable.

One way or another we will be forced to comply. Either we obey the dictates of our conscience, or we will decide to go along with business as usual and obey the dictates of our rulers, in which case and we disobey our unfolding as full human beings. In times of crisis, seemingly impossible ideas become possible. What seems an impossibility today may become all too possible tomorrow. As sovereign individuals, we are not compelled to do good in the world. We might cope by keeping our heads down and avoiding the gaze of Sauron, breathing a sigh of relief when he plucks someone else from the crowd. Yet resisting "evil" is the mark of a virtuous life, regardless of outcome. "All we have to decide is what to do with the time that is given us."[400] There are many things we *can't* do in this world, and we can spend our time dwelling in that fact. However few our options, what *can* we do?[401] What doors are open to walk through? What is meaningful to you?

Despite what has happened to our world, despite the missteps of our species and the mistakes made, despite what has been done to us, we still have virtue at our core.[402] We must enlighten ourselves and multiply our effect so that all conscious men become more powerful than the

400 Gandalf. *The Lord of the Rings* movie (2001-2003). New Line Cinema/WingNut Films.

401 James Corbett (January 11, 2021). *"Introducing #Solutionswatch."* The Corbett Report. https://www.corbettreport.com/introducing-solutionswatch-video/

402 Virtue means the kind of social disposition we carry in us that affects the quality and texture of our life in society as a whole, rather than just isolated actions that we can abstract from that life and say, "Is this action right or wrong?"

manipulated "Mass Man" in directing the course of human affairs. Let us begin our enlightenment.

Disobedience is the true foundation of liberty.
The obedient must be slaves.

— HENRY DAVID THOREAU

Endnote Review Request

If you enjoyed reading this, please leave a review on Amazon/Goodreads. I read every review and they help new readers discover my books.

Please visit me at *michaelronin.net* and sign up for my newsletter.

www.ingramcontent.com/pod-product-compliance
Lightning Source LLC
Chambersburg PA
CBHW062045270326
41931CB00013B/2955
* 9 7 8 1 7 3 6 7 0 4 6 0 8 *